SPORTS ENTREPRENEURSHIP
THEORY AND PRACTICE

SPORTS ENTREPRENEURSHIP: THEORY AND PRACTICE

Dorene Ciletti and Simon Chadwick, Editors

FiT

Fitness Information Technology
a Division of the International Center
for Performance Excellence
West Virginia University
262 Coliseum, WVU-PASS
PO Box 6116
Morgantown, WV 26506-6116

Library of Congress Card Catalog Number: 2011936286

ISBN: 978-1-935412-25-0

Cover Design: Bellerophon Productions
Cover Images: Wimbledon courts image courtesy of London 2012; motorcycle image © Przemysław Rafa | Dreamstime.com; all others courtesy of Yumiko Tamaro Photography
Australia map, page 67 © ymgerman, istockphoto.com
Production Editor: Matt Brann
Copyeditor: Danielle Costello
Proofreader: Maria E. denBoer
Indexer: David C. denBoer
Typesetter: Bellerophon Productions
Printed by: Data Reproductions Corp.

10 9 8 7 6 5 4 3 2 1

Fitness Information Technology
A Division of the International Center for Performance Excellence
West Virginia University
262 Coliseum, WVU-CPASS
PO Box 6116
Morgantown, WV 26506-6116
800.477.4348 (toll free)
304.293.6888 (phone)
304.293.6658 (fax)
Email: fitcustomerservice@mail.wvu.edu
Website: www.fitinfotech.com

Contents

Acknowledgments

An edited collection such as this would not be possible without the contributions of many individuals. We owe a debt of gratitude to Fitness Information Technology's former director, Steven Pope. This work would not have been possible without his vision and guidance, and his recommendations have been invaluable. He believed in this project, providing us the opportunity to contribute to ongoing inquiry in sport. He also provided us with exceptional editorial support through senior editor Matt Brann. This collection has benefitted immensely from Matt's talent and advice, and we thank Matt for his dedicated work and gentle nudges along the way to completion. We are also grateful to the team at Fitness Information Technology who transformed the information we provided into this printed volume.

We enthusiastically thank the authors who contributed to *Sports Entrepreneurship: Theory and Practice* for their participation in this volume: Carlos Pestano Barros, Nicholas Burton, Coyte Cooper, Joris Drayer, George Foster, Samantha Gorse, Stephen Hardy, David Hoyt, Carol Irwin, Richard L. Irwin, Maryellen Kelly, Conway Lackman, John M. Lanasa, Heath McDonald, Mark Nagel, Anna Semens, Kenneth L. Shropshire, Deborah J. Southall, Richard M. Southall, Constantino Stavros, Mário Teixeira, and Rodoula H. Tsiotsou. Their collective aim has been to examine the inherent connection between sport and business from the lens of entrepreneurship, and we value their unique contributions. Standing behind each of these authors is a support group of colleagues, families and friends, and we thank them as well.

We gratefully acknowledge the generosity of the North American Society for Sport History for permission to reprint Stephen Hardy's "Polo at the Rinks" piece, which first appeared in the *Journal of Sport History* in summer 2006. We also thank Yumiko Tamaru for permission to use three of her engaging photographs on the cover of this book.

There is a final acknowledgment necessary. The efforts spent on a project such as this require sacrifice, and we value and appreciate the support of our families, friends, and colleagues. Special thanks goes to Dorene's family, especially her husband, James Don, and daughter, Sabrina, and her colleagues at Duquesne University, and to those among Simon's family and friends who have helped throughout the work on this book.

—Dorene Ciletti and Simon Chadwick

Preface

Sport is a multi-billion dollar industry with global impact. Sports leagues bring in millions of dollars in revenues, sports-related brands are among the most recognized global brands, and professional athletes are among the most sought-after celebrity endorsers. While sport as an industry is not new, fields of study related to the business of sports, such as sport management and sport marketing, are still relatively young. Nauright and Pope (2009) remind us that most academic programs date back to the 1990s, and professional societies have only emerged in the last two to three decades, beginning with the North American Society for Sport Management (NASSM) in 1985, the European Association for Sport Management (EASM) in 1993, the Sport Management Association of Australia and New Zealand (SMAANZ) in 1995, and the Sport Marketing Association in 2002. The history of sport, however, reaches back over centuries.

Sport is inherently entrepreneurial, though few formal connections exist in academic literature, and this volume aims to address this. Sport is inherently connected to business, as sport historians Stephen Hardy (1986) and Dilwyn Porter (2009) note. Porter suggests that sport and business have an intimate and long-standing connection, noting that the links between sport and business have become progressively more systematic and visible over the course of the 20th century, though sport, and sport business as well, have been challenging to define. Porter refers to Hardy's (1986) triple commodity conception of sport, including sport experiences, sports-related services, and sports goods as well as Sage's (2004) three segments of commercialized sport—performance, promotion, and production—for guidance.

Porter (2009) provides a basis for consideration of the role of entrepreneurs in sport history. After addressing definitional problems relative to entrepreneurship, including the characteristics of entrepreneurship, the variety of individuals who may engage in entrepreneurial behavior, and the function of organizations, he suggests that "entrepreneurial activity occurs when individuals or firms combine two or more parts of the sports product, or when they combine part or parts of the sports product with a non-sports product to create something new" (2009, p. 210). This is consistent with Schumpeter's (1965) view that that entrepreneurship does not occur only with the development of a major innovation; entrepreneurial activity involves new combinations as well.

From the formalization and commercialization of sports, to ongoing developments and enhancements in sports organizations, sport clothing and equipment, sport in the 21st century warrants study from an entrepreneurial perspective. Entrepreneurs worked tirelessly to make sports an integral part of our culture, creating leagues that formalized professional sports competition and commercialized it as entertainment, developing new products and services relative to sports, and spurring the growth of other industries including media. Sports entrepreneurs recognized the importance of promoting sports competitions, and utilized media to advance interest in the events. These entrepreneurs developed innovative approaches to media utilization as well as establishing media organizations focused on sports, and today, media companies comprise nearly half of Fast Company's 2010 list of the 10 most innovative sports companies (http://www.fastcompany .com/mic/2010/industry/most-innovative-sports-companies).

Sport historian Hardy (1996) suggested entrepreneurship as a lens through which sport, and thus sport research, could be explored, and, as Ciletti points out in Chapter 1, James Santomier in 2002 argued that opportunities for entrepreneurs exist in sport, yet their contributions have largely been undervalued. His call for sport ventures to be considered as a research focus by those in entrepreneurship and small business has largely gone unanswered. In this volume, we attempt to bridge that gap, including chapters by notable sports academicians covering both conceptual and case examples highlighting sports entrepreneurship. This volume examines sports entrepreneurship from numerous perspectives, including marketing, broadcasting, sponsorship, and social entrepreneurship.

The chapters included in this volume address the innovation, risk-taking, and proactiveness inherent in entrepreneurship. Many chapters rely heavily on examples from one or more sports organizations, and the organizations represent sports teams, sports associations, and sports-related products from the U.S., India, Europe, and Australia. As the entrepreneurial nature of sport is examined, we consider such broad areas as marketing, social impact, and opportunity-seeking.

Morgan and Summers (2005) suggest that the uniqueness of sport should be considered in marketing initiatives. Additionally, increased competition for entertainment dollars has increased the need for sport marketing (Mullin, Hardy, & Sutton, 2007). An entrepreneurial approach to sports marketing may provide value, as Mullin et al. (2007) note that the needs of sports consumers have become more complex and competition for sports consumers' time and attention has increased.

Burton, Chadwick, and Gorse argue in Chapter 2 that an entrepreneur can exploit the opportunities presented by utilizing innovative marketing strategies, philosophies, or techniques, and that the use of this method may distinguish sports entrepreneurs from entrepreneurs in other industries.

Hardy, in his seminal "Polo at the Rinks" piece included as Chapter 11 in this volume, also notes the contributions made by sports entrepreneurs in marketing and promotion, and Cooper, in Chapter 12, acknowledges the importance of marketing initiatives for the sustainability of collegiate wrestling.

Cooper further explains the role of the National Wrestling Coaches Association in developing an entrepreneurial mindset in collegiate wrestling programs, suggesting that this mindset would support the success and longevity of such programs. This is again considered in Chapter 6 by McDonald and Stavros, who explore entrepreneurship and its role in the establishment of two new Australian Football League franchises in new markets, highlighting the entrepreneurial spirit of the AFL. A market leader, it continues to develop new products and programs. Within sports leagues, Porter (2009) suggests that the scope of entrepreneurial activity may be limited by the unique competitor/collaborator relationship that exists between teams, and still the AFL demonstrates an entrepreneurial perspective exploring untapped markets and expanding the brand while building a strong relationship with both fans and the community.

The social impact of sport is significant, and this volume considers the social impact of sports entrepreneurs in Chapter 3 by Shropshire, as well as social entrepreneurship and sport sponsorship in Chapter 5 by Irwin, Irwin, and Drayer. Shropshire examines the social impact of sports entrepreneurs, introducing four types of entrepreneurial sports ventures with social impact: for-profit social impact entrepreneurship, not-for-profit social impact enterprises, athlete as social impact entrepreneur, and government as entrepreneur. He suggests that increased brand equity impacting profitability or the altruistic desire to "do good" may be the motives for those in sports intending to have social impact.

Entrepreneurial spirit connects sports sponsorship and social entrepreneurship in Irwin et al.'s chapter detailing the Memphis Grizzlies' "Get Fit with the Grizzlies" initiative. Entrepreneurs such as Peter Ueberroth (*TIME Magazine*'s Man of the Year for 1985) have made their mark on sport sponsorship, as Ueberroth oversaw the sponsorship of the 1984 Summer Olympics in Los Angeles by Coca-Cola, which spent nearly $30 million dollars to become a corporate sponsor of the event (Reich, 1986). Chalip (2004) notes that "sponsorship has long been a core element of the entertainment industry" (p. xiii), and the connection to social entrepreneurship in the "Get Fit with the Grizzlies" program illustrates the Grizzlies' entrepreneurial spirit. The innovative and proactive development of a social program that fulfilled previously unmet needs, and the incorporation of sponsors into the program were key elements of its success.

Innovation is at the heart of entrepreneurship, and in Chapter 4, Hoyt and Foster explore the Indian Premiere League, one of Fast Company's 2010 most innovative sports companies (http://www.fastcompany.com/mic/2010/industry/most-innovative-sports-companies). Fast Company describes the IPL's inclusion on its list by explaining that "[t]he IPL has transformed cricket, establishing a new model that shows how a nearly 500-year-old game can be revamped, restructured, and tailored to today's short attention spans and entertainment infrastructure—and succeed wildly."

Identifying and acting on opportunity is commonly associated with entrepreneurship, and many definitions of entrepreneurship reference opportunities (Morrison, 1998; Wennekers & Thurik, 1999; Shane & Venkataraman, 2000; Spencer et al., 2008). Entrepreneurs seek out opportunities, and in Chapter 7, Semens considers the entrepreneurial role of sports agents as they bridge the gaps created by structural holes in the network of sports stakeholders, and in Chapter 13 Barros and Teixeira examine the factors that provide an opportunity for career longevity in tennis. In Chapter 10, Lackman, Ciletti, Lanasa, and Kelly suggest that an entrepreneurial approach to ticket pricing may provide opportunities for additional revenue generation for small-market MLB teams, and in Chapter 8, Tsiotsou explores opportunities in sports broadcasting due to the development of the new media, presenting an entrepreneurial sports broadcasting model. In Chapter 9, Southall, Nagel, and Southall detail the entrepreneurial journey undertaken by the founders of the College Sports Research Institute (CSRI) as they uncovered an opportunity, developed a means to address that opportunity through the CSRI, and engaged in innovative initiatives to grow the Institute.

Austin, Stevenson, and Wei-Skillern (2006) connect social impact and opportunity, suggesting a social value framework that considers people, opportunity, and capital relative to the entrepreneurial venture. Sports organizations can effect social change, noted in the United Nations General Assembly's 2003 special resolution suggesting "sport as a means to promote education, health, development, and peace" (Goss & Alexandrova, 2005, p. 54), and Irwin et al. remind us in Chapter 5 that many believe sports organizations have a responsibility toward corporate social action.

Sports Entrepreneurship: Theory and Practice seeks to advance the understanding of sports entrepreneurship with the hope of informing sport research and practice. The chapters included in this volume provide insight into the integration of entrepreneurship and sport, building on existing, often distinct, research from both fields, and exploring the innovation, risk-taking, and proactiveness that connect them. We hope that this volume responds to Santomier's call for the intertwining of sports and entrepreneurship research, serving as a basis for wider discussion and reflection on sports entrepreneurship.

References

Chalip, L. (2004). Beyond impact: A general model for host community event leverage. In: B. Ritchie & D. Adair (Eds.), *Sport tourism: Interrelationships, impacts and issues* (pp. 226–252). Clevedon, UK: Channel View Publications.

Fowler, A. (2000). NGDOs as a moment in history: Beyond aid to social entrepreneurship or civic innovation? *Third World Quarterly, 21*(4), 637–654.

Goss, J., & Alexandrova, A. (2005). HIV/AIDS prevention and peace through sport. *Lancet, 366,* S3–S4.

Hardy, S. (1996). Entrepreneurs, organizations, and the sport marketplace. In S. Pope (Ed.), *The new American sport history* (pp. 341–365). Champaign, IL: University of Illinois Press.

Hardy, S. (1986). Entrepreneurs, organizations, and the sport marketplace: Subjects in search of historians. *Journal of Sport History, 13*(1), 14–33.

Morgan, M., & Summers, J. (2005). *Sports marketing.* Melbourne: Thomson.

Morrison, A. (1998) Entrepreneurs or intrapreneurs. In C. Lashley & A. Morrison (Eds.), *Franchising hospitality services* (pp. 68–91). Oxford: Butterworth-Heinemann.

Mullin, B., Hardy, J., & Sutton, W. (2007). *Sport marketing* (3rd ed.). Champaign, IL: Human Kinetics.

Nauright, J., & Pope, S. (2009). Introduction. In J. Nauright & S. W. Pope (Eds.), *The new sport management reader* (pp. xvii–xxv). Morgantown, WV: Fitness Information Technology.

Porter, D. (2009). Entrepreneurship and sport history. In S. W. Pope & J. Nauright (Eds.), *Routledge companion to sports history* (pp. 197–215). New York: Routledge.

Reich, K. (1986). *Making it happen: Peter Ueberroth and the 1984 Olympics.* Santa Barbara, CA: Capra Press.

Sage, G. H. (2004). The sporting goods industry: From struggling entrepreneurs to national businesses to transnational corporations. In T. Slack (Ed.), *The commercialization of sport* (pp. 29–51). Abingdon: Routledge.

Santomier, J. (2002). Sport business entrepreneurship. *New England Journal of Entrepreneurship, 5*(1), 5–7.

Shane, S., & Venkataraman, S. (2000). The promise of entrepreneurship as a field of research. *Academy of Management Review, 25*(1), 217–226.

Slack, T. (2009). Foreword. In J. Nauright & S. W. Pope (Eds.), *The new sport management reader* (pp. xi–xii). Morgantown, WV: Fitness Information Technology.

Schumpeter, J. (1965). Economic theory and entrepreneurial history. In H. G. Aitken (Ed.), *Explorations in enterprise* (pp. 121–142). Cambridge, MA: Harvard University Press.

Spencer, A., Kirchhoff, B., & White, C. (2008). Entrepreneurship, innovation, and wealth distribution: The essence of creative destruction. *International Small Business Journal, 26*(1), 9–23.

Tripodi, J. (2001). Sponsorship: A confirmed weapon in the promotional armoury. *International Journal of Sports Marketing and Sponsorship,* (Mar/Apr), 1–20.

Wennekers, S., & Thurik, R. (1999). Linking entrepreneurship and economic growth. *Small Business Economics, 13,* 27–55.

Sports Entrepreneurship: A Theoretical Approach

DORENE CILETTI

INTRODUCTION

Sport is a dynamic and unique industry that is inherently entrepreneurial on numerous fronts, and while entrepreneurship literature has expanded to include various categories of entrepreneurship, including social, community-based, and corporate entrepreneurship, few connections between sport and entrepreneurship exist in current literature. Santomier (2002) argues that the uniqueness of sport in the U.S. provides "dynamic opportunities for sport entrepreneurs" and yet entrepreneurial contributions "have been undervalued and underemphasized" (p. 5). Plunkett Research (2009, para. 1) notes that "sports provide a lucrative and continually growing marketplace worthy of immense investments," providing not only economic impact, but also entertainment for millions of people globally.

Entrepreneurship is pervasive, crossing industries and organizations, and its role in sports in creating competitive advantage and delivering value to consumers is significant. Entrepreneurship is a necessary component of a successful industry and a healthy economy (Gorman, Hanlon, & King, 1997; Hisrich & Peters, 1998; Jack & Anderson, 1998; Morrison, Rimmington, & Williams, 1999; Henry, Hill, & Leitch, 2003). As competition for consumer dollars increases and globalization presents challenges and opportunities within a complex, changing environment, an entrepreneurial approach may offer insight for sports organizations.

THE IMPACT OF SPORTS

The sports industry is extensive and growing, worth an estimated $600 billion globally. While the global recession impacted sports, opportunities continue to exist, particularly "exciting, high-value opportunities for sports fans" (Plunkett, 2009, para. 13). In the United States alone, the sports market is valued at approximately $400 billion, including the revenue derived from professional sports, sports equipment sales, sports apparel and athletic footwear (Plunkett, 2009, para. 2). PricewaterhouseCoopers estimates global sports spending to increase nearly 4% from 2009 through 2013, from $114 billion to $133 billion (Clark, 2010).

Numerous factors have impacted the consumption of sport. Standeven and DeKnop (1999) refer to the "sportification of society" by changes in social attitudes and values (Jackson, Batty, & Scherer, 2001; Redmond, 1991) as well as politics and economics (Nauright, 1996; Cooper, Fletcher, Gilbert, & Wanhill, 1993; Collins, 1991). Forces that have shaped the consumption of sport include globalization (Bernstein, 2000), democratization (Standeven & DeKnop, 1999), the role of sport and sport events in urban renewal (Getz, 1998), including implications for civic pride and economic development (Groothuis, Johnson, & Whitehead, 2004), and technological advances, including satellite television (Halberstam, 1999).

Sports-related organizations are business enterprises, contributing to the economy and forging connections with multiple stakeholders, including employees, government, consumers, competitors, and the community. Hardy's (1986) conception of the sport industry acknowledges "the dynamic nature of the industry" comprised of "a game form, services, and goods" (p. 19). Porter (2009) addressed the dissolving boundaries between sport and business, suggesting sport history and business history compare notes, as commercialization of sports occurred along with industrialization and urbanization. It has been suggested that lessons learned in sports can be applied in areas such as politics and business (Dyreson, 1999), and that a connection exists between athletic experience and business and politics (Cronin, 2003).

The sport product can be differentiated from other business and consumer products in a number of ways.[1] As a sector, sport is unique in terms of product, market, finance, and promotion (Mullin, Hardy, & Sutton, 2007). Unique concerns impact the business of sports, including the universal appeal and pervasiveness of sport (Mullin et al., 2007); value conceptualized as "more than a mere economic decision" (Wakefield, 2007, p. 3); inconsistency and unpredictability of outcomes (Parks & Zanger, 1990; Mullin et al., 2007); personal identification and deep emotional attachment with athletes and teams (Lever, 1983; Wann & Branscomb, 1993; Sutton et al., 1997; Chalip, 2004; Mullin et al., 2007; Wakefield, 2007); the symbolic nature of athletes and teams in connection with the community (Chalip, 2004); team image and the celebrity status of professional athletes (Mullin et al., 2007);

service elements including perishability as well as its "intangible, ephemeral, experiential, and subjective nature" (Mullin et al., 2007, p. 13); centrality of social facilitation (Mullin et Al., 2007); cooperative efforts between a team and its competitors (Neale, 1964); promotion generated by media, sponsors, and fans (Mullin et al., 2007; Wakefield, 2007); and a long product life cycle curve (Chalip, 2004) coupled with fluctuating, or seasonal, demand (Mullin et al., 2007).

Uniqueness in its relationship with consumers (Mason, 1999) further differentiates sport. Mullin et al. (2007) suggest that people tend to view sport-related experiences as "special" or holding a "special place in their lives," (p. 17) thus consumption is both experiential and emotional. Mason (1999) posits that, while stadium leases, monopolistic broadcasting rights, predetermined geographic territories, and player contracts (Noll, 1974; Zorn, 1994) are distinguishing factors, the relationship sport has with its consumer is the most notable distinction. Richelieu and Boulaire (2005) argue that "with the exception of music, cinema, and religion, there is probably no other field of activity that generates such passion among its customers as sport" (p. 24). Chalip (2004) concurs, noting that unique concerns, including fans' personal identification and deep emotional attachment with athletes and teams, the symbolic nature of athletes and teams in connection with the community, and a long product life cycle curve should be considered.

The uniqueness of sports has lead to the development of specific fields of study related to sport, including sports marketing (Mullin et al., 2007). Irwin, Zwick, and Sutton (1999) concur, noting the unique demands placed on marketers of sport, and this uniqueness requires an approach that may differ from marketing approaches to goods or services. Wakefield (2007) specifically identifies 10 key dimensions through which the marketing of goods and services and the marketing of sports differ, including purchasers, adoption, promotion and media, distribution channel, product, price, facilities, competition, exchange, and employers. Sport has been studied from a variety of different disciplines such as psychology, sociology, philosophy, and marketing (Olivier, 2006); however, less is known about sport in the entrepreneurship discipline, providing an opportunity for study in this area.

CONCEPTUALIZING SPORTS ENTREPRENEURSHIP[2]

Though there seems to be no one universally accepted definition of entrepreneurship (Sullivan Mort, Weerawardena, & Carnegie, 2003; Spencer, Kirchhoff, & White, 2008), it is commonly defined in economic terms related to enterprise (Schumpeter, 1983; Chrisman, Bauerschmidt, & Hofer, 1998; Drucker, 1995). Schneider, Teske, and Mintrom's (1995) market-based model of entrepreneurship addresses the entrepreneurial functions of discovering and meeting unfulfilled needs; assuming risk with uncertainty, including reputational, emotional, and financial risk; and assembling networks capable of undertaking change. Numerous definitions of entrepreneurship include reference to opportunities (Wennekers & Thurik, 1999; Shane & Venkataraman, 2000; Spencer et al., 2008). Morrison (1998) includes both value and opportunity in the definition, acknowledging unique resources. Tan, William, and Tan (2005) develop a definition of entrepreneurship that addresses profits, innovation, and risk. Peredo and McLean (2006) suggest that that earlier entrepreneurship research connects risk taking and innovation to the entrepreneur who strives to create economic value.

Innovation is a cornerstone of entrepreneurship, and commercialization, generally the stage at which opportunity for economic value is pursued, brings ideas, products, services, and experiences to market. Entrepreneurs are characterized by innovation (Timmons, 1978; Schumpeter, 1983; Carland, Hoy, Boulton, & Carland, 1984; Drucker, 1985), and Schumpeter (1983) suggested that entrepreneurial behavior occured when engaging in innovation, and that innovation wasn't simply invention, but rather involved knowledge, resources, and equipment in new ways leading to commercialization. Entrepreneurs "serve as agents of change; provide creative, innovative ideas for business enterprises; and help businesses grow and become profitable" (Kuratko & Hodgetts, 1998). Entrepreneurs recognize and capitalize on opportunities to develop new products and services, establish new ventures, expand on existing offerings, and commercialize ventures. Entrepreneurs tend to seek financial rewards (such as wealth) as well as personal rewards (independence, opportunities) (Boyd & Gumpert, 1983; Burch, 1986). Dees (2001) notes that "being an entrepreneur is associated with starting a business" further addressing the role of entrepreneurs succinctly: "Entrepreneurs create value" (p. 1).

Connecting Sports and Entrepreneurship

Sports and entrepreneurship have been infrequently connected in academic literature. Sport historians Stephen Hardy (1986) and Dilwyn Porter (2009) address sports entrepreneurship in the context of the interrelated histories of business and sport, acknowledging the role of entrepreneurial activity that informs sports. While Stephen Ball connected entrepreneurship to hospitality, leisure, tourism, and sport (2005), his focus was on tourism more so than sports. James Santomier (2002) notes the lack of value and emphasis placed on the development of the sports industry in the United States, suggesting that his brief article on sport business entrepreneurship appearing in the *New England Journal of Entrepreneurship* serve as inspiration for researchers in entrepreneurship and small business to consider sport as a research focus. It does not appear that a steady stream of research in sports entrepreneurship resulted, though in 2010 a special issue on sport entrepreneurship appeared in the *International Journal of Sport Management and Marketing*.[3]

In terms of the potential impact of a connection between sports and entrepreneurship, consider the recent global recession, which has not left the sports industry unaffected (Plunkett, 2009; Clark, 2010). Business cycles, including the recent global recession, present challenges to the sports industry, as "crisis in financial markets is sending a chill through the sports industry. . . . as the upheaval in global markets, mounting job losses in the U.S. and other signs of a worsening economy continue to undermine consumer confidence" (Futterman, 2008, p. B1). An entrepreneurial approach can provide a mechanism for weathering economic crises, as "challenging situations or declining economies" serve as catalysts for the emergence of entrepreneurs (Peredo & Chrisman, 2006, p. 312) and entrepreneurs are more likely to be alert to opportunities and willing to assume risk (Schneider et al., 1995). Entrepreneurial sports organizations may be more likely not only to endure difficult situations but may emerge ready to move forward with new opportunities, thus engaging in value creation.

Bailey (in Ball, 2005) directly connects sports to entrepreneurship, noting, "Entrepreneurship is critical to the hospitality, leisure, sports, and tourism sectors, as with rapidly changing consumer demands and expectations, constant innovation by businesses is vital to meet and, hopefully, exceed these evolving demands and expectations" (p. 5). Discussing the commoditization of the sport product, Sports historian Stephen Hardy (1986, p. 20) notes a move from sport's "rural ethos" to one of "spectacle and profit" along with and the activities of entrepreneurs. Hardy (1996, p. 357) suggests the sports industry should be viewed from the perspective of entrepreneurs "who developed organizations to produce and distribute three-part commodities," recommending that additional research into areas such as life cycles and product development be explored through the lens of the entrepreneur.

While entrepreneurship often includes risk taking and profit seeking, sports entrepreneurs may have been motivated by other factors, such as "civic duty, egotism, and a love of sport as well as a concern for some profit" (Hardy, 1996, p. 348). Sports entrepreneurs, Hardy asserts, more directly fit the model of innovative activity proposed in Schumpeter's seminal work (1983), acknowledging that the oft-associated entrepreneurial activities of risk taking and profit seeking have a place in sports. These early sports entrepreneurs were trailblazers, acting innovatively to bring new entertainment options to market, taking risks in doing so, and proactively moving forward to address unmet needs. This chapter conceptualizes a theory of sports entrepreneurship that, following Ciletti and Ratten (2009), considers the innovation, risk taking, and proactive nature of sports as inherently entrepreneurial.[4]

Innovation in Sports

Innovation has been connected to sport in academic literature.[5] Hardy (1986) notes the importance of innovation in sports entrepreneurship, referring to it as "the hallmark of the sport entrepreneur" (p. 20). Entrepreneurial sports organizations demonstrate innovation in a variety of ways, including technological innovation, product innovation, and promotional innovation. Athletes themselves can also serve as innovators (e.g., Arnold Palmer in golf, Bill Russell in basketball) redefining their sport.[6] Innovation by users has driven technology related to sports equipment (Stricker, 2009), and through competitive events, integration occurs early on for sports equipment users in the innovation process (Desbordes, 2002). Examples of technological innovation can been seen through areas such as sport video and computer games[7] (Mullin et al., 2007), advances developed for sports such as photo finish technology in 1992, and more recently, the use of technology to legitimize the secondary ticket market by organizations such as Ticketmaster and StubHub.

Innovations are also aimed at generating improvements in sport performance, participation, and development. For example, sport-related technological and product innovation has led to new participatory (and often risky) sports such as whitewater kayaking, paragliding, high altitude mountaineering, big wave surfing, and storm chasing (Olivier, 2006) as well as competition opportunities for athletes with differing abilities in the Paralympic Games (Castonguay, 2008). Technological and product innovation has informed the rise of fantasy sports as well, as technology has simplified the formerly labor-intensive statistics involved in fantasy sports leagues (Farquhar & Meeds, 2007). It is estimated that 30 million adults participate in fantasy sports in the US and Canada (Fantasy Sports, 2009, p. 1). Sporting goods manufacturers in golf and snow sports markets continually work with new technologies allowing for adoption of new equipment and clothing (Plunkett, 2009, para. 10). Innovations in licensing have impacted product development (Mullin et al., 2007), including branded clothing and other merchandise bearing likenesses of athletes, sports teams, and sports brands (e.g. Nike, Adidas, etc.).

Innovative promotional approaches have been pioneered by sports organizations (Mullin et al., 2007). Often, technology spurred promotional innovation. Fragmentation in traditional media through the 1990s as well as technological developments led to the use of new media in sports marketing and promotion (Sweeney, 2007), including the World Wide Web, e-mail, blogs, discussion boards and podcasts, as well as social media such as Facebook and Twitter, providing opportunities to both reach and engage sport consumers globally. As noted by Plunkett (2009, para. 11), "Media used to deliver sports and sports-related information is evolving quickly" and further, "sports coverage is one of the most widely viewed categories online." In fact, Fast Company's 2010 list of 10 most innovative sports companies (http://www.fastcompany.com/mic/2010/industry/most-innovative-sports-companies) includes four sports media-related organizations. The list cites ESPN's aggressive expansion and experimentation, Sportvision's technological innovation, MLB Advanced Media's digital streaming and iPhone application, and Turner Sports Interactive's sports sites featuring advanced tools, archives, and advertising strategies.

Proactiveness in Sports

Mullin et al. (2007) suggest that, as a sector, sport is unique in terms of product, market, finance, and promotion, and further that people tend to view sport-related experiences as "special" or holding a "special place in their lives" (p.17). Sport organizations have both direct contact with customers as well as a continuous inflow of new customers (Ioakimidis, 2007), which provides an opportunity to present communications with impact, positioning them to act proactively as change agents. Sports organizations can entrepreneurially demonstrate proactiveness in numerous ways, including addressing areas such as ambush marketing, sustainability, and social change.

Sports organizations have also proactively addressed challenging issues facing businesses. For example, the Olympic organizing committee, according to a spokesperson, was "taking the issue of ambush marketing very seriously. They have been very proactive . . . in a number of cases so far" (Madden, 2007). The National Football League also proactively and publicly spoke out against KFC and what it viewed as ambush marketing prior to Super Bowl 2008. Fast-food restaurant brand KFC offered $260,000 to charity if a player performed the "chicken dance" following a touchdown during the game because they were not an official Super Bowl sponsor. What began as consumer-generated marketing became ambush marketing, according to the NFL, because KFC was not involved with the NFL or Super Bowl as an official sponsor.[8]

Sports organizations have been proactive to some extent in implementing sustainability initiatives into business operations.[9] Sustainability, emerging as an influential concept for organizations and more generally, society, considers people, organizations, and social processes (Elkington, 1998). Eric Falt, Director of Communications for the United Nations Environment Programme, commented for the Global Forum for Sports and Environment (2004), "The choice to look beyond the strict financial bottom line and exercise social and environmental responsibility is one that can be made by everyone involved in sports, including manufacturers, local authorities, event organizers, and even consumers." Jack Groh, environment program director for the National Football League, noted, "What's good for the environment is good for the bottom line," as the NFL works to incorporate environmental responsibility into its bottom line (Falt, 2006, p. A268). Recently, initiatives including the NFL's focus on community, the NHL's focus on the environment, and awareness by professional sports of the benefits of sustainable development relative to sport venues show increased focus on sustainability in sport.

A sport-related organization can serve as a means to development and an agent of social change. Goss and Alexandrova (2005) state this explicitly, referencing the United Nations General Assembly's 2003 special resolution suggesting "sport as a means to promote education, health, development, and peace" (p. 54). In this case, they are asserting the potential for governments to act proactively to include sports in national programs and policies, noting that the UN and non-governmental organizations including Right to Play[10] are using sports to promote peace.

Sports can also play a role as a means to address vulnerable populations. The International Olympic Committee and UNAIDS recognized the power of sports to do this, agreeing to work together to increase HIV/AIDS awareness. Host cities have increasingly utilized the connection to sports, particularly sports events, to address social issues (Kott, 2005). Recognizing the potential impact of sports in social change, Nike has engaged in several initiatives in this realm. Through its Changemakers program, Nike partnered with Ashoka to host the Sport for a Better World competition, seeking innovative ways for sport to affect social change.[11] The competition drew 382 entries from 69 countries that were judged on innovation, social impact, and sustainability.[12] Winning projects included: development of a sport-based curriculum to educate young people about living AIDS-free; making sports coaches available at urban school playgrounds in the United States to teach kids how to play which enhances social development; and the use of text messaging as a vehicle for promoting job and social opportunities grounded in sports due youth having widespread access to mobile phones but limited access to the internet, so text messaging could be used more effectively in Brazil. Nike and Ashoka have continued their partnership. A current competition, Changing Lives through Football, seeks innovative ways to use football for social change.[13]

Nike is also supporting global humanitarian organization CARE International and its Sport for Social Change initiative, harnessing the "power of sport" to create "lasting individual and social change."[14] Programs are currently in place in Rwanda, Sierra Leone, Kenya, Zambia, Uganda, Brazil, and Ghana. The Sport for Social Change initiative is focused on vulnerable populations, using sport to address poverty, deliver HIV/AIDS information, build self-esteem and leadership skills in women and girls, promote teamwork and conflict resolution, and provide a means for economic empowerment.

Risk Taking in Sports

When sports organizations strive to innovate and take a proactive approach, a subsequent level of risk is involved. Athletes also encounter varying levels of physical risk by participating in sports, ranging from relatively low-risk sports such as curling to high-risk extreme sports such as freestyle motocross. The uncertainty of sport contest outcomes also lends an element of risk for the contenders.

From an organizational perspective, Kedar-Levy and Bar-Eli (2008) noted the connection between innovation and risk taking in sports organizations, further connecting business risk and social risk. Business risk includes financial ownership risk, with sports team owners looking for fun and power in exchange for financial risk (Zimbalist, 2003). Sports organizations regularly assume risk regarding a myriad of decisions involving the business of sports including expansion, funding, employee/athlete contracts, and licensing, as well as marketplace risks related to economic (e.g., consumer income and spending) and legal/political (e.g., regulatory and tax changes) issues. Consider the risks assumed by sports team owners offering multimillion dollar athlete contracts while facing the risks involved with on-field performance, off-field behavior, and the impact of the contract on salary caps.

Socially, sport has been utilized as a mechanism for breaking down barriers, serving as a change agent and assuming social risk. For example, Jackie Robinson broke racial barriers and was known as a civil rights pioneer in the United States as the first African American to play major league baseball as a member of the Brooklyn Dodgers, and Gertrude Ederle demonstrated the ability of women to excel in athletics when she became the first woman to swim the English Channel (Smithsonian Institution, n.d.).

Furthering Entrepreneurial Connections with Sports

Contemporary entrepreneurship research considers specific categories of entrepreneurship, and several of these categories of entrepreneurship literature lend themselves to further exploration relative to sport. In community-based entrepreneurship, Peredo and Chrisman (2006) suggest "the community is simultaneously both the enterprise and the entrepreneur," (p. 311) noting the local connection. Julie Clark, author of PricewaterhouseCoopers' global sports market outlook report (2010) suggests that sports organizations should "think globally and act locally" (p. 2). Sports organizations can engage in community-based entrepreneurship in many ways. Johannisson and Nilsson (1989) connected community interaction with development, and Goss and Alexandrova (2005) note the connection between sport and development. CARE International's Sport for Social Change initiative connects sport to designated communities, with a goal of economic empowerment for vulnerable populations.[15] Sports organizations also engage in community development initiatives. For example, the NFL's Pittsburgh Steelers organization is involved in a number of community-related initiatives, including the Arthur J. Rooney Courage House Luncheon benefiting Holy Family Institute; the Steelers Style fashion show and the Taste of the Steelers dinner and auction which both benefit the Thomas E. Starzl Transplantation Institute at University of Pittsburgh Medical Center and the Cancer Caring Center; the Gala Pittsburgh Sports Night event benefiting Cardinal Wright Regional School on Pittsburgh's North Side (the neighborhood in which founder Art Rooney grew up); and the 9th Grade Nation initiative to bring together freshman enrolled in Pittsburgh city schools to motivate them to achieve academically.[16]

Sports organizations connect with the community through the symbolic nature of athletes and teams (Chalip, 2004). Sports organizations can themselves form—or act as the common bond in the formation of—communities, for example Steeler Nation, a name given to Pittsburgh Steelers fan community by NFL Films (Mehno, 2004), and the online communities of fantasy sports (Roy & Goss, 2007). A recent innovation in sports team ownership and formation of a sports community is demonstrated by the development of United Kingdom-based MyFootballClub.com, a Web-based organization that touts itself as the "world's local football club," the first web-community owned venture.[17]

While community-based entrepreneurship makes mention of social needs (De Leeuw, 1999; Dupuis & de Bruin, 2003), the term *social entrepreneurship* is thought to be coined by Ashoka founder William Drayton (Davis, 2002), who asserted that social entrepreneurs solved social problems (Drayton, 2002). A common theme in conceptualizing social entrepreneurship is creation or maximization of social value over private value (Dees, 2001; Davis, 2002; Sullivan, et al., 2003). Another is an emphasis on problem solving (Johnson, 2003). Austin, Stevenson, and Wei-Skillern (2006) propose a social value framework, where social value exists at the intersection of people, opportunity, and capital, with consideration of the external context, or forces, affecting the entrepreneurial venture. Both sports organizations and athletes have engaged in social entrepreneurship initiatives. Ashoka partnered with Nike's Changemakers program to host several competitions seeking social change through sport.[18] Olympic gold medalist Johann Koss founded Right to Play, a global organization that works to improve the lives of disadvantaged youth through sport, using a model that includes athlete ambassadors.[19]

CONCLUSION[20]

The uniqueness of sport and its entrepreneurial nature provide an opportunity to examine it within the context of entrepreneurship. The entrepreneurial effort of both organizations and individuals has been significant in the history of sports, and as sports organizations face challenges—including increased entertainment offerings and the shattering of traditional media by the advent and adoption of accessible digital technology (Sweeney, 2007), the growing economic disconnect between consumers and professional sports teams (Araton, 1998; Dortch, 1996), problematic off-field athlete behavior, consumer apathy (McGraw, 1998), and concern regarding environmental degradation (Sweeney, 2007)—it becomes increasingly imperative to deliver value, and an entrepreneurial approach warrants consideration. Thus, both academics and practitioners can benefit from consideration of sports entrepreneurship. While a direct connection between sports and entrepreneurship is not always noted, examples of sports organizations engaging in entrepreneurial initiatives involving innovation, risk, and a proactive approach are plentiful. Further research can investigate connections between entrepreneurship and various sports disciplines, including sports marketing and sports management.

Endnotes

1. This discussion was initially formulated in Ciletti, D. (2009.) and further in Ciletti & Ratten (2009).

2. This discussion first appeared in part in Ciletti, D. & Ratten, V. (2009). Toward a theory of sports entrepreneurship. Unpublished manuscript in author's possession.

3. See the *International Journal of Sport Management and Marketing*, Vol. 7, Nos. 1/2, guest edited by Ratten and Ciletti, http://www.inderscience.com/browse/index.php?jour nalID=102&year=2010&vol=7&issue=1/2

4. See also Holt, D., Rutherford, M., and Clohessy, G. (2007). Corporate entrepreneurship: An empirical look at individual characteristics, context, and process. *Journal of Leadership & Organizational Studies*, *13*(4), 40–54.

5. As in Mullin, B., Hardy, J., and Sutton, W. (2007) *Sport Marketing* (3rd Ed.), Champaign, IL: Human Kinetics and Schwarz, E. and Hunter, J. (2008). *Advanced Theory and Practice in Sport Marketing*, Oxford, UK: Butterworth-Heinemann.

6. See http://americanhistory.si.edu/sports/exhibit/gamemakers/index.cfm

7. As of 2008, Odyssey reported that sports games were the third most popular gaming category. See Odyssey (2008, October 20). Music simulations come from nowhere to overtake sports as second most played video game genre. *PR Newswire Release*, http://www .prnewswire.com/cgi-bin/stories.pl?ACCT=109&STORY=/www/story/10-20-2008/000490 7661&EDATE=

8. See http://www.bostonherald.com/sports/football/patriots/view.bg?articleid=10 68877 and http://www.mediapost.com/publications/index.cfm?fa=Articles.showArti cle&art_aid=74871

9. This discussion was initially formulated in Ciletti, D. (2009.) and further in Ciletti & Ratten (2009).

10. See http://www.righttoplay.com/In ternational/Pages/Home.aspx

11. See http://www.changemakers.com /node/728

12. See http://inside.nike.com/blogs/ga mechangers-en_US/2008/07/09/sport-for-a-better-world and http://www.change makers.com/node/728

13. See http://www.changemakers.com /football

14. See http://www.care.org/careswork /whatwedo/initiatives/sportforsocialchange.asp

15. See http://www.care.org/careswork /whatwedo/initiatives/sportforsocialchange.asp

16. See http://www.steelers.com

17. See http://www.myfootballclub.co.uk

18. See http://www.changemakers.com /node/728 and http://inside.nike.com/blogs /gamechangers-en_US/2008/07/09/sport-for-a-better-world

19. See http://www.righttoplay.com/In ternational/Pages/Home.aspx

20. This discussion was initially formulated in Ciletti, D. (2009) and further in Ciletti & Ratten (2009).

References

Araton, H. (1998, October 18). Bizball. *New York Times Magazine*. Retrieved from http://www.nytimes.com/1998/10/18/magazine/bizball.html

Austin, J., Stevenson, H., & Wei-Skillern, J. (2006). Social and commercial entrepreneurship: Same, different or both? *Entrepreneurship Theory and Practice*, *30*(1), 1–22.

Ball, S. (2005, May). The importance of entrepreneurship to hospitality, leisure, sport, and tourism. *Hospitality, Leisure, Sport and Tourism Network*, 1–14.

Bernstein, A. (2000). Things you can see from there you can't see from here: Globalization, media, and the Olympics. *Journal of Sport and Social Issues*, *24*, 351–369.

Boyd, D., & Gumpert, D. (1983). Coping with entrepreneurial stress. *Harvard Business Review*, *61*(March–April), 44–64.

Burch, J. (1986). *Entrepreneurship*. New York: John Wiley and Sons.

Carland, J. W., Hoy, F., Boulton, W. R., & Carland, J. C. (1984). Differentiating entrepreneurs from small business owners: A conceptualization. *Academy of Management Review*, *9*, 354–359.

Castonguay, S. (2008). Technology, innovation and grit: Faster, higher, stronger in disabled sports. *WIPO Magazine*, *4*, 3–5.

Retrieved from http://www.wipo.int/wipo_magazine/en/2008/04/article_0002.html

Chalip, L. (2004). Beyond impact: A general model for host community event leverage. In B. Ritchie & D. Adair (Eds.), *Sport tourism: Interrelationships, impacts and issues* (pp. 226–252). Clevedon, UK: Channel View Publications.

Chrisman, J., Bauerschmidt, A., & Hofer, C. (1998). The determinants of new venture performance: An extended model. *Entrepreneurship Theory and Practice, 23*(1), 5–29.

Ciletti, D. (2009). *Marketing otherwise in sports: Exploring the communicative intersection of marketing and sustainability within limits.* Gumberg Library Digital Collections, Electronic Dissertation and Theses & Dissertations. Abstract retrieved from http://etd.library.duq.edu/cdm-etd/document.php?CISOROOT=/etd&CISOPTR=110562&REC=1

Ciletti, D., & Ratten, V. (2009). *Toward a theory of sports entrepreneurship.* Unpublished manuscript in author's possession.

Clark, J. (2010). Back on track? The outlook for the global sports market to 2013. UK PricewaterhouseCoopers. Retrieved from http://www.pwc.com/gx/en/press-room/2010/think-global-win-local-succeed-in-global-sports.jhtml

Collins, M. F. (1991). The economics of sport and sports in the economy: Some international comparisons. In C. P. Cooper (Ed.), *Progress in tourism, recreation and hospitality management* (pp. 184–214). London: Bellhaven Press.

Cooper, C., Fletcher, J., Gilbert, D., & Wanhill, S. (1993). *Tourism: Principles and practice.* Harlow, UK: Longman Group.

Cronin, M. (2003). Playing games? The serious business of sports history. *Journal of Contemporary History, 38*, 435–460.

Davis, S. (2002). Social entrepreneurship: Towards an entrepreneurial culture for social and economic development. *Youth Employment Summit.* Retrieved from ashoka.org/files/yespaper.pdf

Dees, J. (2001). The meaning of "social entrepreneurship." Stanford University: Report for the Kauffman Center for Entrepreneurial Leadership. Retrieved from http://cdi.mecon.gov.ar/biblio/docelec/dp4012.pdf

De Leeuw, E. (1999). Healthy cities: Urban social entrepreneurship for health. *Health Promotion International, 14*, 261–269.

Desbordes, M. (2002). Empirical analysis of the innovation phenomena in the sports equipment industry. *Technology Analysis & Strategic Management, 14*, 481–498.

Dortch, S. (1996, April). The future of baseball. *American Demographics, 1*(4), 22.

Drayton, W. (2002). The citizen sector: Becoming as competitive and entrepreneurial as business. *California Management Journal, 12*(1), 29–43.

Drucker, P. (1985). *Innovation and entrepreneurship.* New York: Harper & Row.

Drucker, P. (1995). *Managing in a time of great change.* New York: Truman Talley Books/Dutton.

Dupuis, A., & de Bruin, A. (2003). Community entrepreneurship. In A. de Bruin & A. Dupuis (Eds.), *Entrepreneurship: New perspectives in a global age* (pp. 109–127). Burlington, VT: Ashgate Publishing Company.

Dyreson, M. (2001). Maybe it's better to bowl alone: Sport, community and democracy in American thought. *Culture, Sport and Society, 4*(1), 19–30.

Dyreson, M. (1999). Nature by design: Modern American ideas about sport, energy, evolution, and republics, 1865–1920. *Journal of Sport History, 26*, 460.

Elkington, J. (1998). *Cannibals with forks: The triple bottom line of 21st century business.* Philadelphia: New Society.

Falt, E. (2006). Sport and the environment. *Environmental Health Perspectives, 114*, A268–A269.

Fantasy Sports Trade Association. (2009). Media Kit. Retrieved from http://www.fsta.org/FSTA_MK_031810_0510.pdf

Farquhar, L. K., & Meeds, R. (2007). Types of fantasy sports users and their motivations. *Journal of Computer-Mediated Communication, 12*(4), article 4. Retrieved from http://jcmc.indiana.edu/vol12/issue4/farquhar.html

Futterman, M. (2008, October 14). As economy weakens, sports feel a chill. *Wall Street Journal* (Eastern Edition), p. B1.

Gartner, W. (1988). Who is an entrepreneur? Is the wrong question. *American Journal of Small Business, 12*, 11–31.

Getz, D. (1998). Trends, strategies, and issues in sport-event tourism. *Sport Marketing Quarterly, 7*(2), 8–13.

Gorman, G., Hanlon, D., & King, W. (1997). Some research perspectives on entrepreneurship education, enterprise education, and education for small business management: A ten-year literature review. *International Small Business Journal, 15*(3), 56–77.

Goss, J., & Alexandrova, A. (2005). HIV/AIDS prevention and peace through sport. *Lancet, 366,* S3–S4.

Groothuis, P., Johnson, B., & Whitehead, J. (2004). Public funding of professional sports stadiums: Public choice or civic pride? *Eastern Economic Journal, 30,* 515–526.

Halberstam, D. (1999). *Playing for keeps: Michael Jordan and the world he made.* New York: Random House.

Hardy, S. (1996). Entrepreneurs, organizations, and the sport marketplace. In S. Pope (Ed.), *The New American Sport History* (pp. 341–365). Champaign, IL: University of Illinois Press.

Hardy, S. (1986). Entrepreneurs, organizations, and the sport marketplace: Subjects in search of historians. *Journal of Sport History, 13*(1), 14–33.

Henry, C., Hill, F., & Leitch, C. (2003). *Entrepreneurship education and training.* Aldershot, UK: Ashgate Publishing.

Hisrich, R., & Peters, M. (1998). *Entrepreneurship: Starting, developing, and managing a new enterprise* (4th ed.). Chicago, IL: Irwin.

Ioakimidis, M. (2007). Green sport: A game everyone wins. *The Sport Journal, 10*(2), 4.

Irwin, R., Zwick, D., & Sutton, W. A. (1999). Assessing organizational attributes contributing to marketing excellence in American professional sports franchises. *European Journal of Marketing, 33*(4/5), 314–328.

Jack, S. & Anderson, A. (1999). Entrepreneurship education within the enterprise culture: Producing reflective practitioners. *International Journal of Entrepreneurial Behaviour & Research, 5,* 110–125.

Jackson, S. J., Batty, R., & Scherer, J. (2001). Transnational sport marketing at the global/local nexus: The Adidasification of the New Zealand All Blacks. *International Journal of Sports Marketing and Sponsorship, 3,* 185–201.

Johannisson, B., & Nilsson, A. (1989). Community entrepreneurs: Networking for local development. *Journal of Entrepreneurship and Regional Development, 1*(1), 3–19.

Johnson, S. (2003). Young social entrepreneurs in Canada. Alberta: *Canadian Centre for Social Entrepreneurship.* Retrieved from http://www.socialinnovationexchange.org/node/105

Kedar-Levy, H., & Bar-Eli, M. (2008). The valuation of athletes as risky investments: A theoretical model. *Journal of Sport Management, 22*(1), 50–81.

Koss, J. O., & Alexandrova, A. (2005). HIV/AIDS prevention and peace through sport. *Lancet, 366,* 53–54.

Kott, A. (2005). The philanthropic power of sport. *Foundation News and Commentary,* January/February, 20–25.

Kuratko, D. F., & Hodgetts, R. M. (1998). *Entrepreneurship: A contemporary approach.* New York: Harcourt Brace.

Lever, J. (1983). *Soccer madness.* Chicago: University of Chicago Press.

Madden, N. (2007, July 23). Ambush marketing could hit new high at Beijing Olympics; Can a country known for piracy problems ensure only official sponsors will be associated with games? *Advertising Age,* 22.

Mason, D. (1999). What is the sports product and who buys it? The marketing of professional sports leagues. *European Journal of Marketing, 33,* 402–418.

McGraw, D. (1998). Big team troubles. *US News and World Report, 125,* 40–46.

Mehno, J. (2004, November). Birth of a nation: Capturing the identity of a region. *Pittsburgh Sports Report.* Retrieved from http://www.pghsports.com/2004-Issues/psr0411/04110101.html

Morrison, A. (1998) Entrepreneurs or intrapreneurs, In C. Lashley & A. Morrison (Eds.), *Franchising hospitality services* (pp. 68–91). Oxford, UK: Butterworth-Heinemann.

Morrison, A., Rimmington, M., & Williams, C. (1999). *Entrepreneurship in the hospitality, tourism, and leisure industries.* Oxford, UK: Butterworth-Heinemann.

Mullin, B., Hardy, J., & Sutton, W. (2007) *Sport marketing* (3rd ed.). Champaign, IL: Human Kinetics.

Nauright, J. (1996). Writing and reading American football: Culture, identities, and sport studies. *Sporting Traditions, 13*(1), 109–127.

Neale, W. C. (1964). The peculiar economics of professional sports. *Quarterly Journal of Economics, 78,* 1–14.

Noll, R. (1974). *Government and the sports business.* Washington, DC: The Brookings Institution.

Olivier, S. (2006). Moral dilemmas of participation in dangerous leisure activities. *Leisure Studies, 25*(1), 95–109.

Parks, J., & Zanger, B. (1990). *Sport and fitness management.* Champaign, IL: Human Kinetics.

Peredo, A., & Chrisman, J. (2006). Toward a theory of community-based enterprise.

Academy of Management Review, 31, 309–328.

Peredo, A., & McLean, M. (2006). Social entrepreneurship: a critical review of the concept. *Journal of World Business, 41*(1), 56–65.

Plunkett Research (2009). Introduction to the sports industry. *Sports Industry Trends.* Retrieved from http://www.plunkettresearch.com/Industries/Sports/SportsTrends/tabid/274/Default.aspx

Porter, D. (2009). Entrepreneurship and sport history. In S. W. Pope and J. Nauright (Eds.), *Routledge Companion to Sports History* (pp. 197–215). New York: Routledge.

Redmond, G. (1991). Changing styles of sports tourism: industry/consumer interactions in Canada, the USA, and Europe. In M. T. Sinclair & M. J. Stabler, (Eds.). *The tourism industry: An international analysis* (pp. 107–120). Wallingford, UK: CAB International.

Richelieu, A., & Boulaire, C. (2005). A postmodern conception of the product and its application to professional sport. *International Journal of Sports Marketing and Sponsorship, 7*(1), 23–34.

Roy, D., & Goss, B. (2007). A conceptual framework of influences on fantasy sports consumption. *Marketing Management Journal, 17,* 96–108.

Santomier, J. (2002). Sport business entrepreneurship. *New England Journal of Entrepreneurship, 5*(1), 5–7.

Schneider, M., Teske, P., & Mintrom, M. (1995). *Public entrepreneurs: Agents for change in American government.* Princeton, NJ: Princeton University Press.

Schumpeter, J. (1965). Economic theory and entrepreneurial history, In H. G. Aitken (Ed.), *Explorations in enterprise.* Cambridge, MA: Harvard University Press.

Schumpeter, J. (1983). *The theory of economic development: An inquiry into profits, capital, credit, interest, and the business cycle.* New Brunswick, NJ: Transaction Books.

Shane, S., & Venkataraman, S. (2000). The promise of entrepreneurship as a field of research. *Academy of Management Review, 25*(1), 217–226.

Smithsonian Institution (n.d.). *Sports: Breaking records, breaking barriers.* Retrieved from http://americanhistory.si.edu/sports/exhibit/firsts/ederle/index.cfm.

Spencer, A., Kirchhoff, B., & White, C. (2008). Entrepreneurship, innovation, and wealth distribution: The essence of creative destruction. *International Small Business Journal, 26*(1), 9–23.

Standeven, J., & Deknop, P. (1999). *Sport tourism.* Champaign, IL: Human Kinetics.

Stricker, C. (2009, September 14). A mutual finish line. *Public Service Review: Science & Technology, 4.* Retrieved from http://www.publicservice.co.uk/article.asp?publication=Science%20and%20Technology&id=397&content_name=Research%20across%20Europe&article=12648

Sullivan Mort, G., Weerawardena, J., & Carnegie, K. (2003). Social entrepreneurship: Towards conceptualization. *International Journal of Non-Profit & Voluntary Sector Marketing, 8*(1), 76–88.

Sutton, W. A., McDonald, M. A., Milne, G. R., & Cimperman, J. (1997). Creating and fostering fan identification in professional sports. *Sport Marketing Quarterly, 6*(1), 15–22.

Sweeney, J. (2007). Sportscast: 10 controversial issues confronting the sports industry. *The Futurist, 41*(1), 35–39.

Tan, W.L., Williams, J., & Tan, T. M. (2005). Defining the "social" in "social entrepreneurship": Altruism and entrepreneurship. *International Entrepreneurship and Management Journal, 1,* 353–365.

Timmons, J. (1978). Characteristics and role demands of entrepreneurship. *American Journal of Small Business, 3*(1), 5–17.

Wennekers, S., & Thurik, R. (1999). Linking entrepreneurship and economic growth. *Small Business Economics, 13,* 27–55.

Wakefield, K. L. (2007). *Team sports marketing.* Oxford, UK: Butterworth-Heinemann.

Wann, D. L., & Branscombe, N. R. (1993). Sports fans: Measuring degree of identification with their team. *International Journal of Sport and Exercise Psychology, 24,* 1–17.

Wiggins, R., & Ruefli, T. (2005). Schumpeter's ghost: Is hypercompetition making the best of times shorter? *Strategic Management Journal, 26,* 887–911.

Yusuf, A., & Schindehutte, M. (2000). Exploring entrepreneurship in a declining economy. *Journal of Developmental Entrepreneurship, 5*(1), 41–57.

Zimbalist, A. (2003). Sport as business. *Oxford Review of Economic Policy, 19,* 503–511.

Zorn, S. (1994). Couldna done it without the players: Depreciation of professional sports player contracts under the Internal Revenue Code. *Seton Hall Journal of Sports Law, 4,* 337–395.

2

Building an Entrepreneurial Sports Empire: The Case of Red Bull

NICHOLAS BURTON, SIMON CHADWICK, AND SAMANTHA GORSE

INTRODUCTION

Bill Gates. Richard Branson. Phil Knight. They are three of the world's most famous and recognizable entrepreneurs. Each has built their fortune on a foundation of risk, uncertainty, and daring, taking advantage of opportunities presented to them (or indeed that they create themselves), where others fail to see potential. These individuals have become renowned for their business acumen and success, becoming celebrities in their own right, and gaining near brand status of their own. Yet few would include the name Dietrich Mateschitz—the man behind one of the world's most recognizable brands, Red Bull—on a list of the world's top entrepreneurs. Much like Knight and Gates before him, Mateschitz capitalized on an opportunity, and now commands over 70% of the energy drink market, in over 100 countries around the world (Gschwandtner, 2004). As such, this case explores how Mateschitz, a former toothpaste salesman from Austria, built an international brand based on an innovative and controversial marketing strategy, and what role sport has played in giving the Red Bull brand its wings.

Understanding Mateschitz's success, the entrepreneurship behind the man, and the growth of the Red Bull brand, should begin by first assessing what entrepreneurship actually entails. The idea of entrepreneurial spirit can be traced back to the Roman Empire, yet the actual term "entrepreneur" was first utilized by international banker Richard Cantillon, in 1755, defining it as "self-employment of any and every sort" (Long, 1983). Over time, others have contributed to the debate of what an entrepreneur is, with a particular economic focus. However, with little consensus of a definition achieved, Howorth et al. (2005) suggested that many of the existing definitions of entrepreneurship are "insufficient" and need to be combined to fully reflect the complex nature of and influential factors on an entrepreneur. Bygrave & Minniti (2000) suggested that "entrepreneurs are people who show initiative, imagination, creativity, and flexibility. They are willing to think conceptually and to see change as an opportunity."

Equally, a number of ways in which individuals can pursue this entrepreneurial spirit have been suggested, including: (a) new products or services, (b) new methods of production, (c) new markets, (d) new sources of supply, and (e) new forms of organization, or through a combination of these (Schumpeter, 1974). Whilst there is no denying the importance and relevance of these ways of demonstrating entrepreneurial spirit, in this case study it can be argued that a sixth method has emerged by which an entrepreneur can exploit the opportunities presented—by utilizing innovative marketing strategies, philosophies, or techniques—and that it is the use of this new, sixth method that could be used to distinguish sports entrepreneurs from entrepreneurs in other industries.

RED BULL TAKES FLIGHT . . .

In 1982, while working for the toothpaste company Blendax, now part of Proctor & Gamble, businessman Dietrich Mateschitz stumbled across a Thai energy drink called Krateng Daeng. Excited by the product, and recognizing a gap in the global marketplace for such a drink, Mateschitz licensed the formula for Krateng Daeng (directly translated as "Red Water Buffalo") from TC Pharmaceuticals, a Blendax licensee. In 1984, following negotiations with TC Pharmaceuticals and Krateng Daeng's creators, Red Bull GmbH was founded in Mateschitz's native Austria, after the original beverage was diluted and carbonated (it was thought that the original drink was too sweet and thick for a global market). Thai partners, Chaleo and Chalerm Yoovidhya, from TC Pharmaceuticals, retained 49% ownership of the new company (Mateschitz also owns 49%; the other 2% is held in trust).

In 1987, three years after establishing the company, and following extensive product testing and market research, the newly formulated Red Bull was approved and launched in Austria. Five years were spent concentrating on establishing the product and building its brand identity in the Austrian market, and on developing marketing and expansion strategies for the company's European growth. Red Bull was launched in Hungary and Slovenia in 1992, followed by Germany and Switzerland two years later. Mateschitz then targeted the lucrative North American market, first introducing the energy drink in California in 1997.

By 2004, Red Bull had achieved worldwide distribution in an industry worth more than €2.5 billion. The decision to enter markets in this order was an early indication as to the nature of Mateschitz's business development plan, and how he subsequently marketed the core product. There are a number of pertinent questions that could be asked here that will be answered in this chapter: why didn't Red Bull launch straight into the lucrative but highly competitive North American market, which would potentially lead to greater rewards more quickly than some of the smaller markets chosen? Would this have led to a wider, more mainstream appeal of the brand? Did Mateschitz want mainstream appeal or did he set out to establish a counterculture or "antibrand" ideology? Was the order of market entry a deliberate attempt to develop this ideology before the core product was widely available to consumers across its target markets?

Ultimately, the success of Mateschitz and of Red Bull to date lies in the strategy behind its growth, and the slow build that guided the brand's early years. Red Bull is marketed as a brand and an ideology, not as an energy drink—its core product. It is how Mateschitz decided to market the brand, by targeting particular groups of consumers in the market to build an antibrand, or counterculture ideology (discussed later in this chapter), that distinguishes him from the likes of Branson or Gates, whose successes have been achieved largely through the mainstream. Mateschitz recognized the power of sport as an industry to access and engage with many of the target markets identified by the company, and defined the energy drink sector as an industry leader and pioneer. The sport industry, today worth an estimated $141 billion (Klayman, 2009), offers massive potential for revenue generation on a global scale for all parties involved; Red Bull, in building a brand based on extreme sports and fast living, has capitalized on this global marketplace.

In analyzing Mateschitz and the case of Red Bull, we set out here to identify the brand positioning and marketing strategies underlying Mateschitz's entrepreneurial success as well as to highlight key constructs in the strategies employed, with the intent of providing benchmarks for prospective sport entrepreneurs.

THE RED BULL BRAND

Red Bull as a sport entrepreneurship case study begins with the development of the Red Bull product and brand, and the underlying image and identity bred within the organization since its introduction. Built on foundations of perseverance, masculinity, identity, credibility and authenticity, the Red Bull brand has become a prime example of the potential that antibrands have in today's marketplace. Through intelligent marketing, and patient, strategic growth from local distribution to international market dominance,

Red Bull has defined the energy drinks industry and succeeded in building a brand ubiquitous in popular culture and action sports, as well as making strides into traditional media and sports over time.

Faced with legal barriers and difficulties in launching the product internationally during its early years, Mateschitz and his team conducted extensive market research between 1984 and 1986 while awaiting product approval, testing over 200 packaging options prior to their Austrian launch in 1987, which laid the foundation for the company's brand identity (Keller, 2002). The logo concept for the new brand, two charging bulls, was taken from the existing Krateng Daeng product, as was its name, translated into English. As well as differentiating the brand from other canned beverages, such as Pepsi or Coca-Cola, the distinctive colors, the can's shape and dimensions, and its general design served to emphasize the difference between Red Bull and other carbonated drinks. Red Bull also sought to stand out from the crowd by setting higher prices than competing brands, seeking to reinforce the product's efficacy and status, and establishing the company as a premium brand in the eyes of consumers. In avoiding direct competition with industry leaders in carbonated and caffeinated drinks, Mateschitz succeeded in positioning the new product as something different, something unique, with which to present consumers.

More importantly, however, was the innovative, and yet simplified, marketing undertaken by the brand in its development and expansion through markets across Europe. Mateschitz is quoted as saying "We don't bring the product to the people. We bring the people to the product" ("Selling energy," 2002), highlighting the fundamental principles of marketing utilized by Red Bull in the development of the brand's ethos and mystique. Rather than approaching marketing from a universal, top down approach as typified by larger, broader reaching companies like the big two soft drinks marques, Red Bull employed decentralized sales and marketing teams, building the Red Bull brand from the ground-up. Regional sales and marketing representatives established awareness amongst cultural icons, focusing on local and influential DJs, clubbers, ravers, and social trendsetters, growing the brand's identity through word of mouth. Spurred on by the influence and added awareness provided by early adopters and the social elite, combined with its growing popularity as a mixer drink for vodka, Red Bull succeeded in entering new markets on the back of a known and authentic presence amongst consumers, further defining the brand, and affording the company the opportunity to dictate supply and drive demand. Students and truck drivers, too, soon discovered and spread the product's awareness, offering authoritative evidence of its ability to provide energy and keep consumers awake. Such control over the product's release and availability, although partially necessitated by legal complications and the gradual entry of the drink into different countries, added to Red Bull's mystique and created an exaggerated demand in student and bar-hopping circles, defining the brand as a

Generation X standard, and earning the title "the poor man's cocaine" (Gschwandtner, 2004).

Eventually, Red Bull's early focus on influential, night-life enjoying European Generation Xers as a means of entering new markets and creating brand awareness across borders, evolved Red Bull into a generation-defining product for Generation Y. Immensely popular and visible throughout popular culture, sports—both traditional and extreme/adventure—and nightlife (bars and clubbing), Red Bull emerged in North America during the late-1990s and early 2000s, slowly crossing the continent in much the same way European markets were conquered. Beginning with regionalized sales and buzz marketing strategies in California similar to those used in its European expansion, Red Bull took five years to establish a sales presence across the United States, again building the brand's name and identity slowly and organically through what the company referred to as a 'seeding program.' Targeting specific stores, bars, clubs, and gas stations in order to restrict and control access to the product, Red Bull secured added 'cachet' to the brand, a mystique and intrigue that drove Red Bull's brand in its early years. Again focusing on building an attachment to trendy nightlight spots and student life, regionalized marketing and sales directors focused on bars and stores near universities, and specifically employed students as brand representatives, as means of establishing a presence within the Generation Y community.

RED BULL ENTERS SPORT

As well as cementing Red Bull's place with trendy, influential Generation X and Yers, Red Bull soon sought to establish the brand as a sports property, beginning with its early marketing as a provider of energy and added stamina. Credited with creating the energy drinks market as we know it today, Red Bull avoided competing directly with both established carbonated drinks, such as Pepsi or Coke, as well as better-known sports drinks like Gatorade, while establishing a presence in both sport and popular culture all the same.

Red Bull's place in sport, as well as positioning its energy drink as being beneficial for athletes and a driver of performance, has led to the creation both of new and innovative sports properties, and of the sponsorship and eventual ownership of mainstream sports properties. The first such involvement came in 1991, with the creation of the Red Bull Flugtag event, first hosted in Vienna, Austria. The Flugtag, which calls on participants to design and build flying contraptions to be launched off a 9.1 m high ramp, signalled Red Bull's intentions as a brand both in building a repertoire in sport, and perhaps just as crucially, in developing the brand as a prominent figure in the world of extreme sports. Aligning perfectly with Red Bull's "Gives You Wings" slogan and ethos, the Flugtag event opened the sports market to

Mateschitz and the Red Bull brand, and offered the company a place in the emerging extreme sports industry.

Since the advent of the Flugtag event, Red Bull have been ever-present in adventure and 'new-age' sports, spending an estimated $300 million per year on sport marketing (Curtis, 2006); sponsoring and heavily branding over 500 action sport events and athletes, including free-runners, snowboarders, and sky-divers; and further solidifying their reputation as a counter-culture brand with new events, such as Red Bull Crashed Ice and the Red Bull Air Race. As with the company's initial marketing activities and the establishment as a Generation X icon, Red Bull's involvement in, and support of, extreme sports and sub-cultural events has reaffirmed the brand's values and identity, and highlighted the company's unique interests, and its relationship with consumers. Moreover, Red Bull's involvement in newly created sports and non-traditional adventure sports that were on the margins of mainstream popularity in the 1990s, opened the door for Mateschitz to enter more traditional, high-profile sports with a degree of authority and authenticity—key elements of Red Bull's brand identity—both as an established drinks company, and as a brand with a successful sporting history.

Dating back to the creation of the Red Bull Crashed Ice event in 2000, Mateschitz, under the Red Bull name, has amassed an arguably unrivalled international sporting empire, boasting ownership of, among others: EC Red Bull Salzburg (Erste Bank Hockey League, Austria), FC Red Bull Salzburg (Austrian Bundesliga), Formula One teams Red Bull Racing and Scuderia Toro Rosso, Major League Soccer's New York Red Bulls, NASCAR's Team Red Bull, Red Bull Brasil FC (Segunda Divisão Paulista, Brazilian second division), and most recently, fifth division German football club SSV Markranstädt, to be renamed RB Leipzig. Outside the realm of sports, Red Bull have maintained a presence in the consciousness of Generation X and Y, as well, operating a Red Bull Music Academy for up and coming DJs worldwide, creating the Taurus World Stunt Awards, and actively participating in urban art, underground nightlife, street parades, and music festivals. This growth, although staggered over the past decade, has equally seen a pronounced shift in Red Bull's direction as a company. Now a mature product in the energy drinks sector, with an estimated 70% market share around the world (Curtis, 2006), Mateschitz's extension of the brand into sport has signified a new era as a sports empire for Red Bull, with even further growth expected and no signs of slowing.

SPORT WITH WINGS

While Red Bull's sports properties appear at first glance to be rather varied and unrelated, the company's attachment to sport has in fact been undertaken with considerable, and focused, strategic intent. In much the same way as Mateschitz and his partners meaningfully branded and designed Red Bull as a means of differentiating both its product and product category from better established rivals in the drinks industry, in all of Red Bull's sporting ventures such branding efforts have been major factors in the corporation's success. Unlike, for instance, Rupert Murdoch's News International Corporation, or New York sports empire Cablevision, who own and operate massive sports empires across a variety of platforms, each of Red Bull's properties—be they purchased or created—bear the Red Bull name in some way, and have been branded or re-branded to fit the company's colour scheme and identity. While in certain cases this redesign has angered fans and alienated supporters, Red Bull has nevertheless guaranteed itself a visible and highly recognizable presence in the sports market, in much the same way as it did in building the energy drinks market.

Perhaps most vocal in opposing the growing branded empire of Mateschitz, FC Red Bull Salzburg fans fought vehemently against the renaming of the club and the changes to the team's colours and history. Bought in 2005 by Mateschitz under the Red Bull name, a division between fans of the club, and discord over Red Bull's running of the organization led to a fan group forming their own club, SV Austria Salzburg, named after the original club prior to Mateschitz's arrival.

First founded in 1933, SV Austria Salzburg survived a number of changes throughout its history to both its name and ownership, though amongst supporters the name SV Salzburg withstood. The club's original colours, violet and white, were abandoned upon Red Bull's purchase of the team, just as each of Mateschitz's properties have been rebranded in the company's colours, and the club's emblem was adorned with Red Bull's trademark wings. Fan groups protested against the changes and sought support from soccer fans throughout Europe. However, following five months of resistance, supporters of SV Salzburg relented when no agreement could be reached, as 1,500 disenchanted fans walked out on a match against Austria Vienna, never to return. The fans subsequently formed their own club, named for the original SV Salzburg, in much the same way as Wimbledon (AFC Wimbledon) and Manchester United (FC United) supporters have launched new clubs in opposition to ownership issues in English soccer.

Despite the issues faced in Salzburg, such controversy and notoriety has in many ways simply reaffirmed Red Bull's reputation as an icon of the counter-culture, and the flag-bearer of antibrands. Playing in Red Bull-named arenas and stadia, hosting new and unrivalled sporting events, and decorating everything the company touches with the red, blue, and white colours of the brand, as well as wings and the familiar charging bulls logo, Mateschitz has succeeded in building one of the most visible sporting empires in the world. Few sporting entities have enjoyed such visibility across a multitude of sports and platforms, many owners content to respect the traditions and history of sport, and the typically behind-the-scenes nature of sports ownership. Mateschitz, though, has shown a new way in which to build a brand through sport, and is evidence of the potential marketing and brand building vehicle sport provides.

MANAGEMENT IMPLICATIONS: FLYING HIGH

Despite the controversy which seemingly follows Red Bull in all of its endeavours—health concerns over the company's core product, allegations over its contents and effects, fan alienation and unrest over team re-branding, and the re-invention and subsequent commercialisation of extreme sports—Red Bull has succeeded in building one of the most pre-eminent counter-culture brands in history, as well as amassing one of the largest and most diverse sporting empires around. By strategically targeting Generations X and Y, Mateschitz has been able to ensure the longevity of the brand in just five years from the point when the core product achieved worldwide distribution, becoming highly sought after both in bars and dorm rooms around the world.

However, the success of Red Bull as a brand, and Mateschitz as a sport entrepreneur, extends further than their success in building on the extreme sports counter-culture ethos that emerged in the 1980s and 1990s. Mateschitz and his partners took their time in developing the core product, its brand image, and marketing and extension strategies, in order to best build the brand. When the product was launched in the United States, it was first sold in California and then, over a period of five years, it became available across the rest of the country. This expansion into the US market led to a rapid increase in revenue for the company, with the US market accounting for approximately 40% of the company's turnover in 2003. Yet throughout the company's move across the country, the same marketing and sales philosophies that guided the brand through Europe were maintained, leaving the distribution and key sales in the hands of local representatives, more in touch with the market, and better positioned to spread the company's name and image.

Extensive product design and market research has ensured that the company has enabled and empowered Mateschitz's overall corporate strategy. This, importantly, has allowed Red Bull to operate within a budget, maintaining a level of cost awareness throughout its sport involvement and in developing its sports portfolio. To date, Red Bull has yet to invest in the Manchester United's or New York Yankees of the sporting world, the company rather focusing on building a property in their own design, from its foundations up. There appeared to be genuine surprise in the media when it became apparent that the Red Bull Racing team could be a realistic title contender, in a sport traditionally dominated by big spending teams like McLaren, Ferrari and, Williams. Mateschitz has proved that success in sport, as in business, can be built and not just bought, an impressive feat in the brand's short tenure in sport.

Perhaps more important, Red Bull has equally proven to be a pioneer in utilising sport to develop and enhance its brand as an extension of the core product, rather than merely an associated property. Even though the company has sought to extend its sporting portfolio into more mainstream sports, they have chosen sports befitting the company's own brand image.

Adventurous, at times dangerous, and generally ambitious, Red Bull's sports empire reflects the company's own interests and identity; would Red Bull be interested in sponsoring a cricket event? At first glance, it would seem unlikely. However, for a brand whose start in sport was an event as creative and daring as the Red Bull Flugtag, to have entered traditional sports such as soccer and ice hockey may have seemed ambitious only a decade ago. It is with this success in mind that entrepreneurs aiming to build a strong sports portfolio could not ask for a better example than Mateschitz of the possibilities and potential present in sport.

WINGS CLIPPED?

Despite the undeniable success Red Bull has achieved since its emergence in Austria, controversy and notoriety have become part of the Red Bull brand, perceptions not always aided by the company's own actions. When Red Bull bought Austrian football team SV Salzburg, there was uproar amongst fans and the media due to the arrogance displayed by Mateschitz towards the club's history and traditions, as it was dismissively taken over and rebranded. This alienated many fans and it has taken time for the problem to be rectified. Mateschitz was considerably less cavalier in the changes imposed on the New York Red Bulls, despite the American side's much shorter history and legacy as a club and part of a much younger league. Whether or not this was a sign of Mateschitz and his team having learnt from the Salzburg experience, or merely a different approach taken by the company, there is nevertheless some indication that Red Bull could do more in managing its fan relations as it continues to builds a strong presence in sport.

Unlike many of his contemporaries, Mateschitz has managed to remain almost an unknown figure behind the Red Bull brand; Branson and Gates, by contrast, have become in many ways the faces of their respective Virgin and Microsoft brands. Mateschitz, though, prefers to remain behind the scenes, encouraging greater attention on the brand and the properties themselves, a strategy which to date has paid dividends. However, in this same context, it could be suggested that in fact, Red Bull's extreme sports properties have become the image most associated with the brand, rather than Mateschitz or even the energy drinks market it popularized. However, Red Bull's presence in other sports, such as ice hockey, has yet to lead to the same associations and in-roads into the sports market. Beyond Red Bull's ties with adventure sports, the brand is best known as an alcoholic drink mixer, or owner and sponsor of sports teams, rather than as an energy drink or sports drink. In order to gain greater authority and identity in the traditional sports Mateschitz has entered recently—soccer, motor racing, ice hockey—Red Bull must do more to tie the energy drink to more mainstream sports, without damaging the long-standing brand equity built through an involvement in the extreme sports market, which would alienate the company's core target market.

Finally, in investigating and analyzing Red Bull and its strategies for success, it has become apparent that there needs to be a balance between exposure in mainstream media and its ethos as an antibrand. While the company already boasts a successful and long-standing print and television campaign, centred around its trademarked 'Red Bull Gives You Wings' theme, there remains considerable potential in expanding awareness of the brand and enhancing the organization's status as a sports empire through increased media exposure. To this end, Red Bull must do more to utilize the mainstream media, in order to generate greater attention, attracting an increased fan base to their many sporting events and teams, and potentially increase sales of Red Bull's slowly expanding product line. Unfortunately, to date much of their marketing strategy has centered on basic but effective word-of-mouth advertising campaigns, which has proved incredibly beneficial for them in the extreme sports genre; however, media coverage has become a vital means of attracting consumers to mainstream sports, particularly in sports such as soccer and ice hockey whose revenues are driven by ticket sales. As such, in order to continue the Redbull brand's staggering growth over the past decade, and to further expand into traditional sports, Mateschitz can follow the lead of more well-known entrepreneurs, including Gates and Branson, and embrace the popular media, while remaining true to the company's overarching identity and culture.

CONCLUSION

Ultimately, the success of Mateschitz as a sports entrepreneur is in many ways unparalleled. Although other entrepreneurs have achieved similar success, and other sports owners and innovators have perhaps achieved greater success within the sporting realm, few companies rival Red Bull's innovation and perseverance in utilizing sport as a key driver of business and extension of the core brand. Remaining true to the company's core values and identity, Mateschitz has used sport to further promote and grow the Red Bull brand and reach a broader audience of fans and consumers internationally. By stressing authenticity and establishing the brand as an icon of the extreme sports subculture, the company pioneered not only the energy drinks market, but also the use of sport as a brand extension. Given the success Red Bull has achieved over the past twenty-five years, and what we know about entrepreneurship and the role it plays in sport, there can be little doubt of Mateschitz's place amongst sports elite, alongside more famous names like Phil Knight, Adi Dassler, and Mark McCormack. Notwithstanding possible extensions and endeavours in the future, Red Bull's present position as a fixture within youth culture and sport should ensure the brand's enduring market dominance and visibility.

References

Bygrave, W. & Minniti, M. (2000).The social dynamics of entrepreneurship. *Entrepreneurship: Theory and Practice*, Spring, 25–36.

Curtis, B. (2006, October 29). Herr Mateschitz wants to juice you up. *New York Times*. Retrieved from http://www.nytimes.com/2006/10/29/sports/playmagazine/1029play_juice.html

Gschwandtner, G. (2004). The powerful sales strategy behind Red Bull. *Selling Power*, September 2004:60–70

Howarth, C., Tempest, S., & Coupland, C. (2005). Rethinking entrepreneurship methodology and definitions of the entrepreneur. *Journal of Small Business and Enterprise Development*, *12*(1), 24–40.

Keller, K. L. (2002). *Best Practice Cases in Branding* (3rd ed.). New York, NY: Prentice-Hall.

Klayman, B. (2009). *Global sports market to hit $141 billion in 2012*. Reuters. Retrieved from http://www.reuters.com/article/newsOne/idUSN1738075220080618

Long, W. (1983). The meaning of entrepreneurship, *American Journal of Small Business*, *8*(2), 47–59.

Schumpeter, J. A. (1974). *The Theory of Economic Development*. Oxford, UK: Oxford University Press.

Selling energy—Red Bull's Dietrich Mateschitz. (2002, May 11). *The Economist*. Retrieved from http://www.economist.com/business/displaystory.cfm?story_id=E1_TTNDPSP

3

Doing Good While Doing Well in Sports: Sports Entrepreneurs and Social Impact

KENNETH L. SHROPSHIRE

INTRODUCTION

Doing good while doing well. The adage covers a portion of what I address in this chapter. For example, a sure way to have a substantial social impact is to make as much money as possible and then give a good portion of it away to address the issues that you consider appropriate. Think of the foundations funded by athlete greats Andre Agassi and Tiger Woods. But for their individual wealth these athletes would not have been able to contribute such generous funds to educational academies.[1] The academies were established and are sustained primarily due to the wealth of these individuals. The entrepreneurial earnings of these athletes allow them to have a social impact. Playing tennis or golf is not entrepreneurial; however, by applying their wealth toward starting entities with a social purpose, these men have become *social impact entrepreneurs*. Like Bill Gates or Richard Branson, although on a much more modest scale, those who earn large sums in sports have a huge opportunity to have a social impact.

On the other hand, there are entrepreneurial sports ventures that are created specifically to have a social impact. In these ventures, assuming there is no wealthy founder, locating alternative financial sources for sustainability may be the responsibility of the entrepreneurial founders and those who follow the inaugural leadership of the enterprise. Some of these enterprises have built-in methods of sustainability, via a business operational revenue plan or a strong funder development plan, but differ from athlete-funded foundations because they are not dependent on funds from a star athlete or two. Some of these not-for-profit ventures, like Peace Players International and Right to Play, are entrepreneurial in their origins.

In this chapter I'll discuss four types of social impact ventures or entities in the entrepreneurial context. I'll begin with a discussion of the decision to be involved in social impact ventures. The next section will look at ventures formed by entrepreneurs specifically to have a social impact. Next, I'll look at existing ventures and some steps they have taken to have a social impact. Then, I'll focus on the concept of athletes as social impact entrepreneurs, as in the case of Agassi and Woods. Finally, I'll examine broad-based involvement in sport by a government, with entrepreneurial features that have a social impact. There are entrepreneurial lessons from this governmental fourth form as well.

SPORTS ENTREPRENEURSHIP AND SOCIAL IMPACT

Entrepreneurs are more than just business creators. Kuratko (2008) presents a classic view of entrepreneurs and entrepreneurship, one that incorporates innovation, integration, risk, and tenacity, in this explanation:

> Entrepreneurship is more than the mere creation of business. Although that is certainly an important facet, it's not the complete picture. The characteristics of seeking opportunities, taking risks beyond security, and having the tenacity to push an idea through to reality combine into a special perspective that permeates entrepreneurs. . . . Thus entrepreneurship is an integrated concept that permeates an individual's business in an innovative manner. (p. 3)

It is clear that this set of characteristics is important whether the focus is on the bottom line or on social impact; in fact, many entrepreneurs are focused on both.

Entrepreneurs create value, and that value can take many forms. Rather than focusing on value as the monetary bottom line exclusively, social impact entrepreneurship focuses on societal benefit through positive social impact. It may also focus on brand impact. There are two basic reasons for entrepreneurs to become involved in ventures that have a social impact: brand and altruism. Great American boxer Sugar Ray Robinson provides a bit of insight on this issue. He is a good starting point to understand the "why" of being a social impact entrepreneur.

Brand

First, the not-so-altruistic rationale. A columnist, Dan Parker, was relentless in writing stories about whether the then-famed boxer, Sugar Ray Robinson, was a military deserter. The story began during World War II when Robinson mysteriously missed getting on board a ship headed to Europe. Robinson always contended that he suffered an injury and missed the ship that was scheduled to take him overseas. Parker persistently raised questions about the accuracy of Robinson's account, alluding that he was a deserter and was seeking to avoid combat zones. Around this same time Robinson became a major contributor to the Damon Runyon Cancer Fund. The president of that fund was that same reporter, Dan Parker. The stories about Robinson being a deserter began to disappear.

While the Robinson story is an extreme example, the practice of using positive societal action to improve a "brand"—be that of an individual or a company—is fairly common. Consider these examples: A large donation to a charity that gets an individual a great placement on the society page, or the NFL advertising its involvement with the United Way. These are less direct methods of improving a brand; the Robinson story is one of protecting a brand. But they are related in terms of their motivation.

Altruism

On the other hand, Robinson was known to be generous to the extreme, particularly on the individual level. His autobiography begins with a story of his giving at a time when his finances were barely enough to sustain him and his family. He gave half of a bout's purse to the mother of Jimmy Doyle, a boxer he killed in the ring. It is also significant to note that Robinson was one of the first athletes to establish a foundation. He founded the Sugar Ray Robinson Youth Foundation in California. This was long after his retirement and all indications are that he did it because it was simply a positive step that he wanted to take (Shropshire, 2007, p. 165).

FOR-PROFIT SOCIAL IMPACT ENTREPRENEURSHIP

If we use the classic definition of entrepreneur, then there are few sports ventures that lack entrepreneurial roots. At some point there was an individual or individuals that were taking the risk on their own to get the business underway. In that sense it is valuable to focus on social impact involvement of for-profit ventures.

The discussion below is on two for-profit sports ventures and their social impact activities in one case and aspirations in another: the San Diego Padres of Major League Baseball and the Philadelphia Union of Major League Soccer.

San Diego Padres: FriarFit [2]

The experience of concessions at sporting events is relatively universal, whether it's sushi in a ballpark in Japan or hot dogs at an American baseball game. So where is the social impact issue here? One element that threads its way through much ballpark food is the healthiness, or more typically, lack of healthiness. In the United States, the societal childhood obesity problem is unprecedented. One person who had a particular awareness of this was Major League Baseball Hall of Famer Dave Winfield, who approached his old team, the San Diego Padres, with the idea of doing something about it.

Winfield felt it was important for baseball, as a sport, to lead the way in putting the issue of Americans' declining health on everyone's agenda. His view was that baseball could have a major impact not only because of its popularity and the historic place it holds in American culture, but also because of its long season. This was particularly true and important with all of the negative health-related stories that were hitting baseball at the time. Most of the negatives centered on steroid use and accusations of use. Winfield's FriarFit program, apart from being the right thing to do, could assist in getting baseball on the right side of the ledger. This could certainly help the business image of an individual franchise as well. This is a social impact brand enhancer.

The FriarFit program has multiple elements, including offering healthy food alternatives at the ballpark, providing healthy eating and exercise tips, an "instant recess" program (a spontaneous moment of choreographed exercise at the ballpark or elsewhere), and fitness programs for San Diego area schools. The program capitalizes on the celebrity of both the team and the individual players to bring about this fitness social impact.

FriarFit provides a good overview of the types of social impact involvement that established sports enterprises often involve themselves in. The entity chooses a social issue that it has an interest in addressing, and either actively, as with FriarFit, or via monetary contributions, becomes involved.

Philadelphia Union

A group of entrepreneurs came together to launch the expansion Major League Soccer (MLS) Philadelphia Union in 2010. The vice president of operations, Carl Cherkin, makes a clear point about the issues any for-profit organization must weigh when making a determination to become involved in social impact issues: "Our first goal is to be a successful business enterprise."[3] This highlights the social impact conflict and gets back to the "doing good and well" conundrum. This pressure to take on a level of corporate social responsibility is without a doubt more severe for sports-related enterprises than for any other business.

The Union is not actually based in Philadelphia, but in Chester, Pennsylvania, possibly one of America's most economically and socially depressed cities. Like so many, Chester was built on a model that relied on heavy manufacturing. As that industrial sector was replaced by a service-oriented economy, the economic and social status of Chester declined. It is now the host to a casino, an economic move of last resort.

The Union came in with great expectations and great obligations to the community. So far they have focused on enhancing soccer programs in the local area schools, and they are cautiously looking more broadly for other options. In the for-profit world, there has to be a careful focus on the bottom line.

NOT-FOR-PROFIT SOCIAL IMPACT ENTERPRISES

An interesting route to take to avoid having to make the balance between bottom line profitability and "doing good" is to make social impact the primary entrepreneurial purpose. The section below looks at two examples of not-for-profit enterprises designed specifically to have a social impact: Peace-Players International and Right to Play.

PeacePlayers International

Brothers and former college basketball players Sean and Brendan Tuohey find themselves with an enterprise that has grown to a size and impact that they never contemplated after starting PeacePlayers International (PPI) in 2001. It began with the idea of using basketball to promote peace in conflict regions—divided communities. PPI was founded on the premise that "children who play together can learn to live together."

They are now at the next level of entrepreneurship: not quite franchising, but using the skills they've acquired in nine years of operating PPI to help entities with similar goals for social impact. PPI currently operates programs in Northern Ireland, South Africa, Cyprus, and the Middle East that bring together thousands of children to form positive relationships, develop leadership skills, and improve their futures. The bottom-line goal of PPI is to keep the operations going and to meet payroll, not to achieve any extraordinary level of profitability.

There are now probably hundreds of organizations like PPI around the globe. The message is that entrepreneurs can focus directly on the social impact they wish to have by forming an entity to do just that. But the constructed model must also have a strategy for long term funding.[5]

Right to Play[6]

The most basic impact of sport is to serve as a diversion, a focus that prevents negative activities from taking place. Right to Play grew out of an enterprise called Olympic Aid. According to Right to Play's website, "The focus of Olympic Aid during these Games was to show support for people in war-torn countries and areas of distress. Olympic athletes were chosen to be Ambassadors of Olympic Aid to assist in the fundraising efforts" ("History," n.d., para. 1). Working initially with Johann Olav Koss, four-time gold medal winning Norwegian speed skater, more than $18 million was raised to support "five main projects in 1994: building a hospital in Sarajevo, building schools in Eritrea, supporting a mother/child program in Guatemala, supporting refugees in Afghanistan, and a support program for children living with disabilities in Lebanon" ("History," n.d., para. 1). As the organization has continued to grow and go global, the focus is on living up to its name and providing opportunities for youth involvement in sport. Broadly, Right to Play seeks to improve the lives of children by providing opportunities for sport and play.

THE ATHLETE AS SOCIAL IMPACT ENTREPRENEUR

Agassi, Woods, and Robinson are all examples of athletes who became social impact entrepreneurs. Johann Koss, who leads Right to Play as it continues to expand, certainly fits into this category as well.

There is also a growing class of athletes working to raise impactful funds. David Robinson, the former NBA superstar, has long been involved in philanthropic ventures. His Carver Academy School in San Antonio is yet another example of the types of focused educational projects athletes are able to develop.

When Robinson retired, he was confronted with the prospect of continuing to fund the Carver Academy. He also contemplated how to do more. While sustainability may not have been a key concern while earning a lucrative NBA player's salary, how can one make an impact post-career?

Seeking to answer that question, Robinson partnered with a friend, Dan Bassichis, who worked for the investment banking firm Goldman Sachs, to form the Admiral Fund ("Admiral's fund," 2007). The uniqueness of the fund is the multiple bottom line positive impact they intended it to have. The goal of the fund is to seek opportunities for social impact while also providing investors a financial return on their investment. For Robinson's part, one of the uses for those positive returns is the funding of the Carver Academy:

> A friend of mine, Daniel Bassichis, who I got to know through a friend from the Naval Academy, worked at Goldman Sachs Group. He started helping out at the Carver Academy. He understood my mentality, like in basketball, that I see business as a great way to impact the community. And where we invest, we will have partnerships that facilitate investment in the surrounding communities as well. We started Admiral Capital in 2007. At first, the timing seemed awful, with the financial crisis. But we were fortunate. We had a little bit of money out there at work but we weren't hurt. Now there are going to be opportunities galore. Who knows when they are going to be there, but this is a really exciting time. (Corcoran, 2009, para. 26)

Both for-profit and not-for-profit ventures involving sports and social impact have been discussed in the previous examples. Government has also played a role in promoting sport as a channel for positive social impact. The final discussion below takes a look at government in this context.

GOVERNMENT AS ENTREPRENEUR

Royal Bafokeng Sports[7]

This final example, little known before the 2010 World Cup in South Africa, is unique in that it involves a government entity acting in an entrepreneurial fashion. This community is situated on the paved stretch of road about midway between Johannesburg and Sun City, a Las Vegas-like resort in South Africa. After acquiring rights to the world's second largest platinum deposit, the Royal Bafokeng Nation, comprised of 29 villages and 300,000 people, developed innovative approaches to sustainability in South Africa. Led by a kgosi (king), Royal Bafokeng invested its resources to facilitate administration, civil service, and infrastructure for the good of the community.

In addition to traditional investments, Royal Bafokeng believes that sport can be a key tool for development. With that in mind, the previous kgosi built a soccer stadium with a nearly pure field of dreams motivation, and it became a venue for the 2010 FIFA World Cup. It is viewed as the centerpiece to tourism for the region, as it provides a high-altitude training venue for athletes as well as a venue for sporting events and sports tourism.

The entrepreneurial use of sport by Royal Bafokeng is multifaceted. One important point is the effort to use sport for aspiration. The Royal Bafokeng Sports Campus is not only a venue for professional athletes. It will now be in view of children growing up in the region, and they will be aware that the opportunity exists to play in these facilities. This model can be thought of as a pyramid. At the base of the pyramid are mass youth sports activities in which anyone can participate. As the players advance toward higher levels of sports competition (the upper levels of the pyramid), they can actually see professional teams that they can someday join and the facility in which they can play if they participate at the highest level. The governmental investment is unique, as it is an investment in not only the facility, but the development of sport and tourism. In this sense, the government considers the social impact of their entrepreneurial investment in teams and a facility.

CONCLUSION

This chapter has provided multiple examples of various levels of entrepreneurs involved in activities that have a social impact. Many sports enterprises, of course, have an impact without intention. However, those that do intend to have a social impact typically plan to do so for one of two reasons or a blend of the two: increasing brand equity (and presumably having an impact on profitability), or just the altruistic desire to do good.

Entrepreneurs solely focused on social impact, like those involved with PeacePlayers International and Right to Play, have little bottom line profitability pressure, other than achieving their impact goal. For-profit businesses, like the Philadelphia Union, have a different hurdle. Those for-profit businesses may have stakeholders that focus solely on the bottom line impact. In that case the enterprise has to focus not solely on brand but also on corporate social responsibility to have a positive social impact. Sports enterprises are not exempt from this scrutiny and may, arguably, be under greater scrutiny than businesses of a similar size that are outside of sports. Entrepreneurs must be conscious of the role that social impact obligations play in the operation of any sports related enterprise. Finally, governments, such as the Royal Bafokeng Nation, have an opportunity to play a unique social impact role by making entrepreneurial sports investments that have positive impacts on their communities.

Endnotes

1. See the Andre Agassi Preparatory Academy at http://www.agassiprep.org/ and the Tiger Woods Learning Center at http://web.tigerwoodsfoundation.org/programs/twlc/index

2. See the African American Collaborative Obesity Research Network, University of Pennsylvania, "FriarVision Fitness Fanatics Initiative (FriarFit) Stakeholder Interview Business Case Findings," December 2009.

3. Speech, Carl Cherkin, Wharton School, University of Pennsylvania, Philadelphia, PA, March 3, 2010.

4. See http://www.peaceplayersintl.org

5. For a broad look at sports and social impact programs around the globe, visit http://www.sportanddev.org

6. See http://www.righttoplay.com/International/Pages/Home.aspx

7. See generally, Robyn Dixon, "South Africa Has Rich Aspirations," http://articles.la times.com/2009/apr/06/world/fg-rich-tribe

References

Admiral's fund will spur urban growth: Basketball great and Wall St. partner launch fund to invest in inner cities. (2007, June 11). *New York Daily News*. Retrieved from http://www.nydailynews.com/money/2007/06/11/2007-06-11_admirals_fund_will_spur_urban_growth_print.html

Corcoran, G. (2009, September 20). Basketball's admirable admiral. *Wall Street Journal*. Retrieved from http://online.wsj.com/article/SB125322080193420783.html

History. (n.d.). In *Right to play*. Retrieved from http://www.righttoplay.com/International/about-us/Pages/History.aspx

Kuratko, D. (2008). *Entrepreneurship: Theory, Process, and Practice (8th ed.)*. Mason, OH: South-Western Cengage Learning, Inc., 3.

Shropshire, K. (2007). *Being Sugar Ray: America's greatest boxer and first celebrity athlete*. Philadelphia, PA: Basic Civitas, 165.

4

Sports Entrepreneurship: The Case of the Indian Premier League

DAVID HOYT AND GEORGE FOSTER

ENTREPRENEURSHIP

Entrepreneurship is a risky undertaking in any type of business. When founding a sporting league, the chances of success are particularly slim. A study of 205 leagues formed since 1871 found that just 17 had survived through 1997, with 12 more still existing as the result of mergers (Dobbs, Harrison, Zhao, & Wade, 2008). The Indian Premier League (IPL), at least in its first few years, is one of the most stunning success stories in sporting league entrepreneurship. The league rapidly garnered a passionate fan base, as well as lucrative television and sponsorship contracts. Early indicators signaled likely financial success for the league itself and at least some of the team owners. The story of the IPL illustrates important business considerations for entrepreneurs in both sporting and nonsporting industries. It involves identifying an opportunity, leveraging assets, minimizing the impact of inherited liabilities, taking advantage of growth accelerators, and adapting to changes in the business environment. The story also includes ongoing disputes over sharing rules and decision rights by key constituents.

CRICKET, INDIAN TELEVISION, AND THE INDIAN CRICKET LEAGUE

Traditionally, top-level cricket has been played in a format in which matches last five days. While matches lasting many days might have been ideal as a way to pass the time during the British Raj in India, by the end of the 20th century, spectators and television viewers generally had an appetite for games of shorter duration. The first major innovation in the match format was introduced in England in 1963, and enabled games to be completed in one day. An even more compressed format was introduced in 2003, also in England. This version, called Twenty20, allowed games to be completed in about three hours—comparable to an American football or baseball game, albeit somewhat longer than a two-hour soccer game. The Twenty20 format also encouraged high scoring and aggressive play, rather than the more slow-paced style often associated with the classic five-day format. The first Twenty20 World Cup was contested in 2007, in which India defeated Pakistan in the final match. The fan enthusiasm over the event highlighted the format's appeal, particularly in victorious India.

The international governing body of cricket is the International Cricket Council (ICC), which controls the international cricket calendar. Each ICC member (Australia, Bangladesh, England, India, New Zealand, Pakistan, South Africa, Sri Lanka, West Indies, and Zimbabwe) has a governing body. For India, one of the most important countries in the cricket world, the governing body is the Board of Control for Cricket in India (BCCI).

At the turn of the 21st century, India had become the most important economic power in the cricket world. Cricket was the sport most passionately followed by the Indian population. At the same time, Bollywood (the Indian movie industry) and its movie stars had emerged as another key force in Indian culture and life. A combination of these two deep Indian passions—cricket and Bollywood—with a population of about 1.2 billion, a rising middle class of about 250 million, and an economy growing at 6% annually or more, provided a major business opportunity for a new Indian cricket venture.

Indian fans' passion for cricket was a critical element in the success of domestic television channels, with advertising during major matches commanding high prices. In April 2007, this led to the founding of the Indian Cricket League (ICL) by the owners of Indian television network ZeeTV. For years, ZeeTV had unsuccessfully tried to win the rights to televise Indian cricket. Now, they would create their own content, independent of the cricket establishment. The ICL plans initially consisted of six teams, based in Indian cities, using the Twenty20 format. The winner of the first ICL tournament would receive $1 million in prize money. The league planned to eventually expand to 16 teams.

National cricket boards strongly resisted the ICL. Some national boards banned players that signed with the ICL from participating in events, domestic or international, sanctioned by the national boards. As a result, most of the players that initially signed with the ICL were former stars that had already retired from international competition. However, within a few months, the ICL had signed a number of high-profile players to lucrative contracts. The first ICL season ran from November 30, 2007 to December 16, 2007.

FOUNDING OF THE INDIAN PREMIER LEAGUE

On September 13, 2007, the BCCI announced that it was forming a city-based Twenty20 cricket league in India, called the Indian Premier League (IPL). Where the ICL was a renegade league, formed outside the cricket establishment, the IPL had the approval of cricket authorities. Representatives of the ICC and several leading national boards were present at the announcement of the new league. The first season was scheduled to begin in April 2008, with $3 million in prize money. At the same press conference, the BCCI announced the formation of a Champions Twenty20 League, in which top clubs from India, Australia, South Africa, and England would compete.

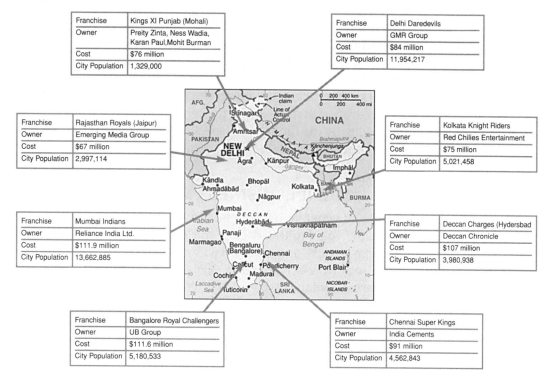

Franchise	Kings XI Punjab (Mohali)
Owner	Preity Zinta, Ness Wadia, Karan Paul,Mohit Burman
Cost	$76 million
City Population	1,329,000

Franchise	Delhi Daredevils
Owner	GMR Group
Cost	$84 million
City Population	11,954,217

Franchise	Rajasthan Royals (Jaipur)
Owner	Emerging Media Group
Cost	$67 million
City Population	2,997,114

Franchise	Kolkata Knight Riders
Owner	Red Chilies Entertainment
Cost	$75 million
City Population	5,021,458

Franchise	Mumbai Indians
Owner	Reliance India Ltd.
Cost	$111.9 million
City Population	13,662,885

Franchise	Deccan Charges (Hydersbad
Owner	Deccan Chronicle
Cost	$107 million
City Population	3,980,938

Franchise	Bangalore Royal Challengers
Owner	UB Group
Cost	$111.6 million
City Population	5,180,533

Franchise	Chennai Super Kings
Owner	India Cements
Cost	$91 million
City Population	4,562,843

FIGURE 4.1. **Map of India, with 2008 IPL franchises.**

Sources: Map from CIA: The World Factbook, https://www.cia.gov/library/publications/the-world-factbook/print/in.html (accessed October 15, 2008); population data for all cities except Mohali is 2008 estimate by World Gazetteer.com, based on 2001 census (http://world-gazetteer.com, accessed October 15, 2008). Mohali is a suburb of Chandigarh, with 2001 census of 123,000. Mohali data in table is the sum of Chandigarh and its suburbs, Mohali and Panchkula, from 2001 census (www.censusindia.gov.in, accessed October 15, 2008), adjusted for growth according to estimated growth for Chandigarh city by World Gazetteer.

The IPL was designed to operate on a franchise basis, a common form of sporting organization in the United States, but a novelty in India. Eight franchises would be sold through an auction to be held in January 2008. The league would sell media rights and sponsorships, with the revenue shared between the league and franchise owners. Teams would be staffed with a combination of Indian and international players, who would be selected through an auction to be held in February 2008. Each of the eight teams would play every other team twice—once at each franchise's home city. The top four franchises would then play semifinal matches, with the winners advancing to play for the league championship. The entire season, consisting of 59 matches, would last 44 days, with the semifinals and finals being played in one weekend. The two finalists would play in the newly announced Champions Twenty20 tournament.

One of the critical steps taken by the BCCI to make the IPL a reality was hiring the marketing and event management firm IMG, which had been involved in the original conception and development of the league. Among the many responsibilities taken on by IMG was to develop the sporting, commercial, and financial structure for the IPL. IMG also drafted all significant contracts, handled the marketing and sales of commercial assets (including media and sponsorship rights) and the sale of franchises, and was responsible for planning and managing the IPL tournament.

In December 2007, the BCCI and IPL published a prospectus for potential franchise owners. This included data on the overwhelming popularity of Twenty20 cricket, noting that it was the preferred form of the game for 76% of cricket spectators. By the time the prospectus was issued, the league had already contracted with at least 48 international players.

THE IPL BUSINESS MODEL

IPL franchises would generate revenue from two sources. First, they shared in "central" revenues paid to the league. These included a share of league media rights, sponsorships, and money paid by league official suppliers. For instance, franchisees were scheduled to receive 80% of television revenues (after production costs) for the first two years, gradually decreasing to 50% for year 11 and beyond. Franchisees would receive 60% of league sponsorship revenues for the first 10 years, and 50% thereafter. In addition to the revenues distributed to all franchisees, BCCI would pay $3 million in prize money.

The second source of franchisee revenue was from locally generated sources. In the first 10 years, the period in which the financial arrangements between franchises and the BCCI were most well defined, each franchise kept 100% of these revenues. This included match tickets, franchise sponsorships, licensing, merchandising, concessions, and other local-source revenue. Teams were responsible for leasing stadiums for their home games. Stadiums were generally owned by cricket associations, which would receive 20% of the tickets for each match. The remaining 80% of tickets would be sold by the host teams, who kept all the revenue from these tickets.

Each franchise owner would pay its franchise fee in equal installments over 10 years. Franchisees also paid player salaries, franchise management salaries, stadium leases, match day costs such as stadium staffing and security, and other franchise-specific costs.

On January 14, 2008, the IPL announced that it had sold worldwide media and production rights to the Singapore-based sports management company World Sport Group for 10 years, for just over $1 billion, of which $108 million was to be used for promotion. $306 million would be paid for the first five years, with the balance paid over the following five years. As part of the deal, Sony Entertainment Television (SET) received the right to televise IPL matches in India for five years.

Franchise Auction

By the time the media rights sale was announced, 32 organizations had purchased the Invitation to Tender document, specifying conditions of the franchise sale, with more following suit before the bid opening on January 24. Interested bidders included companies, private equity funds, and consortiums of individuals (several of which included Bollywood stars). The minimum bid was $50 million. Eight franchises were to be awarded from a pool of 12 cities that met the IPL eligibility criteria, which included access to a stadium seating at least 25,000 and the capability of lighting the stadium for night games.

The franchise auction generated $718 million. The top bidder was the Reliance Group, headed by India's wealthiest man, Mukesh Ambani, which won the coveted Mumbai franchise for $111.9 million. The lowest winning bid was by Emerging Media, a consortium that included Lachlan Murdoch, son of News Corp. Chairman Rupert Murdoch, which bid $67 million for the Rajasthan franchise. Two Bollywood stars, action hero Shah Rukh Khan and actress Preity Zinta, were key members of groups that won franchises, and were the public faces for their franchises.

On February 13 the league announced another large cash infusion, as it sold exclusive title sponsorship rights for five years to property developer DLF at $10 million per year. DLF had been an unsuccessful bidder for an IPL franchise, but still wanted television exposure to the IPL audience, particularly the growing middle class of 250 million consumers. During the first year, third parties estimated that teams split about $30 million in central sponsorship and raised nearly $38 million in team sponsorship (Pande & Behl, 2008).

Player Auction

Cricket players were contracted by their national boards. In leading cricket countries, local teams consisted of a mix of professional, semiprofessional, and amateur players. The national cricket boards had first priority on their contracted players—if a national team had a match or international tour, players were required to participate. This system did not provide a free market for players, and it suppressed their salaries. The World Series Cricket league of the 1970s had been the first attempt to create a market for players, but had long since passed by the time the IPL was launched.

Not all national cricket boards allowed their players to participate in the IPL. In particular, the England and Wales Cricket Board (ECB) required its contracted players to participate in county matches that were scheduled during the IPL season, and would not release its players—a stand that was not well received by the players. The English team captain commented, "We're naïve if we don't think England players are going to end up playing in the IPL. It's exciting, and we shouldn't see it as a threat" ("IPL is too appealing," 2008).

Despite the ECB's refusal, the IPL had contracted with 80 top players from other countries prior to the auction. The league designated five Indian players as "iconic": Rahul Dravid, Yuvraj Singh, Sourav Ganguly, Sachin Tendulkar, and Virender Sehwag. These players were not included in the auction, but were assigned to their home city teams in an attempt to foster local fan excitement. The iconic players received salaries 15% higher than the next-highest player on their teams.

Each franchise was required to have at least 16 players. All players on the Indian national team were eligible. Teams could sign players from other countries, but only four international players per team could participate in any individual match. Each team also had to include at least four players who were under 21 years of age, and four from the franchise's local region.

The total player payroll for each team, for the six-week season, was required to be at least $3.3 million, with a cap of $5 million. The minimum player salary was set at $50,000. In addition to their salaries, players could be paid bonuses from their owners, and a portion of any prize money, but this was left up to each franchise owner.

The first player auction was held on February 20, 2008, with 75 players selected. The total annual salary of these players was $40 million, or an average of $534,000. The top bid was $1.5 million, paid by the Chennai team for Mahendra Singh Dhoni, a top Indian batsman. The next-highest bid was for Australian Andrew Symonds, who went to the Hyderabad team for an annual salary of $1.35 million. These salaries were for a season that lasted just six weeks. A second player auction was held several weeks later to allow teams to add players, using any money still available within the $5 million salary cap.

The six-week salaries of IPL players were substantially higher than salaries paid by their national cricket boards, whose pay structures were not based on market considerations. The IPL auction had an immediate impact on the cricket world. Shortly after the IPL auction, New Zealand Cricket announced a 40% pay increase for its contracted players. This still left the annual top salary well below the average amount bid at the IPL auction, which was for just six weeks of work.

PROMOTING THE LEAGUE

By the end of February 2008, just a few months after the IPL concept had been announced, and six weeks before the start of the season on April 18, eight teams had been formed and staffed with players. The league had sold worldwide media rights, and had a title sponsor. Yet, success was far from assured. Many questioned whether franchise owners would ever recoup the large franchise fees and player salaries, or if fans would embrace the league.

To promote their teams, most franchises incorporated the Indian passion for Bollywood into their marketing programs. All but one of the IPL teams hired Bollywood stars and other celebrities as "brand ambassadors." When Bollywood action hero Akshay Kumar was introduced as the brand partner for the Delhi Daredevils, he "made a grand entry on the stage with a cricket bat and helmet and performed a martial art dance before vouching his loyalty for the team" ("Akshay hopes," 2008). The Daredevils' team captain commented that "Twenty20 is pure entertainment and there are no bigger entertainers than Bollywood stars" ("Akshay hopes," 2008). IPL matches were more than sporting events; they were over-the-top entertainment extravaganzas, embracing Bollywood and other spectacles. Teams typically budgeted $500,000 to $1.25 million for entertainment during home matches.

The one franchise that did not hire a brand ambassador and did not spend lavishly on marketing was the Rajasthan Royals. The team's owners had spent the least of any successful franchise bidder, and also stayed away from high-priced stars at the player auction. Their approach was to focus on the team, rather than individual star players, and to make their statement on the field.

THE FIRST SEASON (IPL-I)

The first day of the inaugural IPL season, April 18, 2008, set the stage for the orgy of cricket and entertainment that was to dominate Indian attention for the following six weeks.

The first match was played in Bangalore, between Shah Rukh Khan's Kolkata Knight Riders and Vijay Mallya's Bangalore Royal Challengers. There were terrible traffic problems, as 40,000 fans tried to get through 16 gates, and there was virtually no parking available. Police said they had not been contacted about parking and traffic management, and streets within 2 kilometers of the stadium were turned into parking lots ("Traffic management," 2008).

Despite these problems, the show began at 6:30 on a raised stage draped in red and orange. A packed stadium "shrieked, screamed, and cheered" as singers performed popular Bollywood songs. The Washington Redskins cheerleaders performed, accompanied by a live band. There were trapeze artists and a laser show, ending with fireworks "going up in [the] air from all corners of the stadium, creating a ring of fire" ("IPL off to electrifying start," 2008). The visiting Knight Riders won the opening match.

The next day, in New Delhi, the Delhi Daredevils played their first match against the Rajasthan Royals. The pregame show included trick cyclists and gymnasts, culminating in a "breathtaking stunt" by a Bollywood action star ("Akhya thrills," 2008). The home team won the match.

While most of the opening matches were well attended, the first home match for the Kings XI Punjab, played on April 19, had disappointing attendance. The franchise owner, actress Preity Zinta, attributed the poor attendance to a local culture of free passes, particularly for VIPs, few of whom came to the match. The home team lost to the visiting Chennai Super Kings.

As the tournament progressed, the IPL became a sensation in India. Attendance at matches was generally strong throughout the tournament, although toward the end of the season, attendance fell off for matches between two teams at the bottom of the standings.

On May 13, 2008, India was rocked by a series of terrorist bombings in crowded markets, tourist sites, and a temple in Jaipur, the capital of Rajasthan and home to the Rajasthan Royals. The bombs killed dozens of people. The team's next home game was scheduled for May 18, and there were suggestions (which were rejected) that it be moved to Bangalore. Two Australian stars of the team, Shane Warne (who also served as the team's coach) and Shane Watson, considered returning home, but stayed with the team. A team manager from Australia and a player from South Africa refused to return to Jaipur ("Bombings may force," 2008). The league, franchises, and league sponsors donated about $1.5 million to the bombing victims.

The season reached its climax when the semifinals and championship match were played in Mumbai on the weekend of May 31 and June 1. Even though the Mumbai team was not participating, local fans were excited. The final match, between the Rajasthan Royals and Chennai Super Kings, was held at the 55,000-seat DY Patil stadium outside Mumbai before a sold-out crowd. The match included a 45-minute entertainment spectacular on four mobile stages, including performances by Bollywood stars and international artists. There were folk dancers, acrobats, and trampoline athletes. The songs for all eight IPL teams were performed. There was a laser and light display, and fireworks ("Salman for the closing," 2008).

The Rajasthan Royals, the team that had spent the least for its franchise and had the lowest player payroll, scored a dramatic last-minute victory.

Following the match, tournament director and IPL commissioner Lalit Modi reflected on the league's first season:

> India fulfilled a dream in an unbelievable manner and made the inaugural event a reality. The people of India and the rest of the world embraced this tournament with their hearts and I feel really proud that we have taken the game of cricket . . . to a new level. It was a difficult road for all of us involved in this venture to walk, there were skeptics . . . the success is there for all to see (Delport, June 2, 2008).

The Situation at the End of the IPL's Inaugural Season

The final match of the inaugural IPL season took place on June 1, 2008, just nine months after BCCI announced the league's formation. Those nine months had been filled with activity—franchise auction, player auction, team formation, event planning, sponsorship sales and activation, and the successful completion of 59 matches. Initial skepticism about the financial viability of franchises had been reduced. The landscape surrounding the salary structure for top cricket players around the world had been dramatically changed.

This was accomplished through a combination of sport and entertainment, what Shailendra Singh, managing director of an event organizing firm, called "a potent mix with 20 percent soap opera, 40 percent Bollywood, and 40 percent cricket" (Roy, 2008).

Immediately after the first season ended, *SportBusiness International* observed, "The IPL has shown what can be achieved in sport through innovation, creativity and a dynamic approach. But we shouldn't forget that the particular set of circumstances which existed at its inception are unlikely to be entirely replicated anywhere else anytime soon" ("The sport business debate," 2008, p. 62).

The first season generated tremendous television viewership and high advertising revenues in India. The matches became "must-see" viewing in India, with the country fixated on the tournament. The media rights agreement with WSG was renegotiated, increasing the rights fee from $1 billion over 10 years to more than $1.5 billion for the remaining nine years of the original term.

The franchise owners did better financially than had been expected for the first year, with at least two teams believed to have been profitable, and two more thought to have broken even. There was considerable interest in the press about the financial performance of franchises. While this information was not disclosed, most observers believed that franchise owners did better. The financial prospects for franchisees were illustrated in February 2009, when the champion Rajasthan Royals sold an 11.7% share of the franchise for about $15.4 million. This transaction valued the franchise at about $140 million, more than twice the team's $67 million franchise fee (Gollapudi, 2009).

Off-Season Developments

The environment for the IPL changed dramatically after the end of the 2008 season. First, the global financial crisis struck in September. As the 2009 season approached, teams found it difficult to sell sponsorship. Sony struggled to sell advertising time. One of the league's major sponsors withdrew. In addition, the rupee declined against the dollar, causing franchises to pay substantially more for their foreign players, who were paid in U.S. dollars, in contrast to Indian players who were paid in rupees at a fixed conversion rate.

The other significant issue was security. In November 2008, terrorists conducted a three-day attack on Mumbai, laying siege to several of the city's finest hotels and killing more than 170 people. One of the focal points was the Taj Mahal Palace Hotel, the hotel of choice for visiting cricket teams.

The Mumbai attacks reemphasized the terrorist threat in south Asian countries, and some foreign cricket players expressed concern for their security. The inaugural Twenty20 Champions League tournament, scheduled for December 2008, was cancelled. However, the cricket world could take some solace in the fact that while the game was extremely popular in some dangerous countries, cricket itself had never been the target of a terrorist attack.

That changed three months later, on March 3, 2009. The Australian national team had been scheduled to tour Pakistan, but had canceled due to security concerns. The Sri Lankan team agreed to make the tour in place of Australia. As it headed for a match against the Pakistani national team in Lahore, Pakistan, it was struck by a dozen heavily armed, masked attackers armed with rifles and rocket launchers. In a 15-minute battle with police guarding the team, the attackers killed five Pakistani police and wounded several of the Sri Lankan players and officials.

The second IPL season was due to start in mid-April, just weeks away. There was one additional potential security concern—the Indian general election was scheduled to be held during the IPL season, and law enforcement personnel would be fully engaged with election security. The Indian government requested that the season be rescheduled, but the international cricket calendar did not have an open window sufficient to hold the tournament. The season would either have to be cancelled, held in India amid serious security concerns, or moved to another country. This had the potential for serious implications to television and sponsorship contracts.

On March 23, the IPL announced that it would conduct its 2009 season on schedule, beginning three weeks later, on April 10. The following day, it announced that the tournament would be held in South Africa.

THE SECOND SEASON (IPL-II)

Despite the last minute change of venue, the 2009 season was a success. The tournament was embraced by its South African hosts, and matches played to enthusiastic crowds. The matches were also avidly followed in India, as they had been during the first season. More people watched more games on television than in the first season, but ratings were down slightly as they watched for shorter periods. This may have been partially due to more matches being played during afternoon working hours to accommodate a five-week tournament rather than 2008's six-week schedule. Analysis of viewing patterns indicated that fans had developed allegiances to their home teams.

While franchise financials were not publicly disclosed, observers believed that by the end of the second season franchises were ahead of their initial

TABLE 4.1. Estimated IPL franchise profit/loss for first two seasons (2008 and 2009)

All values in Rs crore (translated in May 2008 at approximately Rs 1 crore = $0.25 million, and in May 2009 at Rs 1 crore = $0.20 million).

Central Revenues consist of Television (20.0 in 2008; 28.0 in 2009) and Central Sponsorship (15.0 in 2008; 13.0 in 2009).

	Mumbai Indians	Bagalore Royal Challengers	Hyderabad Decan Chargers	Chennai Super Kings	Delhi Daredevils	Punjab Kings XI	Kolkata Knight Riders	Rajasthan Royals
Revenue—2008								
Central Revenue	35.0	35.0	35.0	35.0	35.0	35.0	35.0	35.0
Local—Team Sponsors	11.0	1.4	17.0	14.0	19.8	14.0	28.0	13.4
Local—Gate Receipts	14.0	10.0	12.0	12.8	15.4	9.0	20.0	8.0
Total Revenue	60.0	46.4	64.0	61.8	70.2	58.0	83.0	65.4
Expenses—2008								
Franchise Fee	45.0	48.0	45.0	36.0	34.0	30.4	31.0	27.0
Team Costs	20.0	22.0	24.0	24.0	23.0	25.0	25.0	13.0
Advertising	14.0	12.0	7.0	7.0	14.6	7.0	14.0	7.0
Administration	6.0	6.0	6.0	6.0	6.0	6.0	6.0	6.0
Total Expenses	85.0	88.0	82.0	73.0	77.0	68.4	76.0	53.0
Profit (Loss)—2008	(25.0)	(41.6)	(18.0)	(11.2)	(6.8)	(10.4)	7.0	3.4
Revenue—2009								
Central Revenue	41.0	41.0	41.0	41.0	41.0	41.0	41.0	41.0
Local—Team Sponsors	20.5	1.5	3.0	17.0	20.7	14.0	23.0	12.5
Local—Gate Receipts	4.8	4.8	4.8	4.8	4.8	4.8	4.8	4.8
Total Revenue	65.8	47.3	48.8	62.8	66.5	59.8	68.8	58.3
Expenses—2009								
Franchise Fee	45.0	48.0	45.0	36.0	34.0	30.4	31.0	27.0
Team Costs	20.0	22.0	24.0	24.0	23.0	25.0	25.0	13.0
Advertising	3.0	1.0	1.0	2.0	1.0	1.0	2.0	1.0
Administration	10.0	10.0	10.0	10.0	10.0	10.0	10.0	10.0
Total Expenses	78.0	81.0	80.0	72.0	68.0	66.4	68.0	51.0
Profit (Loss)—2009	(12.2)	(33.7)	(31.2)	(9.2)	(1.5)	(6.6)	0.8	7.3

Sources: 2008 data from Shamni Pande and Tejeesh N.S. Behl, "Will Cricket's New Czars Make Money?" *Business Today*, May 14, 2008. Online at: http://businesstoday.digitaltoday.in/index.php?option=com_content&task=view &id=5206&issueid=28, (accessed October 15, 2008). Team sponsorship data for 2008 was taken from the source for 2009 data. 2009 data from Pande, "Economics of IPL-2," loc. cit. Online at: http://www.scribd.com/doc/20718863 /Economics-of-IPL-2 (accessed January 8, 2010).

financial expectations and moving toward profitability (Pande, 2009). The biggest losers were Indian-based sponsors, who lost the opportunity for marketing activities because the matches were held in South Africa.

Following the second season, BCCI terminated its relationship with IMG due to concern over high fees. This was highly controversial, and the company was quickly reinstated to manage key areas of the IPL, albeit with reduced compensation. The initial arrangement had called for IMG to receive 10 percent of the IPL's gross revenue. This led to fees reported to be Rs 429 million for IPL-I, and Rs 330 million for IPL-II.[1] Eventually, the BCCI reinstated IMG for eight years, at a fixed Rs 270 million per year.[2]

The third season, scheduled to begin March 12, 2010, would be played over six weeks, and would again take place in India.

SUCCESS INDICATORS

After just two seasons, one of which was moved out of India at the last minute, it seemed clear that the IPL had achieved success. The tournament was hugely popular in India, and closely followed throughout the cricket-playing world. The television rights had proven to be extremely valuable, attracting lucrative advertising fees, as demonstrated by the substantial increase in the renegotiated rights contract. *SportsPro* magazine estimated the IPL to be the world's sixth most valuable sports property, at $1.6 billion, in a study published in July/August 2009, behind only the NFL, Major League Baseball, the NBA, NASCAR, and the FIFA World Cup. They estimated the IPL to be more valuable than properties such as Formula One racing and the Summer Olympics ("The world's most valuable," 2009, p. 73).

Franchises dramatically increased in value. The league was planning an auction for two new franchises to participate in the 2011 season, with minimum bids set at $225 million—more than four times the minimum bid in the 2008 auction, and twice the amount of the highest 2008 bid (Gollapudi, 2009).

Players benefited tremendously, generating higher salaries for the short IPL season than they received for a full year from their national cricket boards. Allowing the market to set player salaries illuminated the degree to which salaries had been depressed by the traditional restrictions on player mobility.

The sport of cricket also benefited, as the tournament attracted worldwide interest and allowed fans from all cricket-playing countries to see their best players compete against each other in the fast-paced, viewer-friendly Twenty20 format of the sport. This also posed challenging questions for both the sport's global governing body (ICC) and other national cricket boards. How should they adjust their schedules and contracts to enable their contracted players to participate in the IPL? How could they take advantage of the excitement generated by the IPL, without losing control of their players and without jeopardizing their financial situations due to demands for increased player salaries?

DRIVERS OF SUCCESS

The success of the IPL was greatly enabled by the league's ability to leverage its assets and minimize its inherited liabilities. It also benefited from a number of growth accelerators, and was able to effectively deal with growth inhibitors. In addition, the IPL was nimble in addressing unanticipated problems as they arose.

Leveraging Assets

The IPL had a number of assets that it was able to leverage for success. One was the position of the BCCI. As an important member of the cricket establishment, BCCI was able to attract top players. The ICL, by contrast, was outside the cricket establishment, and could only attract players who were willing to jeopardize their ability to play for their national teams. As the national board for cricket in India, BCCI was also able to gain access to stadiums. A renegade league that opposed the cricket establishment would have had difficulty in both attracting players and securing facilities for their matches.

A second critical asset that the IPL leveraged was the players. Top players had high interest in the league for two reasons. First, the weekly pay they received from their national boards was low compared to what they could receive from the IPL. Secondly, they relished the opportunity to compete with the best players in the world, regardless of what country those players were from. As a result of these factors, national boards that resisted the IPL fostered discontent among their best players, as seen in the case of the England and Wales Cricket Board, which made its players available for the second IPL season.

A third important asset the IPL leveraged was its connection to the other Indian passion, Bollywood. Two franchise co-owners were Bollywood stars, and franchises used Bollywood to promote their teams as well as to transform IPL matches from mere sporting events to entertainment extravaganzas. This helped drive fan excitement.

A fourth critical asset was the partnership with IMG. *SportzPower* reported: "The IPL was conceptualized, marketed, managed, and conducted professionally by IMG. . . . At the conclusion of IPL II, commissioner Lalit Modi was effusive in eulogizing the global sports management company" (Narula, 2009).

Minimizing Inherited Liabilities

Though BCCI was one of the leading national boards and part of the cricket establishment, the ICC controlled the international cricket calendar. The first IPL season was scheduled to take advantage of a relative lack of competing events during late April and May 2008, but some players still had to miss part of the IPL season due to national team commitments. The success of the IPL, and enthusiasm among players to participate, created pressure for the ICC to reduce the amount of schedule conflict with the IPL season. Thus, although not having control over the international calendar, the IPL was able to exert influence.

Growth Accelerators

The IPL benefitted from a number of factors that accelerated its growth. An important growth accelerator was the original $1 billion media contract. Having this in place prior to the franchise auction provided a measure of value to potential franchise bidders, and signaled that the league would be a serious economic power. This was amplified by the early sponsorship agreements signed by the league.

Signing key international cricket stars prior to the franchise auction also accelerated growth. The league's prospectus included many marquee players, signaling to the cricket world that the league was real and should be taken seriously. This was in stark contrast to the ICL, whose players were regarded as past their prime, or disgruntled.

Another key growth accelerator was innovation. The IPL innovated in many ways. One was the player auction. This established a market value for players, attracted enormous attention among cricket fans, and highlighted the quality of talent that the new league offered. A related innovation was building teams using the best players from many countries, mixed with local players. While common in most sports, this was less used at the elite level of cricket where competition had mostly been between national teams.

The league also innovated in marrying sport with entertainment. This enabled the league to appeal to a broad audience within India, attracting far more attention than if it had focused solely on the cricket matches.

Growth Inhibitors

There were a number of factors that might have inhibited the growth of a new cricket league, but which the IPL was able to avoid or minimize. These included inability to get access to stadiums, inability to get television time, and lack of interest on the part of top players. As we have seen, the IPL was able to avoid these problems.

Another potential growth inhibitor was the politics associated with the world of cricket. One political minefield was the ICC-BCCI relationship. The first IPL season was scheduled to take advantage of a relative lack of competing events during late April and May 2008. As of 2010, the ICC had not increased tensions by scheduling ICC events that would preclude most star players from playing in the IPL seasons.

Another political minefield was the politics of the BCCI. *SportzPower* noted in late 2009 that "Lalit Modi . . . is battling for survival within the murky world of BCCI politics" ("Lalit Modi to face," 2009). Although Modi was confirmed in late 2009 as chairman and commissioner through 2012, the media continued to report rifts within the BCCI. Any such ongoing tensions could well reduce the effectiveness of the IPL management team.

In April 2010, Lalit Modi was suspended by the BCCI. The suspension was based on accusations of corruption related to the sale of new franchises and the awarding of broadcast rights. Allegations of fraud and side payments have been part of the storyline in many global sports—the International Olympic Committee and the world of soccer are but two examples. The cricket world also has lived with such allegations on an ongoing basis. In some cases the allegations also extend to on-field match fixing associated with gambling groups. All such allegations hit the integrity aspect of either the on-field or off-field aspects of a league, and can be an important growth inhibitor, at least in the short run.

Yet another potential inhibitor was the difficulty in maintaining strong working relationships with key partners. Tensions between IMG and BCCI have been described previously. Franchise owners were also reported to be upset at not being heavily consulted about key decisions, such as the decision (later reversed) to terminate IMG. The media reported that four franchise owners opposed this decision ("IMG Ouster," 2009).

ADAPTATION AND FLEXIBILITY IN PROBLEM SITUATIONS

The first IPL season involved many challenges, in part due to the short time between league formation and the start of the season. Quick action and responding rapidly to emerging needs are common to all early stage ventures. The IPL and its franchise owners knew that the first season would involve learning as they went, and effectively meeting those challenges.

However, they also found that some of their plans needed changing, and adapted accordingly. This was clearly seen in the matter of the cheerleaders recruited by some IPL teams. The original concept, innovated by the Bangalore Royal Chargers and quickly adopted by others, was to use NFL-style cheerleaders to promote the teams and enhance the entertainment value of the events. The Royal Challengers hired the NFL's Washington Redskins cheerleaders to perform and to recruit and train local women to be cheerleaders. This attracted immediate, intense opposition as being inconsistent with Indian cultural norms, and dominated coverage in the Indian press. Franchises responded by changing the cheerleaders' uniforms from the highly revealing attire common in the NFL to outfits that were more consistent with Indian sensibilities.

The most dramatic problem that required effective adaptation was the security crisis that faced the league prior to the second season. The league and its franchise owners demonstrated considerable flexibility in making its last-minute change of venue for all 59 matches from India to South Africa. A successful second season was important in solidifying the league's first season success, delivering on contract commitments with media and sponsor partners, and maintaining its momentum with fans. With its nimble adaptation to the security challenges in 2009, the league achieved financial success in the short term and positioned itself well for the long term.

CONCLUSION

After two years, the IPL was one of the most successful start-up leagues in sports management history. The IPL leveraged key assets such as India's passions for cricket and Bollywood. However, as success brings inevitable tensions, it also brings differing claims as to the father(s) of that success, disputes over previously agreed revenue sharing rules, and ongoing decision rights. This is seen in BCCI's change of IMG's compensation from a revenue share to a fixed fee model (at a rate well below its fee for the first two years). A number of the franchise owners whose support was vital to the IPL's success felt they had a limited say in key decisions affecting the value of their investments.

After two seasons, cricket governing bodies in other countries, as well the ICC, were still feeling their way as to how to coexist with the high-profile IPL. These bodies must balance the value of the IPL to the world of cricket—including its value to players—with the league's potential to intrude into their own decision rights and the value of their own sports properties.

Endnotes

1. Approximately $10.7 million and $6.6 million, respectively.
2. The dispute between BCCI and IMG was extensively reported, particularly in the Indian online publication *SportzPower*. See articles published throughout September 2009.

References

Akhya thrills Kotla as Delhi Daredevils take on Rajasthan Royals. (2008, April 19). *United News of India*.

Akshay hopes to be lucky mascot for Delhi Daredevils. (2008, March 31). *Indo-Asian News Service*. Retrieved from http://www.thaindian.com/newsportal/sports/akshay-hopes-to-be-lucky-mascot-for-delhi-daredevils_10033075.html

Bombings may force Warne, Watson to go home. (2008, May 15). *Asian News International*.

Delport, D. (2008, June 2). IPL ends on glittering note. *Daily News*, p. 1.

Dobbs, M.E., Harrison, J.R., Zhao, X. & Wade, J.B. (2008, July). Going, going, gone: Niche characteristics and mortality of professional sports leagues. *European Group for Organizational Studies*, Amsterdam.

Gollapudi, N. (2009, December 17). $225M Base Price for Two New IPL Franchises. *ESPNCricinfo.com*. Retrieved from http://www.cricinfo.com/ipl2010/content/story/440027.html?CMP=OTC-RSS

IMG Ouster: BCCI meets Wed. to decide action plan. (2009, September 2). *Sportz Power*. Retrieved from http://www.sportzpower.com/?q=content/img-ouster-bcci-meets-wed-decide-action-plan

IPL is too appealing. (2008, April 16). *Metro*, 48.

IPL off to an electrifying start. (2008, April 19). *Financial Express*. Retrieved from http://www.financialexpress.com/news/ipl-off-to-an-electrifying-start/298772/

Is there life outside cricket? (2008, April). *SportBusiness International*, 58.

Lalit Modi to face the heat in Dec. 17 IPL hearing. (2009, December 15). *Sportz Power*. Retrieved from http://www.sportzpower.com/?q=content/lalit-modi-face-heat-dec-17-ipl-meeting

Narula, S. (2009, September 1). More than money behind IMG's ouster. *Sportz Power*. Retrieved from http://www.sportzpower.com/?q=content/more-money-behind-imgs-ouster

Pande, S. (2009, May 30). Economics of IPL-2. *Business Today*. Retrieved from http://businesstoday.intoday.in/index.php?option=com_content&task=view&id=11551&issueid=5206

Pande, S. & Behl, T.N.S. (2008, May 14). Will cricket's new czars make money? *Business Today*. Retrieved from http://businesstoday.intoday.in/index.php?option=com_content&task=view&id=5206

Roy, S. (2008, June 3). Withdrawal symptoms for fans, cheer for businesses. *Mint*. Retrieved from http://www.livemint.com/articles/2008/06/02211150/Withdrawal-symptoms-for-fans.html?atype=tp

Salman for the closing of IPL. (2008, June 1). *The Times of India*.

The sport business debate. (2008, June). *SportBusiness International*, 62.

The world's most valuable sports properties (2009, July/August). *SportsPro Magazine*, 71.

Traffic management goes for a toss. (2008, April 19). *The Hindu*. Retrieved from http://www.thehindu.com/2008/04/19/stories/2008041961820300.htm

5

Get Fit with the Grizzlies: Application of Entrepreneurship in Sport Sponsorship

RICHARD L. IRWIN, CAROL IRWIN, AND JORIS DRAYER

INTRODUCTION

Similar to the sport industry, sponsorship—specifically, sport sponsorship—inherently possesses attributes characterized as entrepreneurial in nature. This may be best illustrated by the 1984 Summer Olympic Games, hosted by Los Angeles, widely viewed as the most significant catalyst for growth in American and perhaps global sport sponsorship. Prior to the 1984 Games, Olympic financing primarily came from government funding, lotteries, and donations. However, due to numerous economic challenges confronting the International Olympic Committee and prospective host communities, as well as significant losses incurred by previous host communities Montreal and Moscow, The Olympic Committee began researching a new form of funding. Responding to this challenge, Peter Ueberroth, chairman of the Los Angeles Olympic Organizing Committee, devised an innovative plan, minimizing the burden placed upon California tax payers, and relying extensively on private corporate support for generating the funds necessary to host the Games in L.A.

The 1984 Games undoubtedly fulfill the market-based model of entrepreneurship advanced by Schneider, Teske, and Mintrom (1995) with three basic functions performed by entrepreneurs: (a) discovering and meeting unfulfilled needs; (b) assuming risk with uncertainty, including risk related to reputational, emotional, and financial considerations; and (c) assembling networks capable of undertaking change and the most commonly cited characteristic—innovativeness (Spencer, Kirchhoff & White, 2008); Holt, Rutherford & Clohessy, 2007).

While Peter Ueberroth and his management team not only recognized a unique opportunity through discovering the need to generate appropriate funding, it was not without significant opposition. Many saw this revolutionary change, or commercialization of the Olympics, counter to the Olympic mores. Lastly, the change in policy could not have succeeded without involvement from a multitude of key stakeholders including the International Olympic Committee, the United States Olympic Committee and its individual national governing bodies, the local organizing committee, and the collection of global companies recognizing the opportunity to salvage one of the world's greatest sporting events from potential extinction as well as leverage the unique marketing platform for self-promotional purposes.

Through use of this risk-taking funding strategy, corporate sponsorship of the Olympic Games specifically, and sport in general, has flourished. In the subsequent quarter of a century, as sport sponsorship experienced exponential growth worldwide the entrepreneurial nature of the relationship between rights sellers and rights buyers has likewise remained intact. Several sponsorship trends reflect key entrepreneurial characteristics embraced by sport properties endeavoring to sustain, if not improve, sponsorship value as well as maintain economic performance in a challenging economy. For example, European football's Championship League, the National Collegiate Athletic Association (NCAA), and NASCAR have proactively adopted an ambitious "less is more" philosophy, reducing the number of sponsors, in an effort to shift the emphasis away from a sales-focused perspective toward a service-focused emphasis, with the intent of delivering increased value to the limited number of remaining sponsors.

Additionally, a number of American professional sport leagues are innovatively viewing sponsorship as an opportunity to explore for-profit business development partnerships. For instance, as a result of successful, million-dollar deals with Reebok and Sirius Satellite, the NFL includes stock warrants or options in sponsorship rights negotiations whenever possible. Likewise, performance-based agreements, a practice embraced by the NHL following the 2004–05 lockout, have become more prevalent within sponsorship. As a means of attracting sponsors back to the league after the seasonal sabbatical, the NHL offered sponsorship agreements with compensation tied to metrics such as media ratings, website hits, game attendance, and product sales. This approach, which has subsequently become more popular, unquestionably demands that the rights holder or sponsorship seller assume a significant amount of risk in an effort to achieve a set of predetermined performance standards.

Similarly, a number of sport organizations have found substantial benefit in assuming the role of sponsor or rights buyer as opposed to the more traditional role of sponsorship seller. For instance, Major League Baseball has initiated an aggressive portfolio of music tour sponsorships in order to penetrate a new market of licensed apparel consumers ("MLB scores," 2004).

The entrepreneurial spirit associated with sponsorship has not been limited to sport properties or sport marketers. Sponsorship has continued to thrive because it provides sport marketers a brand extension vehicle that is not only cost effective but impacts consumers individually and directly, unlike traditional media advertising. Sponsorship also serves as a resource for both rights holder/seller and rights buyers to enhance organizational image, reputation, and culture, thereby providing properties and sponsors alike with a distinguishable competitive advantage. Such was the case when Santander, a Spanish banking firm, chose sponsorship of a Formula One racing team as a key platform to illustrate the company's global identity.

As such, corporations and sport properties endeavor to use sponsorship, much like other marketing and media channels, for the fulfillment of marketing and communications objectives ranging from enhancing organizational position with the marketplace through increased brand awareness and sales to the fulfillment of public service initiatives. In fact, it could be argued that the most meaningful sponsorship attribute is its inherent, integrative results-based orientation capable of simultaneously fulfilling one or more institutional marketing objectives.

Within the context of this chapter, the relationship of greatest interest is that between sponsors seeking to achieve public service-oriented objectives and entrepreneurship. Researchers found a strong relationship between a corporate sport sponsor's interest in pursuing public service-oriented outcomes—including corporate community engagement and social responsibility initiatives—and innovative, emerging sponsorship opportunities such as naming rights, grassroots initiatives, and start-up ventures such as women's professional sport (Lough & Irwin, 2001).

For instance, a number of corporations, headquartered in a community offering the prospect of a new facility via the recruitment or retention of a professional sport franchise, have earned "hometown hero" status by purchasing facility naming rights, essentially ensuring project completion through the provision of contractually obligated income. While perhaps not the typical "social good" most would expect of the rights buyers, corporate motives for engaging in this innovative funding and branding tactic typically focus on enhancing the community's quality of life, hence, performing a notable public service. This was clearly the case when Federal Express Corporation committed nearly $100 million to build an arena as part of the community's quest to lure an NBA franchise to Memphis, Tennessee, home to the company's world headquarters.

Corporate social responsibility represents an opportunity for the business sector to unite with the public and address joint responsibilities associated with critical social issues challenging the community (Lewis, 2003). More-over, consumer attitudes toward a firm have been found to be more favor-able when the initiative involves a local social cause as opposed to one that is national (Ross, Patterson, & Stutts, 1992). This undoubtedly relates to the psychological contract between a community and its corporate citizens whereby all parties work collectively to achieve a common set of goals (Burke, 1999).

With many corporations employing a business-driven approach to their corporate social responsibility affiliating with the local professional fran-chise through sponsorship makes good business sense. Typically, the team possesses a star power that results in the effective transmission of values (Roy & Graeff, 2003) and engenders high levels of identification or emo-tional involvement—attributes capable of attracting attention and influence positive change within a community (Babiak & Wolfe, 2006; Underwood, Bond & Baer, 2001).

Many believe that sport, particularly professional sport, has a similar re-sponsibility to not only actively pursue but also take the lead in corporate social action (Babiak & Wolfe, 2006; Zeigler, 2007). Similarly, a majority of residents polled within professional team markets strongly believe that a sport franchise is obligated to address local community issues (Irwin, Sutton & McCarthy, 2002; Roy & Graeff, 2003). Therefore, it is important that pro-fessional sports teams embrace public service and socially responsible ac-tions in order to address key issues confronting their community, especially those associated with challenges facing youth, primarily within the areas of education, recreation, and health.

Generally speaking, these social action programs embody the character-istics used to define entrepreneurship—specifically, social entrepreneurship, which can be a vehicle for attempting to solve social problems (Ball, 2005), and can be achieved through the use of sport (Cilleti & Ratten, 2009). Like-wise, Cilleti and Ratten (2009) propose that community-based entrepreneur-ship in sport is achieved through sporting teams partnering with local com-munity organizations, such as schools, to create collaborative programs. Social agenda collaboration makes good sense given the public's expecta-tions of both parties.

GET FIT WITH THE GRIZZLIES

The purpose of this chapter is to highlight how a professional sport fran-chise, the NBA's Memphis Grizzlies, used an entrepreneurial spirit to secure as well as execute sponsorship of a community-based social responsibility initiative called "Get Fit with the Grizzlies." The program embodies the ba-sic constructs found within the market-based model of entrepreneurship (Schneider, Teske, & Mintrom, 1995): discovering and meeting unfulfilled needs, assuming risk with uncertainty (including risk related to reputational, emotional and financial), and assembling a network capable of undertaking change.

The "Get Fit with the Grizzlies" program was the brainchild of Andy Dolich, the Grizzlies' president of business operations at the time. He became aware of the startling national statistics regarding childhood obesity and was personally disturbed by the data. Using this as motivation, he discussed the problem with school district administration and found that Memphis childhood overweight rates were higher than the national levels. Discussions between the two networks were fodder for the genesis of the entire Get Fit program, which soon became reality.

The Get Fit program was based on a six lesson (6 week) instructional curriculum delivered to all MCS fourth and fifth graders by the elementary school's physical education (PE) teacher during their PE class, which took place once a week for approximately 30–45 minutes. The two grades chosen (fourth & fifth) were identified as having the highest overweight rates by school district data. Veteran elementary PE teachers within MCS, who had great understanding of the childhood obesity dilemma in Memphis , were chosen to write the innovative, integrated curriculum. The lessons focused on exposing children to the basic components of fitness; nutrition and body composition, cardiovascular endurance, muscular strength and endurance, and flexibility. Participating students kept track of their weekly physical activity minutes and servings of different food groups using a special Get Fit activity and food log, which their parents were required to supervise and sign. Parents were also included in homework assignments, some as simple as going outside and playing with their child.

Students completing most of the program received logical and logoed incentive prizes, such as jump ropes and water bottles. Individual schools, upon completing all requirements, were visited by the Memphis Grizzlies' mascot, Griz, along with spirit team members who hosted special assemblies that communicated healthy choices for participating students. Also, students who consistently completed and turned in their logs were invited to be a part of a special Achievement Day with the Grizzlies at FedExForum, home arena for the Grizzlies. Memphis Grizzlies' players, dancers, and coaches helped to make this day memorable by further educating the group by means of healthy diet and exercise tips, plus actually playing basketball with the students on the Grizzlies' court.

Need Discovery and Fulfillment

Obesity has become an epidemic among American youth as the prevalence of overweight children ages 6–11 years has almost tripled in only 25 years (Ogden, Carroll, & Flegal, 2008). According to the Centers for Disease Control and Prevention (CDC), most densely populated urban areas in the United States have elevated childhood overweight prevalence rates (CDC, 2008). Obesity is also strongly associated with minority populations and with lower socioeconomic status (Wolf & Colditz, 1998). Plus, the South possesses the nation's highest childhood obesity rates, and the large metropolitan area of Memphis, Tennessee, is positioned right in the middle of all these negative conditions.

Results from the Youth Risk Behavior Survey (YRBS), a national self-report surveillance system for adolescent health behaviors, as well as local data sources indicate that Memphis City Schools' (MCS) students have an over-weight prevalence rate significantly greater than the national average (CDC, 2008). Harper (1991) reported that entrepreneurship is often greater during times of economic crises, and the current youth wellness crisis would simi-larly signal a need for an entrepreneurial spirit.

Fundamental to the market-based model of entrepreneurship advanced by Schneider, Teske, and Mintrom (1995) is *discovery of an unfulfilled need*. The excessive volume of overweight children within the Memphis metropoli-tan market was particularly distressing and signaled need for immediate in-tervention by multiple parties. Hence, the wheels were put into motion by the Grizzlies and Memphis City Schools to launch a program to combat this escalating social issue by teaching the students how to avoid the two major causes for obesity: poor diet and physical inactivity. This unique program was the tangible *fulfillment* of the *discovered need*. According to the Griz-zlies' director for community investment, "We see childhood obesity as a big problem. Get Fit with the Grizzlies was born out of our desire to be that other voice that says you need to eat right, exercise, and make healthy life-style choices."

Risk and Proactive Approach

The presence of reputational, emotional, and/or financial *risk* has been cited as an attribute germane to the market-based model of entrepreneur-ship (Schneider, Teske & Mintrom, 1995), and commonly reported in the lit-erature as a characteristic associated with entrepreneurial behavior. In addition to the risk inherent to any social marketing initiative, the Memphis Grizzlies were insistent on the use of a theoretically grounded assessment protocol designed by a third-party academic research team to determine the impact of Get Fit. A team sponsorship representative said, "While most of the costs associated with program have been covered by sponsorship reve-nue I am sure we would have had some sort of program like Get Fit with the Grizzlies. But, as far as risk, it really comes from that proof of performance piece" (personal communication).

The outcome assessment plan was a *proactive approach*, also a noted entrepreneurship feature (Holt, Rutherford & Chohessey, 2007), and further illustrates the entrepreneurial spirit exhibited by the Memphis Grizzlies. Moreover, beneficiary-oriented, change-related outcome assessments ad-ministered by an objective scholarly research team are typically absent from corporate social responsibility initiatives (Babiak & Wolfe, 2006). In the case of the Grizzlies, the evaluation plan potentially exposed the franchise, as its benefactor, to multiple sources of risk, such as disclosure if the program was unsuccessful, and thus, sponsor non-renewal. Such resolute efforts demonstrate the sport organization's willingness to go beyond simply touting its corporate celebrity status and generate authentic measures of accountability for their socially driven initiatives in hopes of enhancing program legitimacy and franchise credibility within the marketplace.

The Get Fit program was principally influenced by the Social Cognitive Theory (Bandura & Walters, 1963; Bandura, 1986), a theory used in research associated with youth learning and acquisition of health behaviors (Glanz, Rimer, & Lewis, 2002). This model focuses on a primary construct called "reciprocal learning," which means that children learn best by integrating many different channels for new information (e.g., other children, parents, community organizations), and not just what happened in their regular classroom. Using this theoretical approach, a pre-post test protocol was designed by a local university research team using an 18-item "Get Fit with the Grizzlies Student Test" drawn directly from the "Get Fit" curriculum lessons and the CDC Youth Risk Behavior Survey (Irwin, Irwin, Miller, Somes & Richey, 2010). Every fourth and fifth grader exposed to the program was given this test before the lesson began (pretest) and then immediately at the conclusion of the program (posttest). Every student's matched pre- and post-test was analyzed to see if they answered each question right or wrong.

It was anticipated that the results would provide useful measures from which to determine "Get Fit" program effectiveness and how to modify the program for the following year. As stated by one member of the Grizzlies management, "As we get the research back each year, we can compare it to the previous year and see if we are doing a good job as well as what we need to work on. We hope to get information out there, and let it be known that we are making a difference in the community" (personal communication).

Network Development

Corporate social responsibility has been identified as part of a responsibility system in which business, governmental, legal, and social actors operate according to a pattern of mutual responsiveness, interdependency, choice, and capacity (Matten & Moon, 2008). Hence, commitment to an appropriately designed localized social responsibility initiative often results in ally-building providing the participating parties with a unique source of power (Kleinrichert, 2008). As previously noted, assembly of such a network, capable of facilitating change, is also a common characteristic of entrepreneurs and entrepreneurial organizations (Schneider, Teske & Mintrom, 1995).

The Grizzlies franchise business managers were intent on *developing a network* of experts by assembling a group of specialists possessing knowledge of, as well as interest in, combating the identified health problem, in order to effectively launch an authentic health knowledge and behavioral change program. The group consisted of health and fitness educators and administrators from MCS, academic research specialists from a local university, and a select group of corporate sponsors, in addition to team representatives. According to a Grizzlies business executive, "We had to bring in a team of experts to guide us as how to best run this program" (personal communication).

THE TEAM'S ROLE

In addition to serving as program benefactor, the Grizzlies provided a unique source of star power frequently cited as capable of attracting attention and influencing change within targeted beneficiaries (Babiak & Wolfe, 2006; Roy & Graeff, 2003; Underwood, Bond & Baer, 2001). It was anticipated that the team's role was to use their celebrity status maintained by the Memphis Grizzlies as the lone major league franchise in the basketball-fanatical community of Memphis, would provide a localized initiative such as the "Get Fit" program early and long reaching strength. As stated by one Grizzlies' business operations staff member: "We felt it was of value to lend our name and brand recognition, because kids unfortunately tend to listen to that a little bit more than what their teachers and parents are saying. We want to use our 'star power' to get kids moving and change the way that kids behave when it comes to healthy eating" (personal communication).

THE SCHOOL DISTRICT

Ciletti and Ratten (2009) propose that community-based entrepreneurship in sport can be achieved through sport teams partnering with local community organizations such as schools to create collaborative programs. Unfortunately, working relationships involving health education and local professional sports organizations are not as common as one might expect. In fact, during a Physical Education Coordinators' meeting at a national convention a poll involving health and physical education coordinators representing school districts from across the nation revealed that fewer than five percent worked with a professional sport franchise on any initiative, typically due to school policy limiting, if not prohibiting collaborative programs with for-profit businesses. Thus, within this context the proposed arrangement between the Grizzlies and Memphis City Schools was viewed as innovative.

Following extensive planning involving the school district as well as school-level administrators and teachers, an innovative, integrated supplemental curriculum focusing on nutrition and exercise involving math, science, and literature courses was written for fourth and fifth grades by veteran MCS elementary physical education specialists. Implementation at the fourth and fifth grade potentially impacted the health knowledge and behaviors of 17,000 Memphis area children.

A week before the lessons were to begin, all MCS elementary PE teachers were required to attend a half-day, special training session focused on the new curriculum supplement, the activity/food logs, and various special services provided by the Grizzlies to help support the delivery of the program. Some of these services were; web site support, school-site assembly visits by Grizzlies players/mascot/dancers, a basketball coaching clinic with Grizzlies' players and coaches, and an all-district "Get Fit with the Grizzlies Achievement Day" at FedExForum, the Grizzlies home arena, at the program's conclusion.

THIRD-PARTY ANALYSTS

A team of academic research specialists from a local university experienced in health-related program evaluation was commissioned as the Get Fit third-party analysts to develop as well as execute an outcome assessment protocol. It was imperative that the objective team not only possess the requisite research skills, but familiarity with the proposed curriculum. A representative from the research team was involved in a majority of planning sessions and was permitted to provide input when appropriate.

SPONSORS

As previously noted sport sponsorships embedded into social responsibility initiatives, tend to highlight a company's exhibiting characteristics found within definitions of entrepreneurship. Consistent with this tendency, sponsors of Get Fit With the Grizzlies were keenly interested in securing membership within a network committed to meeting an unfilled need, that of influencing healthy lifestyle choices among local youth, at the risk of not realizing a direct financial return on investment. In fact, a team sponsorship representative indicated that a primarily interest among more than one program sponsor was the aforementioned assessment protocol, with favorable results serving as their return-on-investment.

This shift did not signal any sense of relief for the team. In fact, these expectations undoubtedly elevated the pressure, and subsequent *risk*, associated with the proof of performance process. As a team sponsorship representative indicated, "The challenge for us is sponsors are buying this because they think they are helping the Memphis community and youth. If we are not really doing that, I think that they will just say, 'Maybe I should do this on my own'" (personal communication).

While sponsors' funding was critical to delivering a more comprehensive Get Fit program it has already been noted that the Memphis Grizzlies were committed to launch Get Fit with or without sponsor involvement. In fact, as opposed to simply seeking financial capital as the exchanged resource from program sponsors, the Grizzlies targeted their search to a select group of companies with a genuine commitment to the program's objective, and, most importantly, willingness to invest the intellectual capital that would provide program guidance. According to a team sponsorship representative, "We are looking for companies that can enhance the program. So having the Memphis Heart Clinic, Cargill, and Turner Dairy involved in this will provide that expertise" (personal communication).

Similarly, the Grizzlies were committed to affiliating with logical corpo-

THANKS TO OUR SPONSORS FOR MAKING
GET FIT WITH THE GRIZZLIES POSSIBLE

rate partners that enhanced program authenticity due to their product or service which was health-related (see inserted sponsor Thank You ad). As can be expected, this too demanded sacrifice on behalf of the team. For instance, the team was approached by a current team sponsor, a global quick service franchise in the midst of operating a healthy lifestyles program. The Grizzlies declined an offer from the company, feeling it best to be cautious and work only with the aforementioned businesses. As stated by a senior team sponsorship representative, "The three companies that were sponsors really fit. You throw (company X) in there and it looks like, okay, now we are just taking money" (personal communication).

PROGRAM OUTLINES

Approximately 17,000 Memphis area fourth and fifth grade students with their parents participated in the Get Fit program. Likewise, close to a thousand students and parents chose to participate one Saturday in the "Get Fit with the Grizzlies Achievement Day" at FedExForum, where they interacted with Grizzlies' players, coaches, and spirit team members. These actual numbers are important *program outcomes* that reflect program effectiveness and potential sponsor product consumption.

The proof-of-performance rendered interesting results that influenced program development. The pre-test/post-test results were the crucial program outcomes. With respect to the knowledge-based questions, students showed significant improvement on almost all survey items. In particular, students showed great improvement in their familiarity with health-related vocabulary, food group categories, and daily exercises. Responses for the behavior-based questions revealed mixed results but showed some positive change. Items relating to consuming appropriate daily amounts of food groups, such as fruit and meat, showed improvement, as did daily time spent on a computer or playing video games. (see Table 5.1)

Unfortunately, reported levels of both moderate and vigorous exercise significantly decreased between the tests and time spent in front of TV actually increased. Exercise opportunities might have been curtailed by inclement weather during the posttest time frame, which took place at the

TABLE 5.1. Pre/Post Test Results For Correctly Answered Survey Items

Question	Pretest	Posttest
Knowledge-Based Questions		
1. A calorie is:	53.8%	71.1%
2. The five food categories are:	46.3%	61.3%
3. How long should a fourth/fifth grader exercise every day?	27.7%	24.0%
4. What kind of exercise should you do every day?	63.2%	75.1%
5. Why should you stretch before/after exercising?	90.9%	93.3%
6. A good stretch for your hamstrings is:	39.7%	59.3%
7. Where on the body is the quadriceps muscle?	26.0%	48.0%
8. What exercise strengthens the triceps?	50.0%	64.6%
Behavior-Based Questions		
9. Yesterday, how many times did you eat fruit?	56.6%	66.1%
10. Yesterday, how many times . . . vegetables/salad?	62.5%	66.7%
11. Yesterday, how many times . . . soda/soft drinks?	51.1%	45.2%
12. Yesterday, how many times . . . milk, cheese, dairy?	65.5%	68.6%
13. Yesterday, how many times . . . bread, cereal, grains?	69.7%	77.3%
14. Yesterday, how many times . . . meat, protein?	67.2%	72.9%
15. Yesterday, length of time watching TV?	60.0%	56.1%
16. Yesterday, length of time on computer/video games?	61.8%	68.0%
17. Yesterday, vigorous exercise?	56.46%	62.1%
18. Yesterday, moderate exercise?	58.3%	64.1%

end of November through December. Nevertheless, the results provide a snapshot of program effectiveness and direction for future program tweaking. Focus groups' interviews with the PE teachers were also accomplished, which revealed strong and weak areas of the program from their point of view. Overall findings from the different evaluation pieces prompted the following comment from one senior executive with the team: "We didn't solve the childhood obesity problem. In fact, some results got worse. Kids are still eating too much and lying around watching too much TV. So, hopefully we can change that in the future" (personal communication).

CONCLUSION

The Get Fit project clearly reflects the entrepreneurial spirit cited to exist within sport sponsorship campaigns associated with public service, including social responsibility initiatives. This innovative initiative addressing a critical local social issue served as a call to action for a network of stakeholders willing to contribute the intellectual and financial capital necessary for its implementation, which included maneuvering prohibitive school district policy while deliberately incorporating an evaluation protocol that could potentially reveal program ineffectiveness and threaten program messaging and continuance.

As speculated by Wolcott and Lippitz (2007), embracing an entrepreneurial spirit throughout the development, execution, and evaluation of Get Fit with the Grizzlies enabled the Memphis Grizzlies to increase the franchise's social and economic performance and attract sponsor involvement. One sponsorship sales representative stated, "We have so many great community programs like Read to Achieve, that we are trying to sell, but others tend to be more difficult. But this particular program stands out from other community programs. It doesn't require as much of a sales process" (personal communication).

The Memphis Grizzlies, recipients of the 2007 Steve Patterson Award for Excellence in Sports Philanthropy, have been cited as one of the most philanthropic professional sport organizations. Yet these efforts, recognized on a national basis, often go unnoticed locally as an aura of distrust surrounds the franchise particularly as it relates to team ownership, prospective relocation, and public funding usage for the Grizzlies' facility FedExForum. Hopefully, Get Fit will help the team improve these relations. As stated by one community investment executive, "You get more buy in from parents when they realize that you are doing good things out there. If they see the Grizzlies doing good things with kids then I think that they are more apt to come around and start supporting us."(personal communication).

References

Babiak, K., & Wolfe, R. (2006). More than just a game? Corporate social responsibility and Super Bowl XL. *Sport Marketing Quarterly, 15*, 214–222.

Ball, S. (2005, May). The importance of entrepreneurship to hospitality, leisure, sport, and tourism. *Hospitality, Leisure, Sport, and Tourism Network, 1*, 1–14.

Bandura, A. (1986). *Social foundations of thought and action: A social cognitive theory.* Englewood Cliffs, NJ: Prentice-Hall.

Bandura, A., & Walters, R. H. (1963). *Social learning and personality development.* New York: Holt, Rinehart & Winston.

Burke, E. M. (1999). Corporate community relations. Westport, CT: Praeger.

Centers for Disease Control and Prevention (2008). Youth Risk Behavior Surveillance —United States, 2007. *Morbidity and Mortality Weekly Report, 57*(4), 1–136.

Chrisman, J., Bauerschmidt, A., & Hofer, C. (1998, Fall). The determinants of new venture performance: An extended model. *Entrepreneurship Theory and Practice, 23*, 5–29.

Ciletti, D., & Ratten, V. (2009). Toward a Theory of Sports Entrepreneurship. Unpublished manuscript.

Glanz, K., Rimer, B. K., & Lewis, F. M. (2002). *Health behavior and health education: Theory, research and practice.* San Francisco: Wiley & Sons.

Goldsby, M., Kuratko, D., & Bishop, J. (2005). Entrepreneurship and fitness: An examination of rigorous exercise and goal attainment among small business owners. *Journal of Small Business Management, 43*(1), 78–92.

Harper, M. (1991). Enterprise development in poorer nations. *Entrepreneurship Theory and Practice, 15*(4), 7–12.

Holt, D., Rutherford, M., & Clohessy, G. (2007). Corporate entrepreneurship: An empirical look at individual characteristics, context, and process. *Journal of Leadership & Organizational Studies, 13*(4), 40–54.

Irwin, C. C., Irwin, R. L., Miller, M. E., Somes, G. W., & Richey, P. A. (2011). Get Fit with the Grizzlies: A community-school-home initiative to fight childhood obesity. *Journal of School Health, 80*(7), 333–339.

Irwin, R., Sutton, W., & McCarthy, L. (2002). Sport Promotion and Sales Management. Human Kinetics Publishers.

Kleinrichert, D. (2008). Ethics, power, and

communities: Corporate social responsibility revisited. *Journal of Business Ethics, 78,* 475–485.

Lewis, S. (2003). Reputation and corporate responsibility. *Journal of Communication Management, 7,* 356–365.

Lough, N. & Irwin, R. L. (2001). A comparative analysis of sponsorship objectives for U. S. women's sport and traditional sport sponsorship. *Sport Marketing Quarterly, 10,* 202–211.

Matten, D., & Moon, J. (2008). "Implicit" and "explicit" CSR: A conceptual framework for a comparative understanding of corporate social responsibility. *Academy of Management Review, 33,* 404–424.

MLB scores licensed apparel sales through music sponsorship. (2004, June 14). *IEG Sponsorship Report,* 8.

Ogden, C. L., Carroll, M. D., & Flegal, K. M. (2008). High body mass index for age among U.S. children and adolescents, 2003–2006. *Journal of the American Medical Association, 299,* 2401–2405.

Peredo, A. & Chrisman, J. (2006). Toward a theory of community-based enterprise. *Academy of Management Review, 31,* 309–328.

Ross, J. K., Patterson, L. T., & Stutts, M. A. (1992). Consumer perceptions of organizations that use cause-related marketing. *Journal of the Academy of Marketing Science, 20*(1), 93–97.

Roy, D. P. & Graeff, T. R. (2003). Consumer attitudes toward cause-related marketing activities in professional sports. *Sport Marketing Quarterly, 12*(3), 163–172.

Schneider, M., Teske, P., and Mintrom, M. (1995). *Public Entrepreneurs: Agents for Change in American Government,* Princeton, NJ: Princeton University Press.

Spencer, A., Kirchhoff, B., & White, C. (2008). Entrepreneurship, innovation, and wealth distribution: The essence of creative destruction. *International Small Business Journal, 26*(1), 9–23.

Turan, M., & Kara, A. (2007). An exploratory study of characteristics and attributes of Turkish entrepreneurs: A cross-country comparison to Irish entrepreneurs. *Journal of International Entrepreneurship, 5,* 25–46.

Underwood, R., Bond, E., & Baer, R. (2001). Building service brands via social identity: Lessons from the sports marketplace. *Journal of Marketing Theory and Practice, 9*(1), 1–13.

Wolcott, R., & Lippitz, M. (2007). The four models of corporate entrepreneurship. *MIT Sloam Management Review, 49*(1), 74–82.

Wolf A.M., & Colditz, G.A. (1998). Current estimates of the economic cost of obesity in the United States. *Obesity Research, 6,* 97–106.

Zeigler, E.F. (2007). Sport management must show social concern as it develops tenable theory. *Journal of Sport Management, 21,* 297–318.

6

Entrepreneurial Market Leaders: Australian Football League Expansion Through New Team Development

HEATH McDONALD AND CONSTANTINO STAVROS

INTRODUCTION

An essay by A.A Philips over 60 years ago explored the controversial term of "cultural cringe" in Australia. The author posited a notion that some Australians lacked self-belief in societal and culture endeavors unless the work had been internationally validated.[1] One exception to this inferiority complex, he noted, was sport.

Irrespective of whether such a cringe did or still does exist, the fact remains that Australians have consistently used sport as a measuring stick of their progression and place on the world stage. As a result, Australia has become a giant on the global sporting stage, boasting an array of medals and accomplishments at major events that belie its relatively small population.[2] A two-time Olympic Games host, Australia also is home to a Grand Slam tennis event, a round of the Formula One Grand Prix and a range of other elite events.

Australians have used an entrepreneurial spirit to become leaders in sport, despite the geographic and demographic boundaries that are prevalent on such a large continent. Many sports coexist in Australia in a healthy, competitive environment. For example, Australia operates four successful professional football competitions—the two forms of rugby (union and league), soccer, and an indigenous sport known as Australian football. Aside from this there are geographically diverse leagues in other sports, including baseball, basketball, cricket and netball; high levels of interest in motor and horse racing, as well as a strong focus on individual sports such as tennis, golf, and swimming.

This chapter focuses on Australian football, a game run by the Australian Football League (AFL). It is the market leader in professional Australian sports, dominating television viewing, news media coverage, and live attendance. In the shadow of global and domestic competitors, the AFL has used entrepreneurship to not only establish itself, but to thrive and prosper. In recent years, anticipating major challenges on several fronts, the AFL has undertaken an unprecedented range of entrepreneurial decisions aimed at maintaining dominance in the generations ahead. This chapter focuses on one of the most recent and complex decisions involving the establishment of two new franchises in new markets.

AFL BACKGROUND

Australian football is played at the elite level only in Australia, making it, with the arguable exception of American Football,[3] the only major professional sporting league to be only played in one market, but to be the most popular sport in that market.

The sport can trace its origins back to the mid-1800s where components of Gaelic football and rugby were combined to provide a means for cricketers to remain fit during their off-season. Australian football is often referred to by the acronym AFL, which stands for the body that governs the game, the Australian Football League. However, the competition began as the Victorian Football League (VFL) in 1897 as it operated in just one Australian state, Victoria. The VFL was comprised of eight local foundation clubs (Carlton, Collingwood, Essendon, Fitzroy, Geelong, Melbourne, St. Kilda, and South Melbourne). This competition added a team (Richmond) in 1908 and then expanded again in 1925 to include three further local entrants (Hawthorn, North Melbourne, and Footscray).

These 12 teams remained in place for over five decades as the game established itself. The latter part of the last century was the next period of team expansion and the league, renamed as the AFL in 1990, grew to sixteen teams in the period between 1987 and 1997. Two teams entered from both Western Australia[4] and South Australia,[5] the South Melbourne team was relocated to New South Wales in 1982 to form the Sydney Swans, and the Queensland capital city of Brisbane was given a team. This organization began as the Brisbane Bears in 1987, but amalgamated with the Fitzroy Lions ten years later to re-brand themselves as the Brisbane Lions.

Of these sixteen teams in the AFL, ten came from Victoria which remains the power base of the AFL. However, the sport is played in an organized manner in every state and territory of Australia. Australian football is the dominant football game in the states of Tasmania, South Australia, and Western Australia, but has a tougher battle against the rugby games which are very popular in the more northern states of Queensland and New South Wales. A map detailing the location of AFL teams is shown in Figure 6.1. It demonstrates the game's strong roots to the southern parts of the country. Figure 6.1 also shows the location of the two new franchises (noted in capital letters) that the AFL announced in 2008 it was to establish. A team from Western Sydney is scheduled to take to the playing field in 2012. The Gold Coast team, which is the main focus of this chapter, commenced play in 2011. As it was to be the 17th team in the competition, the group that orchestrated the introduction of the new team used the operational name GC17, which quickly came into popular usage. However, the new team entered the competition officially known as the Gold Coast Suns Football Club.

All AFL clubs compete annually for the "Premiership," a trophy and title awarded to the team that, after 22 regular season rounds, wins through a series of playoffs that culminate in the "Grand Final." Teams generally play eleven games at home and eleven games away, although ground-sharing arrangements and a predominance of teams from Melbourne makes the

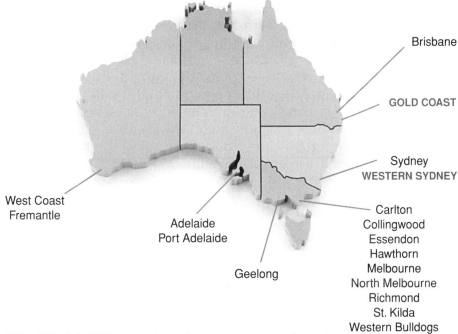

FIGURE 6.1. **AFL team locations (current and new).**
Source: www.afl.com.au

balance between home and away games far more complicated in reality. A national draft and salary cap, along with other equalization measures, have helped make the competition relatively balanced in recent years, with seven different teams having won the eight Grand Finals from 2003 to 2010.[6]

Teams are strongly encouraged, both by the league and historical precedent, to form close relationships to their supporters. One important measure of the degree of fan involvement is through the team's sales of season tickets, which allow the purchaser to typically attend the home games of the team they support. Season tickets in Australian football are referred to as "memberships," as the purchaser also procures certain other rights, such as voting for the club President and board of directors. This is a function of the Australian sporting model which is generally built on community owned and operated teams. Further, season ticket holders have greatly increased communication and social opportunities with the team and other like-minded supporters. Season ticket holders also often receive gifts or merchandise and the ability to access premium or exclusive playoff tickets. In essence, this all serves to move transactional consumers to relational consumers.

Tallies of season ticket holders are prominently highlighted by teams, who all set targets to achieve on a yearly basis and typically communicate this in their promotional efforts. Aside from delivering approximately 20–30% of team revenues, high levels of season ticket sales also equate to a psychological perception of success or strength in the competition, whereas low levels reflect a perception of underperformance.

The AFL also sells its own season ticket package and the success of this, combined with the efforts of the teams' efforts themselves, means that 586,748 season tickets were sold across the 16 AFL clubs in 2009, up 2.2% from 2008, which in turn was up 8% from 2007 (Broad, 2009). This translates to approximately one in every 37 Australians being a season ticket holder of a club. These range in cost from AU$130 to AU$950, depending on reserved seating levels and hospitality options included with game entry.

Despite the strong competitive environment noted earlier, the AFL has been a remarkable success by any measure. Attendance at AFL regular season games totals over 6.5 million, placing it far ahead of other Australian team sports in terms of average and cumulative attendance rates.[7] Its average attendance in 2008 of just over 38,000 people per game eclipsed the English Premier League, Spain's La Liga, and Italy's Serie A, and placed it in the top five of world sport.

The AFL is also the most watched sport on Australian television,[8] with average audiences for regular season games averaging over 1 million viewers. The Grand Final is typically one of the most watched events on television each year, with over 3 million people tuning in.[9]

As can be seen from the figures in Table 6.1, the AFL has performed extremely well on all three of its Key Performance Indicators (KPI) in the past decade in which a greater emphasis has been placed on expanding the popularity of the sport into newer markets.

TABLE 6.1. **AFL key performance indicators**

Key KPIs	1997	2008
Attendance	5,842,591	6,511,255
Membership	382,331	574,091
Participation	428,870	693,052

Source: Australian Football League

GROWTH FOR MARKET LEADERS

Often when entrepreneurial activities are discussed, the story is of an individual rising against the odds to create a new business. These entrepreneurs start small, but end up beating the established competitors through risk taking, cunning, and seizing opportunities others didn't recognize. As much as the oft repeated stories of Richard Branson (Virgin), Nicolas Hayek (Swatch), and Google founders Larry Page and Sergey Brin are inspiring, entrepreneurship by large market-leading organizations is also worthy of examination.

The AFL, by way of example, is a financially strong sport governing body, with a very popular product and widely recognized brand. Sales in current markets are good and growing, and in many ways the sport is the envy of all other professional sports in Australia. The AFL, therefore, could be forgiven for being a conservative and cautious organization focused on consolidation rather than growth.

The AFL continues to be highly entrepreneurial, continually developing new programs and products. These have ranged from national junior development programs featuring modified forms of the game, exhibition matches played in various parts of the world, ground rationalization, and almost annual adjustments to the rules in order to maintain the fast-paced, competitive, and exciting style of the game. Aside from these changes, the AFL has been particularly forthright in recent times in its desire to enter untapped markets, growing the overall category for its sport product. This vision includes markets both domestically in the short-term and internationally in the longer-term.

This is a sound approach, given that growth for market leaders typically comes through growing the overall category (Kotler & Keller, 2009). This strategy works because new customers typically purchase brands according to market share—so most new customers buy the market leader (Hellofs & Jacobson, 1999). Acquisition of competitors and expanding the product range are other tactics used to increase market leader share.

In March 2008, the AFL Commission (the league's governing body), supported by the existing 16 AFL Clubs, announced a plan to create two brand new teams. Both of these teams would be launched in "non-traditional" AFL states: a new team in South East Queensland, located on the Gold Coast and a new team in the Western part of Sydney, Australia's largest city and the capital of the state of New South Wales (NSW). While expansion had occurred previously, this decision was widely regarded as the boldest and most entrepreneurial move the league had made in its 110-year history.

Here we examine the rationale for the launch of these new teams, and focusing on the development of the Gold Coast team specifically, we discuss the tactics used to maximize success.

WHY TWO NEW TEAMS?

The decision to launch two new teams has been questioned by some media commentators (Hinds, 2008) and even an Australian Federal Government report concluded there were "insurmountable" cultural barriers facing the launch of the team into Western Sydney (AAP, 2009). The overriding aim of the expansion was, however, to cement the AFL's position as the number one sport in Australia, as measured by the KPIs shown in Table 6.1, as well as ensuring an increase of matches for the media to purchase in the next round of broadcasting rights.

While one option for growth would have been to encourage greater consumption of the sport through the existing products (teams), this was unlikely given their already high penetration. AFL research suggests that clubs, on average, are converting around 20% of supporters into season ticket holders. Attendance has grown annually, but is reaching capacity in many venues, particularly with stadiums in South Australia and Western Australia. Television viewing of AFL games is also already extremely strong under the current structure, with playoff games and special events among the top-rated shows on Australian television. Real sustainable growth, therefore, seems only possible by increasing penetration into the non-traditional states of Queensland and NSW. While both these states already had an AFL team,[10] the areas selected by the AFL for growth were relatively distinct from these.

The decision to focus the league expansion in these two areas was based on a number of criteria. First, there is significant population growth in these regions. The Gold Coast population was growing at 3.7% annually and was expected to continue to grow at that rate for the foreseeable future, while over 1.3 million people are estimated to live in the Western Sydney region. Initial research by the AFL suggested that 33% of the Gold Coast market was interested in the sport, as was 21% of the Western Sydney market. Of these interested people, around 75,000 on the Gold Coast and 162,000 in Western Sydney claimed they would consider purchasing season tickets for the new clubs in their area. Further to this potential fan base, there was evidence of latent demand for the AFL, particularly on the Gold Coast, which attracts large number of retirees and visitors from southern (AFL-focused) states who would be keen to reassociate themselves with the AFL on a local basis. Aside from regular fans, both regions also have significant local industries, providing a strong commercial base for club sponsors and corporate ticket sales.

In addition, new teams in these regions will ensure live television coverage of AFL games every week, as it is a condition of the AFL's media broadcast contract that team games be shown in their home state live or on very short delay. Two teams would ensure much greater AFL content in prime time in these states, providing an opportunity for further fan development. Finally, and not insignificantly, having at least two teams in every state creates regional rivalry in non-traditional markets (Brisbane vs. Gold Coast, Sydney vs. Western Sydney). These local matches have been big drawcards in both South Australia and Western Australia, and the AFL, which has thrived on these self-proclaimed "blockbusters," has designated one round each season as "rivalry round" as a promotional strategy.

THE DEVELOPMENT OF A NEW TEAM: GC17

The AFL's desire to have a team in a new market began with attempts to convince a Melbourne club to relocate elsewhere. As Australian sporting clubs are generally partially "owned" by season ticket holders, the decision to relocate is often extremely complex and politically charged. Thus, not surprisingly, such a suggestion proved unsuccessful, and was at odds with the aim of creating more "content" for media partners. The attempt to convince an existing club to relocate to the Gold Coast did, however, clearly signal the AFL's intentions to bring a second team into Queensland, thereby setting up an unusual platform for team development. Although the AFL had indicated that Gold Coast and Western Sydney were its preferred locations for new teams, they did invite bids from all over Australia in an effort to get a sense of broader support.

In response to this call, in April 2008 a campaign team was established to manage a formal bid for a new franchise from the Gold Coast. This team comprised an advisory board, a campaign manager, and two marketing/PR staff. The chairman of the bid team was John Witheriff, the managing partner of a large legal firm and the 2005 winner of "Gold Coast Citizen of the Year." The group became known as GC17 almost immediately and set about achieving objectives in seven key areas dictated by the AFL as being essential to the granting of a team license. These objectives (see Table 6.2) covered a range of factors needed to ensure the long-term viability of the team, from building a substantial supporter base to generating interest from potential local sponsors and establishing an agenda for community engagement.

One of the first decisions made was in relation to the name and branding of the bid team. The Gold Coast has been very successful over the past decade in marketing itself as not only a popular tourist destination, but also as a strong local community. The main vehicle for this has been the "Very GC" campaign run over a number of years, which has positioned the Gold Coast as a luxurious and vibrant destination for travelers and business.[11]

The GC17 bid leveraged this highly successful positioning campaign, and with permission of the local marketing officials, used a similar logo and font for the GC17 brand. The obvious synergies between the Very GC campaign and a GC17-based AFL team, in terms of excitement and tourist potential, were clear to both parties. Leveraging the established GC brand in this way played a major role in positioning the new team as something that belonged to, and in, the Gold Coast rather than being seen as an intruder from another state.

The GC17 bid team was supported by the AFL, with senior strategists advising them throughout. Perhaps it is not surprising then, that despite rumors, no other bid team for the Gold Coast area arose to challenge GC17. However, shortly after the GC17 bid team was announced, the State Government of Tasmania, the only Australian state without an AFL team, announced they would also be seeking one of the two new proposed licenses. Tasmania has always had a prominent AFL following, and has produced a large number of elite AFL players from its strong amateur competitions. AFL games are regularly played in Tasmania by interstate-based teams, and the Tasmanian government sponsored one of those teams, Hawthorn, in a deal worth approximately $15 million over 5 years.

The interest from Tasmania, itself an entrepreneurial move, proved problematic for the AFL. The bid had large public sympathy resulting from Tasmania's traditional support for, and contribution to, Australian football. The Tasmanian bid was also required to meet the criteria shown in Figure 6.2, many of which seemed unlikely for a state with a population of only around 500,000. The requirement to provide a suitable playing arena, major sponsors, and adequate support seemed to stymie Tasmania's chances. However, they very quickly accumulated over 20,000 registered supporters, established strong government support, and announced a major sponsorship deal with Mars confectionary.

Despite these impressive achievements, major concerns still existed over the location of the team within Tasmania, given intra-state rivalries and distance between towns, and the limited additional media value that a Tasmanian team would create. Tasmanians were already heavy viewers of AFL, and a local team offered only limited potential to increase that number. Increasingly, senior AFL staff suggested that a Tasmanian team would not happen in the short term. By July 2008, AFL CEO Andrew Demetriou stated: ". . . they (Tasmanian government) are absolutely entitled to put forward their proposal. But the Commission has already decided where the 17th and 18th teams are going" (O'Brien, 2008).

On the surface this appears a confused situation, with bids being encouraged even though the result seemed already determined. The "competitive" bid process served a useful and important function, however. In the Gold Coast area, the GC17 administrators were able to use the concept of a challenging bid process to rally support for the club and to build local connection with the team. Figure 6.2 shows a typical call to action from the GC17 team, including reference to the key targets (20,000 supporters) and a sense that the outcome was very much dependent on what the community did to support the bid. With Tasmania waiting in the wings and running a strong campaign, there was a growing sense that any slipup would see the chances of a team on the Gold Coast evaporate. This galvanized the community.

A multi-channel approach was taken to build a supporter base, as shown in Table 6.3. A database of 7,000 AFL-interested Gold Coast residents had been built over the preceding three years by collecting details of those attending games played in the area, and residents who had participated in AFL-related competitions and promotions. This provided a platform for a number of viral email campaigns that had a supporter-get-supporter focus. The involvement of local schools and some high-profile local celebrities also heightened the word-of-mouth aspect. These efforts were strongly supported by local media, with the local newspaper and a leading FM radio station signing on to be media partners for the bid. Regular updates on progress (particularly the number of supporters signed up) were published and broadcast, build-

FIGURE 6.2. Example GC17 Bid Promotion.
Source: Gold Coast Football Club

ing a sense of excitement and momentum. In all cases, a clear call to action was issued, typically driving people to the website for registration.

As well as using e-mail, online surveys and blogs, Facebook pages and Twitter were used to connect with the public and heighten a sense of connection to the emerging team. Those registering their support were given the opportunity to have input in to the team name, mascot, and colors further enhancing involvement.

In October 2009, the GC17 team presented their submission to the AFL Commission for review. In almost all cases, the GC17 bid had exceeded the set objectives (see Table 6.4). Public support was high with 23,000 committed supporters. Hostplus, a major superannuation (pension) fund for the hospitality, tourism, recreation, and sport industries was signed as a key partner. Other large companies, including Reebok, also pledged support, giving the GC17 bid 111 partners at all levels of business. Tense negotiations with government to secure funding for a new stadium were resolved only after a state election, but resulted in a promised stadium that would be among the best in the country. Finally, the bid team also secured key appointments, ranging from coaching and training staff to commercial operations managers.

On March 31, 2009, after some delays due to the global financial crisis and Queensland state election, GC17 was finally confirmed as the successful bidder for the 17th AFL license. AFL Chairman Mike Fitzpatrick said, "It is also a decision that we have made after a rigorous process to validate the business model for a Gold Coast Football Club. We are confident that we grant the license knowing that you have put in place the foundations to build a strong and sustainable club which will serve well the Gold Coast community."[12]

TABLE 6.2. Seven objectives for a new team

Area	The Challenge	Headline Objectives (Public)	Supporting Objectives (Internal)
1. Supporters	Prove the Gold Coast community can build a strong membership and support base	20,000 committed supporters	•> 50,000 registered prospects •> 20,000 committed supporters
2. Business	Prove the Gold Coast community can generate required levels of corporate support	111 committed business partners	•1 × presenting partner •10 × support partners •100 × business club
3. Foundations	Prove the Gold Coast community can establish first-class training and administration facilities and a positive net asset base	Commitments to long-term training and administration base and financial assets	•Training and Administration base plan—$1m pledges •Plan to achieve > $5m net assets by 2011 •Supported by "high net worth" fundraising
4. Identity	Engage the Gold Coast community in establishing the brand identity of our club	Engage community to define our name, colors, jumper, logo, and values	•Public campaign •Brand strategy process
5. Team	Work with AFL Queensland (AFLQ) to build a competitive football team and strategy for the Gold Coast team entry into AFL competition in season 2011	Appoint key people to execute our football strategy over 2008–10 to enter the AFL competition in 2011	•AFL Queensland alliance •Key appointments •Football Strategy •Preparation for November 2008 draft and season 2009, including interim training and administration base
6. Community	Prove that the Gold Coast community is actively involved in their club, and that the club is actively involved in the Gold Coast community	Engage the entire community to define agenda for social and community programs on the Gold Coast	•Establish community advisory board •Define social agenda/key programs •Local football community engagement •Business, government, other forums •Form partnerships
7. Organization	Prove that the Gold Coast can build the necessary governance structure, management team, and business plan to deliver a long term, successful, community owned, membership-based club	To establish the right governance structure for a successful community-based club	•Business plan (short/term, long/term) •Corporate governance standards and processes •Plan for member voting rights •Board structure and appointments •Management appointments

TABLE 6.3. GC17 fan development actions

Detail	Database	Community	Business	Local Football (AFL)	Public Relations
Overview	•Prior to the launch of GC17, a database of 7,000 AFL supporters had been built—with a combination of e-mail addresses and regular mail addresses. •An integrated EDM and DM campaign was sent to this database. •A supporter referral campaign was also launched	•Local schools involved in AFL were given incentives to sign up pupils and their families.	•Local businesses provided sign-up points within their stores •Partner staff databases were e-mailed	•All local football clubs were given incentives to sign up players, administration staff and families. •Kits were provided to clubs to assist this process	•Strong support from dedicated media partners "Hot Tomato" and "Gold Coast Bulletin" •Competitions to name the team etc. were successful in engaging the community •Constant presence in media of key campaign figure heads supported by promotion of milestones (e.g., signing the 10,000th supporter)
Call to action	•Visit gc17.com .au to register your support •Send in a form •Sign up your friends and family	•Complete a GC17 support form and return it to their school	•Complete a form in store •Visit www.gc17 .com.au to register your support	•Complete a GC17 support form and return it to their school	•Visit gc17.com .au to register your support

TABLE 6.4. GC17 performance against objectives

Area		Headline Objectives	Achieved
1.	Supporters GC17	20,000 committed supporters	•42,000 supporters •23,000 met engaged criteria
2.	Business GC17	111 committed business partners	•1 × presenting partner •10 × support partners •100 × business club
3.	Identity GC17	Engage community to define our name, colors, jumper, logo, and values	•Public were engaged at every stage •Team name was announced
4.	Team GC17	Appoint key people to execute our football building strategy over 2008–10 to enter the AFL competition in 2011	•Key appointment, including senior coach •Football Strategy •Preparation for Nov 2008 draft and season 2009, including. interim training and administration base

ENSURING MARKETING SUCCESS
FOR THE GOLD COAST FOOTBALL CLUB

Having secured the 17th AFL license, the marketing challenge was really only beginning for the new Gold Coast team before its first game in 2011. Sport's nature as a service product means that no amount of pretesting or planning can truly replicate the match-day experience. Not only must the new Gold Coast team ensure acceptance and attendance by the community, it must also ensure that all the entertainment aspects of modern-day sporting experiences create an atmosphere that will lead to greater enjoyment and involvement.

To do this Gold Coast will have to not only engage those fans already familiar with the AFL and its unique sport, but also seek to educate and enthuse those people who see the game as somewhat "foreign." Balancing two such different approaches is difficult for marketers. Hardcore fans might not like the patronizing nature of a team seeking to explain the sport to new users, while those new users might feel challenged by the very complex nature of the game. The Gold Coast team will also have to cope with an onset of comfort that may ensue following the license acquisition. There is a sense within the AFL community that the AFL will, given the importance of this market, not allow the new brand to fail and will provide any support necessary to guarantee its success. While such perceived assurances can be heartening, they can also often lead to complacency. Entrepreneurial strategies to motivate and engage both outside and within the club will thus be required.

One strategy to help ease the club into the community is to carefully balance the team with new, up and coming players from the region with "brand name" players drawn from existing teams. This strategy helps to counter any potential perceptions that the players are highly paid mercenaries, while also giving fans a sense of being able to achieve short-term success on the field. The Gold Coast Football Club made the concept of bringing in a high-profile player a priority, with arguably the league's best player, Gary Ablett Jr., a key signing in 2010. Gold Coast was able to make such a bold move into the market thanks to an increased salary cap in their early years.

The team will also benefit from concessions in the annual AFL draft that gave them unprecedented access to the majority of the top young prospects in the country. The AFL draft is the primary means of entry for talented players into the league, with research[13] identifying that such players reach their peak performance after six years. This priority access to elite young talent will allow the club to steadily build towards on-field success, however, much will be required off the field before then to generate and maintain the local community's support.

Gold Coast Football Club will have to ensure that its strategic objectives stay focused on the organic development of a team from the region, despite the temptation to build a broader brand. Similarly, it will be best for the team to focus on its own processes, rather than seeking to emulate or compare to those of existing clubs. While many businesses like to benchmark against others, an entrepreneurial approach by its very nature suggests new and innovate methods and measures. If the Gold Coast's management, or its fans, were to look down towards Melbourne and compare themselves to teams regularly playing in front of 50,000 fans and with season ticket lists in excess of 40,000, they may quickly grow disillusioned. Thus, the challenge will be to develop their own set of standards and priorities.

One entrepreneurial approach already being utilized is the passion of the growing team being intertwined with the enthusiasm of a local community that has grown significantly itself in recent years. People living on the Gold Coast in Australia appear relatively proud and supportive of their community and have a tendency to take a relaxed and enjoyable attitude to life. The new Australian football team has reflected this in its engagement, professionally and seriously building their brand, but maintaining a sense of pride in the values of the region in doing so. The incorporation with the region's tourism campaign and the fact that the club did not initially impose a name or colors on the team, but rather allowed these to develop over time in consultation with the community, are positive indications of this.

Naturally, as a new market, Gold Coast's challenges and strategies will be shaped by the unique environment that surrounds them. Entrepreneurs are generally not followers, but leaders, so the new team will have to carefully position their product against the significant array of entertainment options available in the region, while seeking to establish a sense of leadership. The mantle of the AFL's place in Australian sport will assist in this, but the relative popularity of other sports in the area will dissipate some of this accrued brand value. While the introduction of the Gold Coast Football Club has been a bold entrepreneurial move by the AFL, other sporting teams have already entered the market in preceding years, pre-empting any ability by the Australian football team to claim the title of the only elite sporting organization representing the region.

CONCLUSION

As with any new sporting experience, much of the background work is geared towards the moment when the gates finally open and customers arrive to experience the entertainment offered. In this instance, Gold Coast's entrepreneurial activities have started the membership experience long before actual game time. By building such involvement before the first game, Gold Coast Football Club put themselves in a strong position of succeeding by embedding the team firmly within the local community and by setting clear goals based on past experience of what determines new team success.

Further, they have been strongly supported throughout by the AFL, who has shown the foresight and level of strategic planning necessary. Acting as most successful market leaders do, the AFL has leveraged all the financial, political, and psychological advantages that come with being a dominant market player to position this new team as a strong new brand. This acts to give the community a sense of team security and longevity—removing a primary source of the risk involved in supporting a start-up franchise. If the on-field performance can match what has happened off the field, it is very likely that Gold Coast Football Club will not only be soon playing in their first Grand Final, but also playing an integral part in the ongoing success of Australia's most popular sport.

Acknowledgments

The authors kindly thank and acknowledge Christina Johns of the Gold Coast Football Club and Shaun Welch of the Australian Football League for their assistance with material in this chapter.

Endnotes

1. Published by Melbourne University Press and titled "A. A. Philips on The Cultural Cringe," the work has become a famous and oft-debated part of Australian culture.

2. As one example, the Australian Olympic team finished fifth in the overall medal tally in the 1996 Summer Olympic Games, then fourth in the overall medal tally for the 2000 and 2004 Summer Olympic Games, and seventh overall in the 2008 Summer Olympic Games.

3. American Football has been played at a professional level in Europe (under various names, including NFL Europe) from 1991 to 2007, and currently a regular season NFL game is played each season in London. A similar game to American Football is also played professionally in Canada.

4. From Western Australia, West Coast Eagles joined in 1987 and the Fremantle Dockers in 1995.

5. From South Australia, Adelaide joined in 1991 and Port Adelaide in 1997.

6. Despite the popularity of Australian football in the State of Victoria, four of the seven teams that won the Grand Final in the eight-year period noted were from outside this State.

7. The Australian Bureau of Statistics (ABS) collects extensive statistical information on Australian sport attendance and participation. See Australian Bureau of Statistics (2007) Sports Attendance in Australia, Catalogue No. 4174.0 as one example.

8. There has been some recent conjecture on which sport dominates television viewing in Australia, with the NRL (rugby league) claiming to have a higher aggregate audience, however their figures (which were only slightly higher) include a range of products in addition to their regular season (e.g., State of Origin). More direct comparisons of audiences for regular season games show AFL is a clear leader. See http://www.smh.com.au/rugby-league/league-news/we-will-fight-them-on-the-couches-league-outrates-afl-for-first-time-20091220-l7i3.html for details.

9. http://www.oztam.com.au/documents/2009/E_20090920.pdf

10. Brisbane Lions in the case of Queensland, and the Sydney Swans in NSW.

11. See www.verygoldcoast.com.au for the positioning campaign.

12. http://www.gc17.com.au/news-and-media/news/gold-coast-football-club-granted-17th-afl-licence/page-1/

13. Work done by statistical agency Champion Data with academics from RMIT University in 2009 was presented to the AFL and its members clubs at an invited seminar. It indicated the value of the first round (first 16 picks) of the AFL draft in ensuring success of clubs in subsequent years.

References

AAP (2009, June 26). *AFL rejects Senate report*. Retrieved from http://www.news.com.au/couriermail/sport/afl/story/0,27046,25694295-5016169,00.html

Broad, B. (2009, 21 July). *Club membership record defies global slowdown*. Retrieved from http://www.afl.com.au/news/newsarticle/tabid/208/newsid/81105/default.aspx

Hellofs, L. L., & Jacobson, R. (1999). Market share and customers' perceptions of quality: When can firms grow their way to higher versus lower quality? *The Journal of Marketing, 63*(1), 16–25.

Hinds, R. (2008, November 20). AFL still wild for west Sydney, even in the face of growing discord. Retrieved from http://www.theage.com.au/afl/afl-news/afl-still-wild-for-west-sydney-even-in-the-face-of-growing-discord-20091124-j837.html

Kotler, P., & Keller, K. L. (2009). *Marketing management* (13th ed.). Upper Saddle River, NJ: Pearson.

O'Brien, B. (2008, July 15). *Hope for Tassie team*. Retrieved from http://au.news.yahoo.com/a/-/newshome/4792704/

7

Bridge, Gate Keeper, Negotiator: The Sports Agent as Entrepreneur

ANNA SEMENS

INTRODUCTION

The role of agents in transfers and contractual arrangements is key to the operation of the player labor markets in professional sport. In soccer for example, FIFA estimates that 95% of transfers involve an intermediary. However, while in practice intermediaries have become key stakeholders, the lack of academic attention on agents contrasts sharply with their role in the labor market.

This chapter considers the role of agents as entrepreneurs. Setting out the sports industry in terms of an extended network of interconnected stakeholders, it is suggested that established agents, through their wide range of contacts, have been able to act as a bridge over structural holes in the network. By acting as a middleman, the agent is able to exploit the informational asymmetries inherent in the market system to add value in performing a search and match function.

Using interview data collected from sports agents, players, and clubs, the agent's role is then further explored with reference to Simmel's analysis of third party transactions. It is demonstrated that elements of both bringing two parties together and keeping them apart are integral to the operation of agents. Further, the connections and networks that develop around agents can often lead to opportunities for the agent to create new business ventures.

Contrary to neoclassical analysis, in which everyone has equal access to entrepreneurial opportunities, it is clear that in the sports industry, knowledge gained through prior experience within the network affords agents the ability to recognize entrepreneurial opportunities and to parlay this position to build their enterprise.

BACKGROUND

Sport occurs on a worldwide scale and comprises global flows in the form of migrant players, global technological developments, and the rapid flow of money. As well as this, the media dimension allows information and images to be distributed worldwide (Maguire, Jarvie, Mansfield, & Bradley, 2002). This globalization has enabled sport to be transformed into big business, with team sports increasingly dependent on revenue generated from broadcasting, sponsorship, and advertising. Interdependent commercial relationships are thus able to increasingly change the nature and character of sport (Athelaid & Snow, 1979; Maguire, 1999; Maguire et al., 2002). From a financial perspective these interdependent relationships between sports organizations, media companies, and marketing agencies have become central to the survival of commercial spectator sports, while players have been transformed into entertainers and at times superstars (Horne, Tomlinson, & Whannel, 2003).

Technological developments have enhanced "the ability of television sport to produce spectacular entertainment," promoting the sporting spectacle to markets around the world (Whannel, 2004, p. 293; see also Hersh, 1993 and Morris & Nydahl, 1985). By the 1980s, sponsorship too had become a major source of revenue at the elite level, and since then agents have become rich and powerful by forging relationships with players, managers, governing bodies, promoters, television executives, and sponsoring companies (Horne et al., 2003).

Sport is now a global business, driven by "maverick entrepreneurs" that filled the positions of agents and constituted the mediation point between themselves and sports organizations, stars, television, sponsors, and advertisers (Horne et al., 2003, p. 267). The willingness of governing bodies to respond to the needs of commercial stakeholders such as broadcasters and sponsors has been heightened by the activities of sports entrepreneurs from outside the governing bodies (Whannell, as cited in Coakley & Dunning, 2004). The practice and consumption of sport can therefore be understood through networks of power and chains of interdependency (Hargreaves, 1986; Sage, 1990; Sugden & Tomlinson, 2002; Sugden, 2002; Maguire et al., 2002).

STRUCTURAL HOLES

Entrepreneurship is recognized as being central to the market process; however, it is not an important consideration in standard economic texts. While neoclassical economics analyzes competitive equilibrium in detail, it contributes little in explaining how this equilibrium is achieved. Tensions exist between different theoretical approaches to modeling this and it can be difficult to reconcile the comparative static analysis in mainstream economies with dynamic markets. The essence of the problem lies in the fact that neoclassical economics makes the assumption that everyone has free access to all information which is necessary in decision making, thus reducing decision making to a mechanical optimization process (Casson, 2005).

Austrian economists, however, assume that markets are composed of people with different information (Hayek, 1945). It is these information differences which are central to entrepreneurial opportunities. While the neoclassical assumptions around free access to information mean that all opportunities must be equally obvious to everyone (Shane, 2000). Austrian economics considers "opportunity exploitation to be endogenous to opportunity discovery" (Shane, 2000, p. 450). Informational asymmetries thus provide opportunities. In market transactions, asymmetric information can lead to a misallocation of resources. A reaction by an entrepreneur to this misallocation of resources can bring the market system back into equilibrium. However, asymmetric information means only a subset of the population is able to recognize the opportunity (Kirzner, 1973).

Social networks are thought to be pivotal in the distribution of information and control, and as a consequence, in the distribution of resources, within markets (Burt, 1992). The process of how an entrepreneurial opportunity is recognized and by whom can be related to the networks in which people operate. Burt (2001) suggests that at any moment in a market, a network exists "in which individuals are variably connected to one another as a function of prior contact, exchange, and attendant emotions" (p3). Structural holes in an imperfect market are thought to emerge where there are gaps in a network so that not all individuals are connected.

In order to trade efficiently, complete information on all goods and services, sellers, buyers, and prices is necessary. However, information will not flow at the same rate, with knowledge expected to circulate more quickly within than between groups. People are therefore not all simultaneously aware of the same information. As the diffusion of information occurs over time, individuals that are informed earlier, or more broadly, have an advantage (Burt, 2003). According to Burt, control of this information diffusion underlies the social capital of structural holes[1]—a concept in which individuals with strong relationships spanning the holes in the network are afforded a competitive advantage (Burt, 1992). As Burt states:

> "Structural holes are thus an opportunity to broker the flow of information between people, and control the projects that bring people together from opposite sides of the hole." (2001, p.5).

The ability of an agent to connect diverse groups (such as football clubs and players) enables him or her to collect more information than those with limited contacts. As well as being able to bring together otherwise disconnected individuals, the agent is able to have an influence over how that information is used and whose interests are served when those contacts engage. Someone who adds value by brokering the connection between others is thus an entrepreneur in the literal sense (Burt, 2001).

Though a structural hole exists between two groups, the groups will often be aware of each other, but circulate in different flows of information. In this way, sports agents have been able to act as a bridge between different stakeholders in order to extract value. As Khurana states, "an actor who is between others is in a better position to extract advantage than an actor who does not occupy such a bridging position" (2002, p. 239). The broker benefits by separating or arbitraging between two parties (Burt, 1992).

Burt's work draws on insights from Simmel (1922) and Merton (1957) on the autonomy generated by conflicting affiliations. Simmel elaborated the relational differences and dynamics between transactions/relations taking place between two parties and those between three, relating three categories of third party interactions: (a) *tertius gaudens*, (b) *divide et impera*, and (c) *mediator*. *Tertius gaudens* and *divide et impera* relate to situations in which third parties are able to gain an advantage by adopting a bridging position between unconnected parties, thus reducing transaction costs. The *mediator* on the other hand is able to bring together parties who may be known to each other but choose to work through an intermediary. The benefit to the intermediary thus is drawn from reaching an agreement between the two parties.

Elements of all of these can come into the relationship between sports agents and other parties (athletes/ players, clubs, sponsors etc).

THE AGENCY BUSINESS

Though agents have existed since the legalization of professionalism, in the 1960s and 1970s a combination of an increasingly liberalized labor market allied to commercial opportunities and an expanded international market for players meant that the use of agents by players grew (Joyce, 1997; Mason & Slack, 2001, 2003; Mason & Duquette, 2005; Shropshire & Davis, 2003; Karcher, 2006). The associated riches from media deals in the 1990s accelerated this process.

Previous research has identified three main roles of sports agents, which occur to a greater or lesser extent in Europe and North America:

1. Contract negotiation—between player and club/ player and sponsor/
2. Matching service (scouting) between players and clubs/players and sponsor or endorser.
3. Brokering deals—between clubs/player and club.

The second two roles differ from the first in that they relate more to the bridging position of structural holes in which entrepreneurial profit can be appropriated by the middleman in introducing two parties, while keeping them separate. Both sides will have separately built up a level of trust with the middleman, who is then is able to occupy the position between the two. These forms of third party interaction would often tend to be more similar to Simmel's *tertius gaudens* or *divide et impera* relations.

CONTRACT NEGOTIATION

The first service of negotiation is perhaps the most common function of agents, in which an intermediary acts between two parties to a transaction. The two parties will likely already be in contact with one another, but choose to employ an intermediary to take care of negotiations. This process relates to Simmel's mediator role.

Market changes in terms of improved labor rights for players and increased commercialization have meant that it is more important for players to receive specialist advice. In the context of the changing sports market, agents have been able to establish themselves in a key role transferring knowledge to players, affording them greater negotiation power in relation to clubs.

In North America, though opportunities for agents have arisen since the 1920s, their widespread use is thought to have begun in the 1960s (Joyce, 1997; Mason & Slack, 2001, 2003; Shropshire & Davis, 2003). As revenues rose for teams throughout the 1960s, experienced managers of clubs were able to keep salaries low because players generally had little business or financial experience and no knowledge of their own worth to the club or the salaries of others (Mason & Duquette, 2005). While in parallel, the reserve clause effectively tied the player to a club indefinitely (Sanderson & Siegfried, 1997). Legal challenges to this system progressively led to increased liberalization in the labor market enabling players to take greater control over their careers.

In the 1960s in England, the retain and transfer system was abolished (Szymanski & Kuypers, 2000; Dobson & Goddard, 2001). While modifications to the labor market were contributing towards a more liberal environment, with the abolition of the maximum wage also allowing players to enter into wage negotiation with their club, the transfer system still denied players the occupational freedom they sought. In Europe in particular, the Bosman ruling in 1995 was a major turning point affording freedom of movement to players and giving them more control over their careers. Allied to the increasingly commercial environment in which sports clubs operate, many opportunities arose for players to improve their contractual terms and conditions. This ability to exercise greater power in negotiations with clubs gave way to a need for specialists to advise players in attaining the maximum possible rewards in deals.

The intention of an agent in representing a player is to negotiate a higher wage for the player as well as bonuses and additional benefits. Because players tend to be unskilled in negotiation and have limited market knowledge, agents aim to balance discussions and try to gain an advantage for the player. The agents interviewed suggested that in many cases the hierarchical structure of sports clubs is such that a player would not necessarily want to speak to the manager and risk a negative outcome. As one player stated, "having an agent makes a nice demarcation line between this is me as a footballer and I will do what you tell me to do as a footballer, but off the park I'm not doing that" (English Premier League Footballer, personal communication, 20th February, 2009). However, agents assert that part of their role lies in making sure that the player is realistic about the level of remuneration he can expect.

In this way, the role of mediator as an arbiter of positive outcomes can be easier to achieve.

SCOUTING AND BROKERAGE

In Europe, as well as representing players in a mediation role agents are able to act in the bridging role identified by Burt. In a study conducted for the European Union it is stated that

> "Sports agents act, first and foremost, as intermediaries between sportspersons and sports clubs/organizers of sports events with a view to employing or hiring an athlete or sportsperson. . . . Finding a job placement for a sportsperson is the central and specific role of sports agents." (KEA-CDES-EOSE, 2009, p. 2)

This middleman position of an agent is common in European sport and is thought to have emerged in the 1970s and 1980s as wealthy soccer clubs in Italy sought to recruit talent from Eastern Europe. In order to overcome the political and legal barriers to such transfers, agents were employed to facilitate deals which clubs acting alone might have been unable to achieve (Holt et al., 2006). Through the network of contacts from the players and clubs they represent, agents are able to transfer knowledge to particular clubs about the potential availability of players. This has largely come about because of the inability of clubs to react to changing market circumstances. According to Magee (2002), "the sport was increasingly unprepared for the increased involvement of agents, their business approach, and their rapid centralization in the transfer and contract process" (,p. 230).

As well as acting in a quasi-scouting role introducing players to clubs, interviews with clubs and agents in Europe suggest that in order to transfer a player a club interested in signing the player would meet with his agent "to see if there's any common ground or anywhere near."(Sports agent, personal communication, September 27th, 2008). One agent states that transferring information between club and player is one of his key roles in the recruitment process to ensure that "the groundwork has been done before round table discussions to ensure the salary demands/ scales are matchable. . . . Though a club could directly approach another club to enquire about their player, the reality of the situation is that no buying club will make a real serious offer for a player unless they know the player is going to accept"(Sports agent, personal communication, September 27th, 2008).

Following the Bosman ruling, the removal of quota restrictions on the number of foreign players, combined with the broadening of the EU, has increased the size of the pool of talent available for clubs to sign, which in turn has provided a role for agents in providing localized expert information and coordination. In the English Premier League especially, foreign players make up an increasing proportion of first team squads.

This role of agents in performing scouting functions is much less evident in North American sport because rather than working for the club, the agent acts solely for the player. Differences in the structure of leagues between the European and North American models also affect the type of opportunities available to agents. Whereas European teams compete with clubs in other markets to attract the top players to their club, in North America there is little competition for players from leagues overseas. Thus, greater fluidity in the European transfer market creates the opportunity for knowledgeable middlemen to occupy the gap between clubs and between players and clubs. Each league also has its own set of regulations governing the domestic market, unlike in North America where there is a single professional league for each major sport (Holt et al, 2006). In the case of soccer for example, though FIFA sets overarching regulations with which all leagues should comply, "cultural differences, and differences in the application of such rules, have created an ambiguous environment in which agents have been able to thrive" (Holt et al., 2006, pp. 4–5).

In addition to the function of agents in matching clubs and players, a myriad of other activities also contribute to the role of an agent in modern sport, including concluding contractual arrangements (image rights contracts, sponsoring contracts, advertising contracts, etc.) or managing the assets of the sportsperson in which agents can again perform a "search and match" role with sponsors. In an increasingly globalized industry where the boundaries between sports, entertainment and media industries have become fuzzy, the reach of sport has been recognized by and emerged as a strategic focus for many international corporations. With this, the potential appeal of "associating with global athletes has intensified, as they attempt to market their products to broader bases of opportunities for consumers" (Mason & Duquette, 2005, p. 97). These changing market conditions have provided another opportunity for agents in sourcing ever more lucrative endorsement and sponsorship deals.

Once the matching service has been performed there is a role for the agent in brokering the deal. As one player states: "The club didn't know too much about me because I'd been playing overseas but my agent was able to fix up a deal because he's moved a lot of players around for them [club] before . . . then he sorted out my package" (Championship player, personal communication, December 17th 2009). Agents are generally able to broker deals between two clubs: between the player and club or between the player and sponsor. The position of the knowledgeable agent in the network affords him the possibility to build up trust between parties involved. Agents also identified that, in some situations if the player's agent is not well known to a club, then another agent who is trusted by the club may become involved as a facilitator—it has been identified by both clubs and agents that trust between the parties to a transaction is very important in arranging a deal.

OPPORTUNITY DISCOVERY AND PRIOR KNOWLEDGE

Since most research on entrepreneurship adopts either the framework of neoclassical economics or psychology, which assume equal access to information, it follows that there is an equal probability of discovering an entrepreneurial opportunity (Shane, 2000). However, as Hayek (1945) proposed, opportunity discovery can be seen as a function of information, and it is clear that in the context of the sports industry different people will discover different opportunities according to the prior knowledge that they possess, and an entrepreneur will only discover those opportunities relating to his own knowledge (Venkatarman, 1997) since differences in information lead people to see different value in different situations. Related to this is the theory that opportunity discovery depends on relative differences in search costs among potential entrepreneurs, as people are able to discover opportunities more readily when they have either superior information-processing ability or search techniques available to them (Shaver & Scott, 1991; Stiglitz, 1994). However, Austrian economists propose that "opportunity, by definition is unknown until discovered" (Shane, 2000). Instead of discovering the potential for profit by searching for it, Kirzner (1997) suggests that entrepreneurial opportunities occur when an individual recognizes the value of information that they receive through other means and, thus, entrepreneurial discoveries can be made without actually searching for them.

This seems to be the case in the sports market where many agents interviewed said they never intended to become an agent but got involved through helping a contact or through a spinoff of another project. As knowledge is generated through experiences, it stands to reason that some people will be exposed to information that is not available to others, and in some cases it is simply through luck that relevant information makes something else develop that you hadn't previously investigated (Nelson & Winter, 1982). As Shane (2000) states,

> "Prior information, whether developed from work experience, education or other means, influences the entrepreneur's ability to comprehend, extrapolate, interpret, and apply new information in ways that those lacking that prior information cannot replicate . . . only a subset of the population will possess prior information that will trigger the discovery of a particular entrepreneurial opportunity." (p. 432)

In this way it is important that in being able to exploit an opportunity, the entrepreneur has prior knowledge of the operation of the market, the way to serve that market, and the problems that customers can face. When technological or regulatory changes are invoked, it can be a conduit for an individual to employ diverse information to exploit a new idea. As users may not recognize that they need a service until it is offered to them, the onus is on the entrepreneur to recognize the gap in the market. Users often struggle to articulate their need for products or services which have not yet been developed (Von Hippel, 1994).

Opportunities can thus arise either through search or recognition, in which case prior knowledge is important in the discovery process. In the case of sports agents, it seems that the latter has been true. Their position in the network has exposed agents to knowledge of different aspects of information related to the market for players in terms of clubs, sponsors, media, and governing bodies. The idiosyncratic information gathered through prior knowledge makes people better able to discover certain opportunities (Fiet, 1996; Venkatarman, 1997).

OPPORTUNITY AND THE CHANGING MARKET PLACE

The agents who are well networked have been able to recognize additional opportunities to enable them to develop their business. As the sports industry developed, different types of representative emerged. While in the early days, agents in both Europe and North America tended to work alone and were often part time agents and full time stockbrokers, lawyers, accountants, or members of any other profession (Shropshire & Davis, 2003), the industry now has become specialized, where successful agents devote their lives to building their place in the network. Financial investment and tax planning advice, for example, have become a necessity for players who wanted to ensure their money was protected after negotiating high compensation packages. One way to manage all of these roles has been to form a full service agency (FSA), which has been the trend in both the United States and Europe over the last 20 years (Shropshire & Davis, 2003). FSAs have changed the nature of the agency business and have become very powerful in the sports market. By offering a holistic service encompassing all of the services a club or player could need, they have been able to develop power by virtue of the people they work with and contacts they have. As well as providing for the business needs of clients, one major advantage for FSAs is that they possesses the resources to develop their own sports academies, further creating a competitive advantage over rivals. IMG, for example, identifies athletes at a young age and then pays for their training at an IMG academy under the assumption that the company will get to represent the athlete in his/her future career (Mason & Duquette, 2005).

In terms of bridging structural holes, FSAs also often have an advantage by virtue of the volume and strength of the agents working together. As well as being able to react quickly to new opportunities, they are also potentially better insulated against adverse shocks to the market.

Restrictions in the way in which agents are able to conduct their business have meant that they have had to diversify their roles. The imposition of transfer windows has, according to one agent, "forced agents into different working patterns" (Sports Agent, personal communication, November 18th, 2008) ensuring they are involved in other aspects of the industry such as match arranging and sponsorship, so as to ensure their cash flow is not limited to two periods per year. Additionally, FIFA's 6+5 rule has meant that more agents seek to recruit players at younger ages and help transfer them around the world. The networked position of agents has enabled them again to act as a central point in transferring information.

In terms of being able to react to shocks, the collapse of ITV digital in the UK led to an increased gap between the Premier League and Football League in terms of revenue generation. The reduction in revenues available to clubs meant that squad sizes in the football league had to be reduced and less money was available to pay players. This had a domino effect, with agents receiving less money in commissions, and as many football league clubs reevaluating their spending. However, while this had an adverse effect in forcing some agents out of business, it also altered the market for playing talent and created a role for entrepreneurial agents in a scouting capacity, instead of clubs having their own internal scouting network. If the agent is trusted, clubs have suggested that this can provide a more cost effective approach to talent identification.

DISCUSSION

By virtue of their key role in the network society, agents are able to transfer knowledge when necessary and also react quickly and appropriately when they recognize opportunities. It is essentially their position in the market and exposure to different aspects of it that allows them to recognize entrepreneurial opportunities.

In many ways, the agent has come to act as a gatekeeper, keeping the two parties to a transaction separate. In this way the agent acts as a broker—usually between the player and club or sponsor. Because often the player is not directly connected to a new sponsor or club, they are likely to approach his agent with whom they may have worked previously. The agents may actively structure their network to include structural holes and are unlikely to introduce similar actors to each other so as to maintain their own control. In this way, negotiations take place through the agent.

Agents with a diverse set of contacts spanning a large number of structural holes (including clubs and academies in different countries, as well as related industries such as sponsors, media and press) are likely to be party to enhanced information. At a simple level, in a network that reaches more people, the volume and diversity of information is likely to be higher (Burt,

1999). Additionally, the person oriented at the center of a network of disparate contacts (which are only linked because of the person at the center), will be the first to see the needs in one group which could be matched to the skills of another. The trend of consolidation between firms as discussed above can relate to this in connecting disparate groups. If the agency lies at the center of social organization, the agent is able to broker deals as well as mediate the image of one party to another and strategically move information between contacts. As Burt states, "the information and control benefits reinforce one another at any moment in time and cumulate together over time" (1999, p. 7). In this way, well connected agents become increasingly attractive, making it even more difficult for unconnected individuals to enter the industry. Individuals with networks rich in structural holes are able to control more rewarding opportunities. As they can quickly move information to where it is needed, they are able to be highly mobile and responsive to the needs of others. Entrepreneurial individuals are thus able to create bespoke solutions according to the specific needs of the individuals involved.

The importance of being well connected and able to build bridges over the structural holes is clear in professional sports, which is an environment that is often thought to be impenetrable to outsiders (Magee, 2002). It is common for agents to work with ex-players who are able to link them to the network of their colleagues and help them gain the trust of younger players.

Traditionally, conflict has often existed between agents and clubs with the bridging role thought to be divisive. But lately, agents have become an accepted part of the industry where it is recognized that they can provide a legitimate and necessary service. In the context of an agent acting on behalf of a player to negotiate his contract, it is clear that the club and player could engage in direct exchange. However, they choose not to. The form of market in the case of professional sports is conducive to the existence of middlemen. In markets where there are a large number of buyers and sellers, two parties are able to interact to transact with each other. However, when there are fewer buyers and sellers, the process can become more difficult (Khurana, 2002). While parties in the sports industry will be aware of each other, there are many considerations for both parties to make before contact is made. Adverse selection arising from asymmetric information will be a concern for any club selecting a new player. An intermediary can help to reduce the risk from uncertainty. Additionally, structures and norms in the industry come into play.

The nature of the market is such that neither side will want to divulge information regarding their current contractual position (player) and needs (club) because it will impact on more than just those parties. The player will not want to divulge the possibility for a move, as it could have damaging effects on career or reputation, whereas the club is unlikely to want to admit that they are looking for a new player to avoid causing discontent among players or identifying weaknesses for competitors to exploit. This element of risk for both sides can make it beneficial for intermediaries to become involved.

Additionally, though to an extent there is a large amount of information available about many players in the well-known leagues, informational asymmetries are still a feature of the market. Although public sources can be used to collect information regarding an athletes playing career, more private sources may need to be engaged to attain specific knowledge about an individual's character and demeanor off the pitch. Additionally, with an international market it is impossible to scout every player, so some information needs to be delivered via the third party.

In terms of acting as a negotiator of salary there are elements of divisiveness evident but also a role for the agent in risk mediation. In the context of the role of executive search firms in acting as mediators between CEO candidates and company directors, Khurana (2002) states:

> "In direct two-person interactions . . . negotiations about sensitive matters such as salary can provoke intense emotions. . . . The employment of an intermediary, however, dampens the feelings that would accompany such demands and represents the demands to the other in a more conciliatory, more objective manner." (p. 247)

A similar viewpoint was put forward in interviews with players, clubs, and agents, in which many stated that not only is it difficult for a player to negotiate a contract when lacking skill in such business matters, but the necessity of a close working relationship with the team's manager presents difficulties in making salary demands. An agent is able to fulfill this role, often without the presence of the player in negotiations so there is no animosity felt between the player and club. The agent is able to act as a buffer, effectively insulating both parties to the discussions and protecting all egos involved.

Final considerations are the rules which surround the signing of players. Most leagues have regulations in place to maintain the stability of the competition and make it difficult for clubs to approach players directly with view to having them join their team. There is thus an institutionalized gap between buyers and sellers in the market.

CONCLUSION

The concept of players being represented by agents was relatively obscure until the 1980s. Though they existed, it wasn't until the 1990s that agents became integral and influential stakeholders in the business of football.

Agents have come to occupy a key role in the transfer market due to changes in the distribution of power and information between clubs and players. While prior to free agency players were exploited, labor liberalization in the 1990s enabled them to take more control over their careers. Unskilled in negotiation, and with increasing amounts of money at stake, players became more likely to employ professional representation. As the market changed and the differences between the elite performers and the average or lower league players became more marked, different roles emerged for agents.

As media interest in sports increased, additional revenue sources emerged, enabling athletes to both appropriate more of the surplus from teams and widen their popularity via the increased media exposure. The market for agents has evolved with the transition from players as sportsmen to becoming entertainers, with high media profiles in their own right. While initially the agent's main source of revenue was derived from the fees clients paid them for contract negotiation, competition in the market from other agents as well as the recent imposition of transfer windows have led agents to seek additional ways to increase their revenues. The services an agent can provide for their client have therefore developed.

The move toward consolidation of different aspects of the industry has been influenced by the impact of global technological development, which has increased the global profile and opportunities available to athletes worldwide (Whannel, 2004). Following the increase in the number of foreign players in the Premier League in particular, the profile of football has risen exponentially. To exploit this potential, large corporations with little experience in the sports agent industry and without elements of the necessary network have established themselves as credible service providers by purchasing top sports agency firms or solo operators who themselves are well connected and can bridge any structural holes. In this way entrepreneurs have been able to exploit the broad range of commercial opportunities available to clients.

While many of the analyses of middlemen focus on information, it is also necessary to consider the context of interactions in reaching a deal (Khurana, 2002; Nohria, 1992). The middleman is able to help create a working relationship between the parties.

Decision making emerges out of social context, and market conditions create an opportunity for an intermediary to bring together two parties, which in turn can bring about a mutually beneficial transaction. Through building trust, the intermediary is able to reduce the uncertainty and risk for all parties involved by controlling the flow of information. In the reality of imperfect markets, clubs have come to rely on personal contacts in player recruitment, while players rely on their agents to match them to clubs and find media and endorsement deals. The same is true of those companies who seek to match their brand to a star athlete. A well-placed intermediary is able to act as a bridge to all of these diverse sectors of the market, acting as a broker and a mediator in transactions, while helping to minimize transaction costs and insure against risk for all parties.

Endnote

1. Social capital refers to features of social organization such as trust, norms, and networks which can facilitate coordinated action (Putnam, 1993, p. 167). Social capital can thus afford better connected people a competitive advantage.

References

Athelaide, D., & Snow. R. (1979). *Media Logic*. London: Sage.

Burt R. (1992). *Structural Holes*, Cambridge, MA: Harvard University Press.

Burt R. (1999). Entrepreneurs, Distrust, and Third Parties. In Thompson L., Levine J., and Messick, D. (Eds.), *Shared Cognition in Organizations: The Management of Knowledge*. Hillsdale, NJ: Lawrence Erlbaum Associates.

Burt, R. (2001): Structural Holes versus Network Closure as Social Capital, In: Lin, N., Cook. K., Burt, R.S. (Eds.), *Social Capital—Theory and Research*, Hawthorn, NY: Aldine de Gruyter.

Burt, R. (2003). The social capital of structural holes. In M. F. Guillen, R. Collins, P. England, and M. Meyer (Eds.), *The New Economic Sociology: Developments in an Emerging Field* (pp. 148–189). New York: Russell Sage Foundation.

Burt R., (2009). *Neighbor Networks: Competitive Advantage Local and Personal*. UK: Oxford University Press.

Casson M. (1982). *The Entrepreneur*. Totowa, NJ: Barnes and Noble Books.

Casson M. (2005). *The Entrepreneur: An Economic Theory*. Edward Elgar Publishing Ltd.

Coakley, J., & Dunning, E. (2004). *Handbook of Sports Studies*. London: Sage.

Dobson, S., & Goddard, J. (2001). *The Economics of Football*. UK: Cambridge University Press.

Fiet, J. (1996). The informational basis of entrepreneurial discovery. *Small Business Economics*, 8, 419–430.

Hargreaves, J. (1986). *Sport, Power and Culture: A Social and Historical Analysis of Popular Sports in Britain*. Cambridge: Polity Press.

Hayek, F. (1945). The use of knowledge in society. *American Economic Review*, 35, 519–530.

Hersh, P. (1993). Media facilities at the 1992 Olympic Games. *Citius, Altius, Fortius*, 1(3), 4–5.

Holt, M., Michie, J., & Oughton, C. (2006), *The Role and Regulation of Agents In Football*. The Sport Nexus.

Horne, J., Tomlinson, A., & Whannel, G. (2003). *Understanding Sport: An Introduction to the Sociological and Cultural Analysis of Sport*. London: Spon Press.

Joyce, K. (1997). The ethics and dynamics of negotiating a professional sports contract. *Texas Entertainment and Sports Law Journal*, 6(2), 7–11.

Karcher, R. (2006). Solving problems in the player representation business: Unions should be the "exclusive" representatives of the players. *Willamette Law Review*, 42, 738–774.

KEA-CDES-EOSE (2009). Syudy on Sports Agents in the European Union: A Study Commissioned by the European Commission (Directorate General for Education and Culture) available at http://ec.europa.eu/sport/library/doc/f_studies/study_on_sports_agents_in_the_eu.pdf

Khurana, R. (2002). Market triads: A theoretical and empirical analysis of market intermediation. *Journal for the Theory of Social Behavior*, 32, 239–262.

Kirzner, I. (1973). *Competition and Entrepreneurship*. Chicago, IL: University of Chicago Press.

Kirzner, I. (1997). Entrepreneurial discovery and the competitive market process: An Austrian approach. *Journal of Economic Literature*, 35, 60–85.

Magee, J. (2002). Shifting balances of power in the new football economy. In J. Sugden & A. Tomlinson (Eds.), *Power Games: A Critical Sociology of Sport* (pp. 216–239). Routledge.

Maguire, J. (1999). *Global Sport: Identities, Societies, Civilisations*. Oxford: Polity Press.

Maguire, J., Jarvie, G., Mansfield, L., & Bradley, J. (2002). *Sport Worlds*. Leeds: Human Kinetics.

Mason, D. S., & Slack, T. (2001). Industry factors and the changing dynamics of the player-agent relationship in professional ice hockey. *Sport Management Review*, 4, 165–191.

Mason, D. S., & Slack, T. (2003). Understanding principal-agent relationships: Evidence from professional hockey. *Journal of Sport Management*, 17(1), 4–5.

Mason, D. S., & Duquette, G.H. (2005). Globalization and the evolving player-agent relationship in professional sport. *International Journal of Sport Management and Marketing*, 1, 93–109.

Merton, R. K. (1957). Continuities in the theory of reference group behavior. In *Social Theory and Social Structure* (pp. 335–440). New York: Free Press.

Morris, B., & Nydahl, J. (1985). Sports spectacle as drama: Image, language, and technology. *Journal of Popular Culture*, *18*, 101–110.

Nelson, R., & Winter, S. (1982). *An Evolutionary Theory of Economic Change*. Cambridge, MA: Harvard University Press.

Nohira, N. (1992). Information and search in the creation of new business ventures: The case of the 128 Venture Group. In N. Nohria and R. G. Eccles (Eds.), *Networks and Organizations*. Boston: Harvard Business School Publishing.

Putnam, R. D. (1993). *Making Democracy Work. Civic Traditions in Modern Italy*. Princeton, NJ: Princeton University Press.

Sage, G. (1990). *Power and Ideology in American Sport: A Critical Perspective*. Champaign, IL: Human Kinetics.

Sanderson, A., & Siegfried, J. (1997). The implications of athlete freedom to contract: Lessons from North America. *Institute of Economic Affairs*, *17*(3), 7–13.

Shane, S. (2000). Prior knowledge and the discovery of entrepreneurial opportunities. *Organization Science*, *11*, 448–469.

Shaver, K. G., & Scott, L. R. (1991). Person, process, choice: The psychology of new venture creation. *Entrepreneurship: Theory and Practice*, *16*(2), 23.

Shropshire, K. L., & Davis, T. (2003). *The Business of Sports Agents*. Philadelphia: University of Pennsylvania Press.

Simmel. G. (1922) [1955]. *Conflict and the Web of Group Affiliations* (K. H. Wolff & Re. Bendix, Trans). New York: Free Press.

Stiglitz, J. (1994). *Whither Socialism?* Cambridge, MA: MIT Press.

Sugden, J., & Tomlinson, A. (2002). *Power Games: A Critical Sociology of Sport* London: Routledge.

Sugden, J., & Tomlinson, A. (2002). Theory and method for a critical sociology of sport. In J. Sugden & A. Tomlinson (Eds.), *Power Games: A Critical Sociology of Sport* (pp. 3–22). London: Routledge.

Sugden, J. (2002). Network football. In J. Sugden & A. Tomlinson (Eds.), *Power Games: A Critical Sociology of Sport*. London: Routledge.

Szymanski, S., & Kuypers, T. (2000). *Winners and Losers: The Business Strategy of Football*. London: Viking Press.

Venkatarman, S. (1997). The distinctive domain of entrepreneurship research: An editor's perspective. In J. Katz and R. Brockhaus (Eds.), *Advances in Entrepreneurship, Firm Emergence and Growth*. Greenwich, CT: JAI Press.

Von Hippel, E. (1994). Sticky information and the locus of problem solving: Implications for innovation. *Management Science*, *40*, 429–439.

Whannel, G. (2004). Sport and the media. In J. Coakley and E. Dunning (Eds.), *Handbook of Sports Studies*. London: Sage.

8

Entrepreneurship in Sports Broadcasting

RODOULA H. TSIOTSOU

INTRODUCTION

Sport broadcasting evolved into a multi-billion dollar business and a major source of revenue for sport organizations (leagues, federations, associations, and clubs) due to increasing viewership demand and value. In 2008, FIFA generated $556 million in revenues from selling its competitions' broadcasting rights while the Union of European Football Associations (UEFA), the governing body of European football (soccer), received 800 million Euros from selling the 2008 European Football Championship ("TV channels," 2008) media rights. According to UEFA, each of the 31 EURO 2008 games was watched live by at least 155 million television viewers whereas the final round of the tournament was broadcast in 231 countries all over the world (UEFA EURO 2008 review, 2008).

Due to the large viewership, sports have become an integral programming content for broadcasters. As Mickael Hagege, Client and Research Manager for Eurodata TV Worldwide has stated: "Sport is leader in the best performing TV audiences ahead of fiction for 2002, thus occupying the first place of the most watched genre by viewers throughout the world" (Eurodata Worldwide, 2002). The sporting events with the largest worldwide audience are the Summer Olympic Games, the FIFA World Cup, Tour de France, Cricket World Cup, Rugby Union World Cup, Super Bowl, and the FIA Formula 1 World Championship.

The competition for the acquisition of sports broadcasting rights, along with the large sums of money spent on them demonstrate the dominant position of sports in television programming. In 2003, the International Olympic Committee (IOC) signed a $155 million contract with the Japanese broadcasting consortium NHK for the television rights of the Athens 2004 Olympic Games ("Japanese TV," 2003). In June 2003, the IOC concluded a $2.1 billion renewal deal with NBC for the U.S. television rights to the 2010 and 2012 Olympic Games. The European Broadcasting Union bought the rights for the same Olympic events for $800 million. Both deals include all television, radio, mobile, video-on-demand, Internet, broadband, and audio rights ("EBU secures," 2004). More than 840 million people in China tuned in to the opening ceremony of the 2008 Beijing Olympic Games, perhaps the largest television audience in history for a single event. China Central TV paid about $17 million for exclusive broadcast rights in China and raised approximately $394 million in Olympic advertising revenue. By comparison, NBC paid $894 million for broadcast rights in the United States and was expected to garner more than $1 billion in ad revenue (Barboza, 2008).

Escalating viewer demand for sport content continues to drive many of the technological advances in broadcasting resulting in changes not only in the way sports are watched but also in how they are delivered. Sport broadcasting constitutes a dynamic business area with rapid developments in the creation and use of new media and technologies that provides several new entrepreneurial opportunities.

THE DISTRIBUTION PROCESS
OF BROADCASTING RIGHTS

Broadcasting is the live or recorded transmission of a sport event via analog or digital method with the usage of ground receivers, satellite, or cable networks. According to the Television Without Frontiers directive of the European Union, "Television broadcasting means the initial transmission by wire or over the air, including that by satellite, in un-encoded or encoded form, of television programs intended for reception by the public. It includes the communication of programs between undertakings with a view to their being relayed to the public" (1997, p. 65).

There are various ways and different distribution channels that are used to broadcast a sporting event (Tsiotsou, 2005). In any case, when discussing broadcasting rights in sports and regardless of the medium used, there are

FIGURE 8.1. The main parties involved in the broadcasting rights process.

three main parties involved: sports rights holders, licensed broadcasters that bought the rights to broadcast the event, and viewers of the event (Figure 8.1).

SPORTS RIGHTS HOLDERS

The Sports Rights Holders (Figure 8.2) could be either main holders or secondary holders. Event organizers such as sport federations (e.g. national sport federations), leagues (Major League Baseball—MLB), committees (e.g. International Olympic Committee—IOC) associations (e.g. Fédération Internationale de Football Association—FIFA), unions (e.g. Union of European Football Associations—UEFA, Rugby Union), school teams (e.g. Florida State University athletic program), and sport clubs (e.g. Juventus, Chelsea) constitute the main sports rights holders. Marketing or sport marketing agencies (e.g. Octagon, SportFive Group, Dentsu Group, Infront Sports and Media, CSI Sports, Sports Marketing Australia) are considered secondary holders because they buy the rights from the main holders in order to sell them to broadcasters.

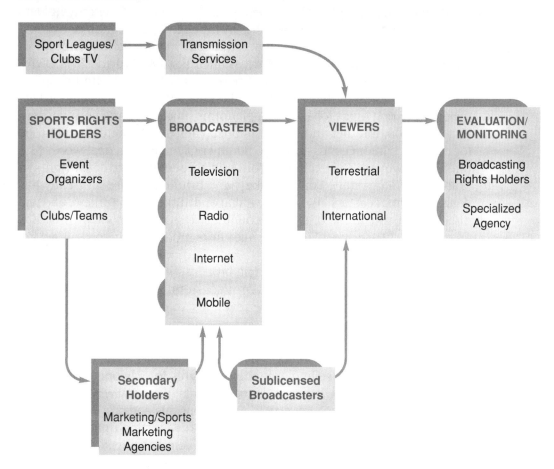

FIGURE 8.2. **Contemporary entrepreneurial broadcasting model in sports.**

The main rights holder is usually the organizer of a sport event and controls its broadcasting because it owns or controls access to the facilities where the event takes place. Thus, only the broadcaster that has bought the rights is allowed admission to the premises of the events and production of the television signal. The right to broadcast a sport event is granted usually for a given territory (e.g., per country) on an exclusive basis. Exclusivity is the main element of the value of a sport program. The number of viewers and the amount of advertising money a sporting event attracts indicate the broadcasting value of a sport program.

Main Sports Rights Holders

Broadcasting rights constitute a major source of revenues for the main sports rights holders. In 2008, FIFA generated $957 million ($703 million) in revenues. The lion's share of its revenues was attributable to the sale of broadcasting rights ($556 million—58% of revenues). Similarly, 60% of UEFA's EURO 2008 revenues came from selling its broadcasting rights (UEFA EURO 2008 review, 2008). The main sport rights holders either sell the broadcasting rights of their events to broadcasters or sell them to secondary holders or combine the above strategies either by broadcasting medium or by territory. For example, the IOC has changed recently its marketing strategy of the broadcasting rights for the Olympic Games. For the 2010 and 2012 Olympic Games, IOC sold its European broadcasting rights to the European Broadcasting Union (EBU) for $800 million. Lately, IOC awarded SportFive the broadcasting rights for all media platforms—including free and subscription television, Internet and mobile phones—across 40 countries in Europe for the 2014 Winter Games and 2016 Summer Olympics in a deal worth $316 million. However, IOC excluded from this agreement broadcast rights in France, Germany, Italy, Spain, Turkey, and Britain because it already has deals with broadcasters in Italy (Sky Italia) and Turkey (Fox Turkey), and will directly negotiate in the other four countries. This strategy will provide IOC an expected 30% increase in its revenues from broadcasting rights, reaching $1 billion (Davis, 2008).

Nowadays, it is very common to split broadcasting rights and sell them to two or more media platforms and broadcasters. From the right holders' standpoint, this is done to increase revenues, to comply with regulations (e.g. the European Union competition law) and mostly, to secure revenues. The collapse of many digital platforms such as Kirch' s Media Group in Germany and Alpha Digital in Greece in the past years has made event organizers more cautious in selling broadcasting rights to only one broadcaster. Leagues and clubs have lost significant amounts of money while their existence in many cases was in question. Championships and professional clubs operations went to a critical point because broadcasting rights is one the main revenue sources for most sport organizations. As a result, many sport organizers have changed their strategy in selling broadcasting rights, splitting them into two or more packages and selling them to different broadcasters. For example, UEFA developed ten different broadcasting rights packages for the Champions League tournament while the German football league split its broadcasting rights into nine packages—four for television broadcasting, two for Internet, and two for mobile phone streaming (German broadcasting deal, 2005).

Secondary Sports Rights Holders

Marketing and sports marketing agencies also have emerged as a main intermediary in the broadcasting rights process. In many cases, sports event organizers sell broadcasting rights to an agency that is authorized to sell those rights to broadcasters. In this case, the event organizers maximize revenues and avoid separate negotiations with individual broadcasters. It is a recommended approach especially when the event organizer does not employ experienced people or does not have the capacity to directly negotiate and sell its broadcasting rights.

In line with this reasoning, Dentsu Group, a Japan based marketing company, has been awarded to sell broadcasting rights for several international sport events. Thus, Dentsu was granted to sell the broadcasting rights in Japan for the 2006 FIFA World Cup, the exclusive worldwide marketing and broadcasting rights (excluding Europe and Africa) of the IAAF World Athletics Series, and the exclusive broadcasting rights in Japan (2004–2009) for Major League Baseball (Dentsu, 2006) .

Sportfive Group, a network of companies based in Europe and controlled by the French media giant Lagardere, marketed and sold the broadcasting rights of Euro Cup 2008 for UEFA. Several television channels across the globe acquired the telecasting rights of Euro 2008. The Sportfive Group took a market-to-market strategy of selling the Euro 2008 broadcasting rights. Thus, it sold the rights to telecast the Euro 2008 soccer matches to more than 60 television channels in 55 countries all over the world ("TV channels," 2008).

Chinese media group, XFMedia, has acquired the free-to-air media rights for the UEFA European League for three years from European football's governing body, UEFA, through the sports marketing agency, Team. Under the deal, which runs from 2009 to 2012, XFMedia will show at least one live match, a delayed match, and a highlights program each match week on NMTV. In addition, XFMedia will show all matches from the competition live on Internet and on mobile through their leading mobile service provider, M-in ("XFMedia," 2008).

Over the last decade, U.S. colleges and universities are changing their strategy from making direct deals with broadcasters to outsourcing most or all of their media rights to sports marketing firms. This approach provides athletic departments more revenues and at the same time lets them focus on ticket sales and fundraising activities. For example, Louisiana State University signed a 10-year, $74.5 million deal in 2005 to consolidate media rights with CBS Collegiate Sports Properties. In this vein, the universities of

Texas, Arizona, Tennessee, and Kentucky have signed multi-year multimillion contracts with IMG College (former Host Communications) for their media rights (McCarthy, 2006).

LICENSED BROADCASTERS

Broadcasters (television, radio, Internet, broadband, and mobile telecommunications) buy the rights to broadcast a sporting event to viewers, the people who desire to watch it. Broadcasters, except from being buyers, can also be the sellers of broadcasting rights. They might sell (sublicense) all or part of the broadcasting rights to another media platform, or they might sell advertising time for the event they have the right to broadcast.

Broadcasters are usually interested in securing broadcasting of sport events for following reasons: to increase their market share and value, and to test new technologies. For example, in 1995, Unity/Arena bought the rights to broadcast the Bundesliga's games (Germany's top-level soccer league) and attracted more than 900,000 subscribers in a few months. At the same time, Premiere, a pay-TV group and the previous owner of these rights, lost 42% of its market value and part of its subscribers (Hatton & Wagger, 2007).

Until recently, television was the dominant medium in airing sports events followed by radio. However, broadband, Internet, and mobile platforms have emerged as new methods for broadcasting sport contents all over the world. This shift to new media channels resulted from the changing needs of consumers.

Thus, Internet residential users decrease their time spent on watching television and turn to personal computer entertainment ("The sport and new media," 2001). For example, U.S. online television viewing has more than doubled within 2 years. Almost a fifth of homes are watching broadcasts on the Internet, according to the survey conducted by the U.S. Conference Board and TNS on a sample of 10,000 American homes. The massive rise is largely due to the flexible viewing times available with online television allowing viewers to choose when they watch the latest hit television shows. Thus, the lack of restriction from schedules and location, ad skipping, and portability were the most important benefits derived from online television. "The shift from appointment TV to content on demand is well underway," said Michael Saxon, Senior Vice President of TNS Brand and Communications. "Fundamentally, consumers expect content to be available when they want it, and on the screen of their choice TV, PC, or mobile. For consumers, PCs enhance content on demand from simply time-shifting to place-shifting. Online content can be viewed in any room in the house, or at work or school." The same survey showed that over 70% watch Internet television sites daily and mainly for entertainment purposes. Sports are one of the most popular shows viewed online along with news, drama, comedy shows, and reality shows ("Massive growth," 2008).

ComScore, a digital market intelligence and measurement service provider, reported recently that Internet television and video watching audience has increased by a 10% margin during the last 12 months to an impressive 29.6 million unique viewers in the U.K. The company estimated 4 billion videos views for January 2009, in the UK. Nearly 100 million of these were viewed on the websites of the top five television networks (BBC, ITV, Channel 4, Channel 5, and Sky TV). ComScore also found that of the entire UK Internet users, 80.1% have watched Internet television and video, this equals around 280 million hours of video streaming for this month ("Ten percent," 2009).

Although when they appeared, new media rights were only partially exploited by sports rights holders, nowadays there is an increasing interest in developing and selling these rights (Table 8.1). New media companies have developed their whole business based on the Internet. For example, Sportal, a fast-growing new media company, has acquired the Internet rights of 50 leading European Football clubs. Worldsport.com, another new media company, bought the Internet rights from 50 international sport federations in 2000 by offering each federation a minimum of $ 300,000 over a five-year period (Laflin, 2001). These new broadcasting platforms are expected to change the landscape of sports broadcasting in the coming years by taking a "niche" marketing approach, reaching global audiences, and dealing with new issues (e.g., online piracy). Moreover, Internet broadcasting will change the way broadcasting rights are sold from a territorial to a worldwide base.

TABLE 8.1. **New media rights deals**

SPORT	EVENT	BROADBAND/ MOBILE	BROADCASTER	TERRITORY
American Football	National Football League	Broadband	Yahoo Sports	Worldwide (except North America) live video
American Football	National Football League	Broadband	Apple iTunes	Worldwide (video highlights)
Canadian Football	Canadian Football League	Broadband	Interactive Netcasting Systems	Worldwide
Cricket	ICC Champions Trophy	Broadband	Star Entertainment India	Worldwide
Cycling	Vuelta a Espana	Broadband	Cycling.tv	Worldwide (except mainland Europe)
Field Hockey	BDO World Cup	Mobile	Vecracom	Pakistan
Soccer	FA Premier League	Mobile	British Sky Broadcasting	UK
Soccer	UEFA Champions League	Broadband and Mobile	Sina.com	China
Tennis	Roland Garros	Broadband	The Tennis Channel	USA

Source: "The sports market media," 2006.

Television

Television broadcasting can be made via either terrestrial, cable, or satellite transmission. Terrestrial television refers to the modes of television broadcasting which do not involve satellite transmission or via underground cables. Cable television is a system of providing television to consumers via radio frequency signals transmitted to television through fixed optical fibers or coaxial cables as opposed to the over-the-air method used in traditional television broadcasting in which a television antenna is required. Satellite television is delivered via a communications satellite and received by a satellite dish and set-top box. Satellite television provides a wide range of channels and services, often to areas that are not services by terrestrial or cable providers. Currently, there are two primary satellite television providers of subscription-based service in the United States (Dish Network and DirecTV), two in Canada (Bell TV and Shaw Direct), two in Australia (FOXTEL and SELCTV), and four in Europe (Astra, EutelSat, SES Sirius, and Hispasat). In the United States, DirecTV offers more than 40 sports channels (e.g., NBA TV, ESPNU, CBS college sports, and Fox Soccer Channel) to choose from, while Bell TV in Canada includes more than 10 sport distributors (e.g., MLB Extra, Setanta Sports, and HPI TV). FOXTEL in Australia offers eight sport channels (e.g., ESPN, Eurosport News, Fox Sport, and Sky Racing) while Astra provides more than 90 sport choices to its consumers in Europe (e.g., Eurosport, Canal+Sport, Extreme Sport, Nova Sport, and Sky Sport). In addition to territorial transmissions, satellite receivers can demodulate and convert their signals to the desired form of outputs such as television, audio, and data.

The development of sports channels.

Sport channels are television specialty channels (usually exclusively through cable and satellite) broadcasting sport events, usually live, and when not broadcasting events, sports news and other related programming. Sport channels have greatly improved the availability of sports broadcasts, generating opportunities such as the ability for one person to see every single game his/her team plays over the course of the season.

The first sports channel was from the SportsChannel networks, which went on the air in 1977 with the original SportsChannel (now MSG Plus). Since the 1970s, many channels have surfaced around the world, several focusing on one sport in particular, or one region of a country, showing only their local team's games.

In the United States, ESPN (Entertainment Sports Programming Network) is the largest dedicated cable television sports network which began broadcasting in 1979. In 1993, ESPN2 was founded and three years later, ESPNews was launched. In 1997, ESPN purchased Classic Sports Network and renamed it ESPN Classic. The latest ESPN network in the United States, ESPNU, began on March 4, 2005. ESPN International began in the early 1990s to take advantage of the growing satellite markets in Asia, Africa, and Latin America. In Canada, ESPN, Inc. purchased a minority share of TSN and RDS (in fact, the current corporate logo of both looks similar to that of ESPN). In 2004, ESPN finally entered the European market by launching a version of ESPN Classic, and in December 2006, it agreed to purchase North American Sports Network. On February 1 2009, NASN was rebranded as ESPN America. ESPN International dominates televised sport, broadcasting on a 24-hour basis in 21 languages to over 165 countries. It reaches the one desirable audience: young, single, middle-class men. ESPN, for example, thinks globally but provides local customization, such that the focus is on soccer in Latin America, table tennis in Asia, and cricket in India (Herman & McChesney, 1997).

In Europe, Eurosport, a sport satellite and cable network, was launched in 1989 as a joint venture between the European Broadcasting Union and Sky Television plc. Eurosport, available in 54 countries and broadcasting in 20 different languages, is owned and operated by the TF1 Group. Eurosport broadcasts a variety of sports such as the Olympics, UEFA Champions League, UEFA Cup football, the Paris Dakar Rally, Monte Carlo Rally, cycling events such as Le Tour de France and Britain's Premier Calendar road racing series, tennis events including the French Open and the Sony Ericsson WTA Tour, World Championship Snooker, Australian Football League, winter sports, and youth sports like skating and surfing. Eurosport is often provided by cable operators as part of their basic package and it is shown in most countries across Europe. Currently there are a number of channels that are broadcasting under the Eurosport name: Eurosport (France, British, Deutschland, Italia, Poland, Nordic, and Asia Pacific), Eurosport 2 (versions for all Eurosport regions except Asia Pacific), and Eurosport News. Sportitalia is also part of the group. In May 2007, Yahoo! and Eurosport formed a cobranded website (www.eurosport.com), which Eurosport uses as its Web portal, including an online TV Guide, in the UK, Ireland, Spain, Italy, and Germany.

Al Jazeera Sports is a Qatar-based Arabic-language sports channel launched in November 2003 by the Al Jazeera network. It is the most popular sports channel in the Middle East, covering a wide range of major sporting events, such as the UEFA European Football Championship and the Summer Olympics. Al Jazeera Sports also owns the exclusive broadcasting rights in the Middle East for major football leagues, like the Spanish La Liga and the Italian Serie A. Al Jazeera Sport currently has opened four additional channels: Al Jazeera Sports +1, Al Jazeera Sports +2, Al Jazeera Sports +3 and Al Jazeera Sports +4 with the intention to open new more channels to cover the UEFA Champions League.[1]

Other well known sport channels are Fox Sports Australia, TVN, and Nine in Australia; TSN, Rogers Sportsnet, Fox Sports World Canada, and Leafs TV in Canada; Sky Sports, Canal+Sport, and Setanta Sports in Europe; ART Sport, ShwoSports, Dubai Sports, Ten Sports, and NEO Sport in the Middle

East and South Asia; Fox Sports Net, MSG Network, and Comcast SportsNet in the United States.

The television landscape is changing substantially due to the growing number of "niche" channels all over the world. Thus, there are channels focusing heavily or exclusively on one sport or on one sport team. Examples of one-sport channels are NBA TV (basketball), Fox Soccer Channel and GolTV (soccer), NFL network (American football), the Golf Channel (golf), MLB network (baseball), NHL network (hockey), NEO Cricket (cricket), and SPEED (auto racing).

NBA TV, a 24-hour digital network of the National Basketball Association (NBA), was launched in 1999. NBA TV televises hundreds of live games, including regular season and playoff matchups from around the NBA, WNBA, and NBA D-League. NBA TV is available to millions of homes throughout the U.S. and in 79 additional countries and territories (Turner, 2008).

NEO Cricket, a Mumbai (India) headquartered cricket entertainment channel, is a part of Neo Sports Broadcast Pvt Ltd. NEO Cricket has the exclusive broadcast rights for all international and domestic cricket events played in India and broadcasts to 30 countries. In 2008 NEO Cricket broadcast six international cricket series, including four featuring India, adding up to nearly 200 days of live cricket. In addition, NEO Cricket airs Cricketainment shows, three of which are daily shows such as Dial C for Cricket, Sportszone, and Encounter. Neo Cricket performance has grown remarkably over the years and today is considered the number one television channel in India. NEO Cricket broadcasts to 30 countries, from Japan, Korea, and Taiwan in the Far East on The New Media Group & Hum Tum TV; from the Middle East and North Africa on the ADD/Pehla platform; from Singapore on Starhub; Hong Kong on ICable; and from Sri Lanka on Dialog TV and Lanka Broadband (Sehgal, 2008).

Moreover, large sport clubs have developed their own channels such as Yankees Entertainment and Sports (USA), S.L. Benfica TV, Real Madrid TV (Spain), Manchester United TV (UK), Sport TV(former Magic TV owned by Olympiacos Football Club, Greece), Milan Channel (Italy). Real Madrid TV is a digital television channel, operated by Real Madrid specializing in the Spanish football team. The channel features Real Madrid football matches, club news, player and coach interviews, as well as news and interviews from the club's successful basketball team, and is available in Spanish, English and French. The English language version of the channel aims to be an information and entertainment portal for Real Madrid fans throughout the world. GlobeCast, a subsidiary of France Telecom and a global provider of content management and worldwide transmission services, delivers Real Madrid TV to the UK, Asia, the Middle East, and other parts of Europe ("Real Madrid," 2006).

The Yankees Entertainment and Sports (YES) Network is a New York City regional cable television channel dedicated to broadcasting baseball games of the New York Yankees and basketball games of the New Jersey Nets. YES was launched on March 19, 2002. The channel is available in New York, New Jersey, Connecticut, and parts of Pennsylvania, nationally on DirecTV and regionally on AT&T U-verse and Verizon FiOS. YES is owned by the Major League Baseball team the New York Yankees, Goldman Sachs Group Inc., and former New Jersey Nets owner Raymond Chambers. In 2001, the network valued $850 million and now it is worth as much as $2 billion. The YES network generated about $340 million in revenue in 2006 based on 11.4 million subscribers while the Boston Red Sox (owned by New England Sports Network) produced $125 million last year, with four million sub-scribers (Sessa and Soshnick, 2007).

Ownership of television channels provides sport leagues and clubs sev-eral benefits such as control over the broadcasting content and its quality, full financial exploitation of the broadcasting rights, and enhanced ability to reach consumers all over the world and build global sports brands.

Internet Television

Internet television constitutes the new medium for broadcasting sports. Several Internet television channels have emerged all over the world. These channels often have a specific focus:

- sport, news, and entertainment contents (e.g., TV7 in France, CCTV online and UUSee in China, Big Pond TV in Australia, TV Taroba and Globo Media Center in Brazil, OKBC TV and 33 MAG in Canada);
- Sports-only (e.g., Band Sports in Brazil, ESPN.com and Fox Sports in Australia, PPLive in China, Eurosport and Pancrace TV in France);
- a single sport (e.g., ATP Rogers Cup—tennis, and British Columbia Hockey League—Hockey in Canada; ATP Masters series Monte-Carlo—tennis in France; MLB TV—baseball, Black Belt TV—martial arts, and MLS Online—soccer in the United States; Sohu.com—soccer in China);
- a college athletic department (e.g., Hoyas All Access—Georgetown University, Gator Vision Online—University of Florida, Maryland Ath-letics—University of Maryland)
- or a team (e.g., ACMilan.com—soccer team in Italy; BenficaTV.com—soccer team in Spain; TFC—soccer team Toulouse in France; Arsenal TV, Chelsea TV online, Manchester United TV—soccer teams in the UK).

Sport Internet television provides live coverage of sport events and video clips. The majority of sport Internet channels are found in the United States (220 websites), followed by the U.K (60 online TVs), Canada (13), China (7), France (7), Australia (5), and Brazil (4).

PPLive is the largest P2P (peer-to-peer) Internet television broadcasting and video streaming media platform in China. PPLive has partnered with many reputable organizations in China and around the world, including CCTV, SMG, NBA, Warner Brother, ESPN, Star TV, MTV, TVB, TVBS, etc. and currently offers a broad range of premium domestic and international sports content online, including matches from the CBA, NBA, English Premier

League, European Champion League, and Germany's Bundesliga, etc. PPLive has also broadcast Olympic sporting events live online.

ESPN.com represents one of the leading U.S. Internet television broadcasters. Recently ESPN.com changed its programming strategy by splitting its products with ESPN360.com. Under the new approach, ESPN360.com is devoted to live coverage of sport events (usually those that are not available via ESPN TV networks), whereas online video on-demand services are available via ESPN.com, ESPNSoccernet.com, ESPNdeportes.com, and ESPNRadio.com. ESPN360.com is a full-time, multi-sport, live sports-driven broadband channel featuring a broad array of live sports events and programming every day, such as NBA games, U.S. and international soccer, college football and basketball games, and NASCAR, Nextel, and Busch Series races. ESPN360.com served more than 3 million streams for the 2006 FIFA World Cup tournament and 500,000 for the FIFA Champions League. ESPN360.com is free to sport fans and available to more than 15 million homes in the U.S. that receive high-speed Internet connection from an affiliated service provider ("New programming strategy," 2007).

In addition to Internet television developed either by sport rights holders or traditional sport channels, new intermediaries have emerged in the broadband landscape by the form of Internet sport broadcasters or producers.

In 2008, JumpTV Inc., a leading broadcaster of live and on-demand sports and international television over the Internet, and NeuLion, Inc. (an end-to-end Internet Protocol TV (IPTV) service of live and on-demand sports and international programming over the Internet and through set top boxes) merged to create a leading enterprise IPTV provider. NeuLion Inc/JumpTV Inc. provides content owners and aggregators with an end-to-end enterprise technology solution which enables content to be monetized and streamed to multiple platforms through browser based devices. Content can be viewed on the computer, the television through the proprietary NeuLion Set Top Box, and mobile devices. With 143,000 subscribers, NeuLion Inc/JumpTV Inc. has partnerships with and provides services to more than 200 leading professional and collegiate sports properties, including the National Hockey League (NHL); more than 150 NCAA colleges and universities; the World Championship Sports Network; and the 2010 South American, African, and Asian World Cup Qualifiers ("JumpTV," 2008).

NeuLion Inc/JumpTV Inc. is one of the largest live streaming companies in the world, having streamed approximately 16,000 live sporting events in the 12 months ended August 31, 2008. In March 2008, ComScore ranked JumpTV as the #1 most engaging website among those in the sports video category with a recorded 40.4 minutes per viewer per month in the United States. Additionally, JumpTV viewers watched approximately 20 million minutes of online sports video in the United States in March 2008, ranking it as #4 in the Sports Video Sites category overall ("JumpTV," 2008).

In addition, Internet television channels usually acquire the services of Internet production companies such as the National Mobile Television (NMT).

NMT is a provider of mobile analog, digital, and high-definition television facilities for the production of television and Internet broadcasts from remote locations such as U.S. stadiums, arenas, and conference halls. NMT currently provides facilities and services for more than 5,000 events annually, including major sporting, entertainment, distance learning, and corporate events.

Mobile Television

Mobile TV is the new medium "on the block" of sport broadcasting that is expected to further grow in the future, although its spread is not consistent all over the world. According to the market research company, Global Telecoms Insights (GTI), the Asian mobile market is booming, more than in the United States and Europe. GTI reports that the use of mobile television in Japan and South Korea has doubled since last year, from 14% to 32%. Mobile television growth in Hong Kong also has doubled, from 18% to 32%. In contrast, in Europe, the mobile sector grew from 6% to only 8%, whereas in the U.K. it increased from 8% last year to 13%. In the United States, the number of mobile users has doubled since last year, reaching 11% (Reiter, 2009). Recently, the Open Mobile Video Coalition (OMVC), an alliance of U.S. broadcasters dedicated to accelerating the development of mobile digital television, announced the first wave of broadcasters that have been committed to launching mobile digital television (DTV) services in 2009. These broadcasters will launch mobile DTV across 63 stations in 22 markets, covering 35 percent of U.S. television households. The new technology will provide live, local, and national over-the-air digital television to consumers via next-generation portable and mobile devices at pedestrian and vehicular speeds. Of the 63 stations, there will be 14 NBC affiliates, nine ABC affiliates, nine CBS affiliates, five FOX affiliates, nine ION Television affiliates, four CW affiliates, and four MyNetworkTV affiliates (OMVC, 2009).

According to Juniper Research, the global market for mobile sports content and services will grow from just over $1 billion in 2006 to $3.8 billion in 2011. "All mobile TV trials to date have shown that sport on mobile TV will be a success story," says Kieran Mahon, media development manager at Vodafone (Wilson, 2006). Nowadays, traditional broadcasters (e.g., Sky, BBC One, ITV1, and Channel 4) are including mobile television in their medium bundles and broadcast live sport events via cellular phones and portable device applications (e.g., iPhones). In 2007, Sky offered live coverage of the Barclays Premier League on mobile for the first time. Sky Sports 1, 2, and 3 were available via Sky Mobile TV as simulcast channels. The coverage included Sky's 92 live Premier League matches (Oatts, 2007). During the 2010 football World Cup, FIFA, for the first time, will have live coverage specifically produced for mobile phones, providing a major boost for mobile broadcasting in Africa ("World Cup prompt," 2009).

The wide use of mobile phones resulted in the development of new broadcasting intermediaries and platforms in the sport broadcasting landscape. MELISA, a cross-media broadcasting platform of sports events, features interactive advertising and sports-related games over digital television and next-generation mobile network infrastructures. The platform provides services for optimal presentation of complex interactive real time video content for advertisement, and an advanced real-time gaming (betting) engine in at least two different client platforms (Papaioannou, Borälv, Demiris, Johansson, and Ioannidis, 2004).

Sports also have been used to test mobile television technology. At the 2006 Commonwealth Games held in Melbourne, Broadcast Australia introduced digital video broadcasting-handheld (DVB-H) mobile television technology. This new technology demonstrated the abilities of DVB-H mobile television by providing up to seven channels broadcasting live the Games to select handheld devices. Moreover, an information channel was also available, providing event-related data (e.g., starting lists and medal tallies) (Kepreotes, 2007). The 2006 World Cup in Germany was also used to test mobile and DVB-H technology by Siemens, a German mobile phone company, and other mobile television channels in the U.K. (Reid, 2006).

Mobile television is currently the only available "unicast" vehicle, which means it can be individually called up onto a mobile phone. As more people become familiar with and use new media and advance technology, distribution and market share of broadcasting rights for sporting events will undergo significant changes.

Radio and Internet Radio

Radio broadcasting remains an important means of communication and advertising all over the world, despite the strong impact of the Internet and television. China is the world's second largest radio broadcasting market, with more than 1,000 broadcasters for the 1.3 billion people in 340 million families, next only to the United States, according to a rating by Nielsen Media Research ("Nation 2nd largest," 2004).

Radio constitutes the first medium used to broadcast sport events. Radio broadcasting is an audio (sound) broadcasting service, traditionally broadcast through the air as radio waves (a form of electromagnetic radiation) from a transmitter to an antenna and a thus to a receiving device. The first radio broadcast of a baseball game was on August 5, 1921, over Westinghouse station KDKA from Forbes Field in Pittsburgh, Pennsylvania, where the Pittsburgh Pirates played against the Philadelphia Phillies. A few months before, in April 1921, the first boxing fight was broadcast over the same radio station. In the early days, radio sport broadcasting was just a part of a radio's programming. However, nowadays many radio stations turn into sports radio stations broadcasting only sports. For example, it has been estimated that there are more than 85 sports radio stations in North America. Specifically, there are 18 in the east, 23 in the southeast, five in northwest, 12 in west, 14 in the Midwest, and 13 in the southwest.[2]

Through the years, radio sport broadcasting evolved via the creation of radio networks and the appearance of Internet radio (Table 8.2). One such as network, Terrapin Sports Network, provides coverage of the athletics at the University of Maryland, throughout Maryland, Washington DC, and Northern Virginia, and reaches into West Virginia, Pennsylvania, and Delaware. Terrapin Sports Marketing, a division of CBS Collegiate Sports Properties, manages the Terrapin Sports Network on behalf of the department of athletics.[3]

TABLE 8.2. International sport radio and Internet radio broadcasters

Country	City	Radio Station	Language/ Theme	On the Internet
Europe				
Italy	Rome	Videolina	Italian/News and Sports	http://www.videolina.it/
Italy	Rome	RAI Sports	Italian/Sports	http://www.rai.it/
Denmark	Copenhagen	4 Sport	Danish/Sports	https://www.4sport.dk:19638 /welcome/
Germany	Berlin	Eurosports	German/Sports	http://de.eurosport.yahoo.com/
UK	London	BBC World Service	English / Sports	http://news.bbc.co.uk/sport/ default.stm
Greece	Athens	Nova Sport FM	Greek/Sports	http://www.sport-fm.gr/
Asia Pacific				
Australia	Sydney	Radio Australia Sports	English/Sports	http://www.abc.net.au/ra/sport/
Australia	Sydney	Roo TV Sports	English/Sports	http://www.rootv.com/
China	Beijing	Sports TV	Chinese/Sports	http://www.smg.cn/Index /Index.aspx
Japan	Tokyo	1242 Radio	Japanese/Sports	http://www.1242.com/
North America				
Canada	Sherbrooke	CHLT 630	French/News and Sports	http://www.1077chlt.ca/
Canada	Montreal	CKGM	English/Sports	http://www.team990.com/
Canada	Ottawa	CFGO The Team	English/Sports	http://www.team1200.com/
Canada	Toronto	CJLC The Fan 590	English/Sports	http://www.fan590.com/
Canada	Vancouver	CKST The Team	English/Sports	http://www.team1040.ca/
USA	Cincinnati	WCPO	English/Sports	http://www.wcpo.com /default.aspx
USA	New York	Fox Sports	English/Sports	http://msn.foxsports.com/
USA	New York	Sirius	English/Sports	http://www.sirius.com/
USA	Seattle	Northwest Cable News	English/News and Sports	http://www.nwcn.com/

Source: http://broadcast-live.com/sports/webcasts.html

SIRIUS satellite radio includes a channel known as College Sports Nation, a U.S.-based college sports radio network. It broadcasts football, basketball and other related college sports events, and became the Official Satellite Radio Partner of numerous teams, including the Alabama Crimson Tide, Auburn Tigers, Florida Gators, Kansas Jayhawks, Kentucky Wildcats, Louisiana State University Tigers, Michigan Wolverines, Nebraska Cornhuskers, Notre Dame Fighting Irish, Ohio State Buckeyes, Oklahoma Sooners, Syracuse Orange, Tennessee Volunteers, Texas Longhorns, UCLA Bruins, and USC Trojans.

In addition to Internet television, the Web provides an alternative transmission medium for radio stations, enabling them to reach a global audience. Table 8.2 presents several sport radio and internet radio broadcasters all over the world.

NEW TRENDS IN SPORTS BROADCASTING

Advances in technology have resulted in rapid and dramatic transformations in the broadcast industry by introducing new delivery and viewing platforms ranging form mobile to the Internet. New media has used broadcasting of sporting events as a vehicle to enter into a market and to introduce new and advanced technology. On the other hand, new media provides new distribution channels for broadcasting sporting events and more revenue sources.

New technology is changing the broadcasting environment of sporting events in terms of quality and quantity. More broadcasters (Internet and mobile companies) are competing for the rights of major sporting events while broadband technologies (via cable, digital, high definition, and wireless connections) provide faster connections and quality transmission, and new advertising technologies (virtual advertising) allow for target marketing. Furthermore, new technology might make the users of new media the producers of their sport program (e.g., interactive sports entertainment: games, gambling). Following, new trends in sports broadcasting are presented.

Smart Watches

In March 2004, Microsoft introduced the Smart Personal Objects Technology (SPOT) initiative and announced the kickoff of sports content for Smart Watches for MSN Direct. Smart Watches, manufactured by Fossil Inc. and Suunto, allow people to conveniently and discreetly receive the information that matters most to them, with just the flick of a wrist by personalizing their watch through an interactive Web site (http://www.msndirect.com/) where they choose the specific information and services they want. Microsoft's strategic alliance with ESPN provides sports fans who subscribe to the MSN Direct service the latest information on their favorite basketball teams, including updated scores, standings, game times, and more. With detailed information and data delivered direct to their Smart Watch, fans can keep a pulse on their favorite teams while on the go, in a restaurant, at a meeting, or wherever they don't have access to a television or radio. Initially, MSN Direct offered content for the National Basketball Association (NBA), the Women's National Basketball Association (WNBA), and men's and women's NCAA basketball (Division I) teams ("MSN Direct," 2004). Live broadcasting of sport events constitutes the upcoming challenge of the smart watch technology that is expected to be tested in the near future.

Virtual Advertising

Virtual advertising refers to the use of electronic (imaging) systems, which alter the broadcasting signal by substituting, or adding, venue advertising in the television picture ("EBU," 2000). Virtual advertising (also referred to as virtual signage or electronic imaging systems or electronic billboards) are real-time video insertions into television broadcasts. This involves overlaying an advertisement into a space in the telecast—either over the top of an existing ground signage, or alternatively in a "free-space" on the field of play or in the crowd. This form of advertising is only visible to the television viewer. The inserted virtual ad remains tied to its field position regardless of camera motion. People at the ground cannot see the imposed sign (Turner & Cusuman, 2000). Virtual advertising is being used increasingly often in the transmission of sports events on television (for example, to allow advertisers and event sponsors to target particular geographical markets with different brand names or messages), but it may also be used in the transmission of other events.

Princeton Video Image, a U.S. COMPANY, introduced virtual advertising in 1995; since that time, new companies such as Sci-Del (United States), ISL Marketing (Europe), and Symah Vision (Europe) have adopted the technology (Turner & Cusumano, 2000). Virtual advertising systems, such as ADVision, EPSIS, or Imadgine have been developed to expand the potential market for sport event advertisers by altering (or adding) the received broadcast of advertising at events to suit different markets. Virtual advertising creates new potential for broadcasters by providing the opportunity to adapt advertising content according to receiving region, to place ads in unique locations within stadiums, and to use animated signage. Thus, one advertiser of an international sport event could target different markets by advertising different brands and products, and by adapting its advertising messages (e.g., in various languages) for each receiving country ("Virtual advertising," 2000). Virtual advertising transforms sport events into advertising media platforms able to generate new revenues for rights holders, broadcasters, and program producers.

The NHL tested virtual advertising for the first time during the Stanley Cup playoff broadcasts on its national TV partners in 2008. This decision was made to drive revenue and enhance branding during the busiest part of the hockey season. "We want to convince corporate America to spend more marketing and ad dollars against hockey," said John Collins, the NHL's senior executive vice president of business and media. The virtual advertising plan was patterned after the same type of advertising behind home plate during televised baseball games. Hockey's version superimposed ads on the glass above dasherboards that protect spectators. The ads, which will not be visible in the arena, will not affect camera angles or live television shots (Mickle and Ourand, 2008).

THE PHENOMENON OF BROADCASTING PIRACY

The proliferation of new media and broadcasting technologies has enabled sports rights holders to generate substantial new revenue streams. Recently, sport rights holders are facing with a new challenge that is threatening the value of broadcasting rights called "broadcasting piracy." Broadcasting piracy refers to the illegal live broadcasting of sports events over the various media such as television, radio, mobile, or Internet. Broadcast piracy causes serious harm to both sports rights holders and broadcasters, requiring content monitoring services and substantial legal protection. Because sports broadcasting rights are usually sold on an exclusive basis the illegal copying and/or retransmission of sports contents, either live or deferred, devalue the broadcasters' costly investments and prevent from their further exploitation (e.g., increased advertising revenue and sublicensing). Furthermore, due to the diminished value, sport rights holders would no longer secure large revenues from broadcasting rights because they cannot guarantee exclusivity, a significant aspect of the rights value.

According to the European Broadcasting Union, there are several forms of broadcasting piracy:

- Retransmission of live or recorded broadcasts by a pirate station operating in a neighboring country.
- Commercial sale to the public of videocassettes of unauthorized copies of a sports program in the broadcaster's country and abroad.
- Cable distribution of complete broadcast sport programs in the broadcaster's neighboring country.
- Rental of unauthorized recordings of a television broadcast by a video club offering the "service" of making an unauthorized copy of a pre-selected television program with a view to the sale thereof in video form.
- Manufacture, importation, and distribution of pirate decoders and/or smart cards specifically designed to permit unauthorized access to encrypted television services.
- Public "large-screen" showing of live broadcasts of international sports events.
- Showing of unauthorized copies of television sport programs to customers in various types of shops, or to the public at fairs or exhibitions.
- Sale to the public of unauthorized recordings of broadcast programs by a dealer in radio or television equipment.

- Broadcasting or cable distribution of pre-broadcast satellite signals, which carry sports programs.
- Publication in newspapers, magazines, and books of still photos taken from the television screen, particularly of broadcasts of news and sports programs.
- Distribution of television and radio broadcasts to hotel rooms by internal hotel cable services.
- Retransmission of live broadcasts of football matches via the Internet, partly "framing" the broadcast images with the pirate's own advertisements.

Online Piracy

Broadcasting piracy over the internet is known as "online piracy" and constitutes one of the most serious threats of piracy due to peer-to-peer programs. Peer-to-Peer (P2P) networking is an application that runs on personal computers and enables files sharing to anyone with an Internet connection. P2P networks connect individual computers together and enable them to share files instead of having to go through a central server. In a P2P network, a television signal can be retransmitted using ordinary computers to broadcast live sport events. The new online P2P distribution technology, called BitTorrent, enables the illegal live broadcasting of sport events to a large number of recipients by spreading the bandwidth load across many computers via file sharing amongst "swarms" of users. P2P technologies have been initially used in the music industry by companies such as Napster, Grokster ,and Sharman License Holdings (owner of the KaZaA file sharing system).

Online piracy is a reality and threatens the traditional sports broadcasting model. For example, in the U.K. English Premier League matches on Saturdays, live broadcasting is not allowed in order to secure fan attendance in sports arenas. It has been found that more than 50,000 people log onto websites broadcasting the games live and illegally. To cope with this issue, FA Premier League took action by identifying the websites offering unauthorized coverage of live football games and succeeding in shutting down several of them (Couchman Harrington, 2006).

Facing Broadcasting Piracy

The evolution of new technologies enabling online piracy and illegal broadcasting of sport content constitute a threat to the value of new media rights and to the value of exclusive and live television, broadband streaming, and mobile rights. The increase of user-generated-content (UGC) and social networking sites are one of the major developments in sport broadcasting rights. Sports rights holders need to ensure that their content is not misused and their intellectual property is protected and leveraged. With a view to combating, in an effective manner, sport broadcasting piracy, sports rights holders and broadcasters can employ several approaches either in isolation or in combination:

a. The Legal Approach: Sports rights holders can use the consultancy of specialized law firms in order to combat broadcasting piracy phenomena by either identifying potential web pirates and/or by taking legal actions against them. For example, Viacom, Seconds Out, and FA Premier League brought a claim against YouTube over footage that has been posted there. In order to face the problem of broadcasting piracy, law firms specialized in new media rights and piracy have emerged. Law agencies such as Couchman and Harrington Associates in Europe are known to specialize in broadcasting piracy.

b. The Technological Approach: Sports rights holders can either utilize new technologies such as monitoring software to identify unauthorized broadcasting or hire specialized agencies to detect and track down broadcasting pirates. They can use new technologies and services such as digital management software and digital watermarking technology in order to gather crucial intelligence on their programming (when and where their content is aired). New companies offering broadcast monitoring and management services have been developed in order to assist sports rights holders in securing the value of their properties (Figure 8.2). One such a company, Teletrax, offers global video broadcast monitoring and video asset management services to sports rights holders since 2002. Teletrax uses video watermarking technologies that enable tracking and monitoring of sport content aired via cable, satellite, and terrestrial broadcasters.[4] Another well known firm, NetResult, works on behalf of right holders such as UEFA, Formula One, and the cricket and rugby union world cups and takes illegal content off the Internet (Wilson, 2007).

c. The Marketing Approach: Recently, new business models have been adopted which empower copyright holders and enable the legal online broadcasting of sport events in reasonable prices. For example, YouTube introduced new measures for fighting online piracy by developing video clip identification technology for its file-sharing site. This new technology allows right-holders who collaborate with YouTube to either take down the clips or monetize them through advertising in a revenue share with the site. Taken another approach, FA Premier League allowed English Premiership football matches to be broadcast live and legally on the Internet by its right holders, Sky and Setanta Sports, from 2007–2010. At the same time, BBC offers legal sport content (recorded highlights of Premiership matches) to U.K. Internet users, and Sky Sports is sending clips to mobile phones (Wilson, 2007).

CONCLUSION

The globalization of sports and the development of new media in combination with improvements in content acquisition, production, and delivery of broadcasting technologies have complicated the process of sports broadcasting. In addition, these advancements lead to the broadcasting of an extraordinary volume of premium-quality sport content that is able to attract the interest of global sport consumers. Developments occur not only in the ownership of broadcasting rights and in the exploitation of new media rights but in all aspects of the broadcasting process and the stakeholders involved. Thus, nowadays, right holders are becoming broadcasters by owning their medium platform, new broadcasting media are reaching global viewers, and viewers are changing the way and the media via which they watch sports.

New digital media such as digital terrestrial television, digital cable, digital radio, Internet television and mobile television have had a significant effect on the way sport is delivered and watched. With the introduction of new broadcasting platforms (e.g., Internet, mobile phones), new media rights are developing and fully exploited by right holders. Thus, new media are gaining additional value in the media sector and compete against other broadcasting media for achieving a larger market share. As a result, television rights might lose their dominant market position and their value diminishes gradually. As the new media have entered the broadcasting market, TV broadcasters are losing part of their market share, which decreases their advertising revenue and, thus, the cost of television broadcasting rights might decrease in the future. Competition among broadcasters has become more intense and has lead to the development of strategic alliances between different media (television, Internet, and mobile companies), infrastructure owners, and sporting bodies (sport clubs) that acquire to buy all the broadcasting rights of a single sporting event.

Traditional broadcasting media provide passive experiences to their viewers while the convergence of broadcasting technologies requires higher involvement from the viewers while incorporating several interactive components. New media have changed viewing habits and turned viewers into active producers of their own entertainment, though the cost of using these new technologies increases the cost of viewing for the consumers (subscribers). Sport consumers have the opportunity to watch sports in high-definition screens (HDTV) and Dolby Digital surround sound, with multiple camera angles and super-slow-motion replays on multiple broadcasting platforms. Moreover, viewers are increasingly requiring more unicast services that will provide more choices—more programs and viewing platforms on demand, and the ability to customize their viewing experience to their specific interests and preferences.

However, new media raise additional copyright issues in sports broadcasting. Broadcasting piracy (especially online piracy), although providing free-of-charge viewing to sport consumers all over the world, is seriously threatening the value of sport broadcasting rights. Current regulatory frameworks of broadcasting rights seem to be insufficient for the existing competitive market, causing uncertainty and likelihood of new developments. New regulatory frameworks need be developed that will include new media and protect broadcasting rights of sport events without distorting and restricting competition by interfering with the supply and demand of broadcasting rights.

All the above developments and innovations indicate the emergence of the new entrepreneurial model in sports broadcasting which will further transform the broadcasting scene in the coming years.

Endnotes

1. Retrieved from http://english.aljazeera.net/sport
2. Retrieved from http://www.jobmonkey.com/sports/html/sports_broadcasting_jobs_links.html
3. Retrieved from http://www.umterps.com/multimedia/md-tv-radio-affiliates.html #sportsnetwork
4. Retrieved from www.teletrax.tv

References

Barboza, D. (2008, August 28). Olympics are ratings bonanza for Chinese TV. *The New York Times*. Retrieved from http://www.nytimes.com/2008/08/22/sports/olympics/22cctv.html?_r=1

Couchman Harrington. (2006). Online piracy threatens the value of sports broadcasting rights [Press release]. Retrieved from http://www.couchmansllp.com/documents/news_press/Online%20Piracy%20&%20Sports%20Broadcasting%20Rights.pdf

Davis, C. (2008). IOC's new gatekeeper strategy could close the door on EBU. *TV Sports Markets*, 12(20). Retrieved from http://www.sportbusiness.com/print-edition/ioc%E2%80%99s-new-gatekeeper-strategy-could-close-door-ebu

Dentsu Inc. (2006). Dentsu concludes agreement to become exclusive agent in Japan and Asia for broadcasting rights covering major Serie A football clubs [Press release]. Retrieved from http://search.dentsu.com/en_all/search.x?q=exclusive+broadcast+rights+in+japan&f=&imgsize=1&pagemax=10&page=1&ie=utf8&mode=en_all&pid=j0t8IYG4nWBEhjm4rHx4lw..&qid=WkOisZZwaSo.#0

EBU memorandum on virtual advertising. (2000, May 25). Retrieved from http://www.ebu.ch/CMSimages/en/leg_virtual_advertising_tcm6-4366.pdf

EBU secures $800M IOC deal. (2004, June 18). *SportBusiness.com*. Retrieved from www.sportbusiness.com/news/index?news_item_id=154920.

German broadcasting deal—EU template for future agreements? (2005, January 26). Retrieved from http://www.euractiv.com/Article?tcmuri=tem:29-134541-16&type=News

Hatton, C., & Wagner C. (2007). Winner takes all: Football rights and competition law. *Global Competition Review*. Retrieved from http://www.hhlaw.com/files/Publication/52f2f3e7-5246-46ac-b413-2c9c0429ce34/Presentation/PublicationAttachment/8efdb35b-53a0-4db9-8034-312afd6f3d18/GCRFootballrightsApril2007.pdf

Japanese TV rights boost IOC. (2003, July 28). *SportBusiness.com*. Retrieved from http://www.sportbusiness.com/news/?news_item_id=151995

JumpTV and NeuLion to Merge and Create Internet Protocol Television (IPTV) and Web Streaming Powerhouse. (2008, June 9). Retrieved from http://www.neulion.com/news/2008/JumpTV_NeuLion_Merge_Press_Release.pdf

Kepreotes, P. (2007, March 3). The revolution of sports broadcasting. Retrieved from http://www.broadcastaustralia.com.au/assets/files/White%20Papers/2007%2003%20-%20The%20Revolution%20of%20Sports%20Broadcasting.pdf

Laflin M. (2001). Sport and the Internet—The impact and the future. In *New Technology in Sports Information and Sports Information Management*. International Association for Sports Information. Retrieved from http://multimedia.olympic.org/pdf/en_report_60.pdf

Massive growth shows USA is loving On-line TV [Web log]. (2008, September 5). *Worldtvpc.com*. Retrieved from http://www.worldtvpc.com/blog/massive-growth-shows-usa-is-loving-online-tv

McCarthy, M. (2006, November 16). Schools, coaches cash in on lucrative media deals. *USA Today*. Retrieved from http://www.usatoday.com/sports/college/football/2006-11-16-cover-coaches-media_x.htm

Herman, E. & McCheshey, R. (1997). The global media: The new missionaries of corporate capitalism (p. 83). London: Continuum.

Mickle, T., & Ourand, J. (2008, March 31) NHL will test virtual ads in playoffs. *Sports Business Journal*. Retrieved from http://www.sportsbusinessjournal.com/article/58509

MSN Direct Introduces Sports Content, First New Channel for Smart Watches. (2004, March 22). Retrieved from http://www.microsoft.com/presspass/press/2004/mar04/03-22sportslaunchpr.mspx

Nation 2nd largest global radio broadcasting market. (2004, May 11). *China Daily*. Retrieved from http://english.peopledaily.com.cn/200405/11/eng20040511_142923.html

New programming strategy for ESPN360.com broadband service. (2007, August 8). Retrieved from http://www.espnmediazone.com/press_releases/2007_08_aug/20070808_NewProgrammingStrategyforESPN360.comBroadbandService.htm

OMVC Demonstrates Future of Mobile DTV and Details Initial Broadcaster Roll-Out Plans. (2009, January 9). Retrieved from www.openmobilevideo.com/_assets/docs/press-releases/2009/01-08-09OMVCDemonstratesFuture.doc

Papaioannou, E., Borälv, E., Demiris, A., Johansson, N., & Ioannidis, N. (2004). User interface design for multi-platform interactive sports content broadcasting. *AVI*. Retrieved from http://melisa.intranet.gr/documentation/publications/User%20Interface%20Design%20for%20Multiplatform%20Interactive%20Sports%20Broadcasting.pdf

Real Madrid TV kicks off in the UK via satellite. (2006, June 12). *SportBusiness.com*. Retrieved from http://www.sportbusiness.com/news/160897/real-madrid-tv-kicks-off-in-the-uk-via-satellite

Reid, D. (2006, June 23). Mobile TV entices football fans. *BBC News*. Retrieved from http://news.bbc.co.uk/2/hi/programmes/click_online/5109582.stm

Reiter, A. (2009, May 19). Global telecoms insights says Asian mobile TV growth drives phone choices [Web log comment]. *Reiter's Mobile TV Report*. Retrieved from http://www.mobiletelevisionreport.com/2009/05/page/2/

Sehgal, N. (2008, November 27). Record ratings propel NEO cricket to top position among sports channels. *TVnext.in*. Retrieved from http://www.tvnext.in/news/142/ARTICLE/1756/2008-11-27.html

Sessa, D., & Soshnick, S. (2007, August 2). New York Yankees TV network might fetch $2 billion. *Bloomberg.com*. Retrieved from http://www.bloomberg.com/apps/news?pid=20601079&refer=home&sid=aTcfoWsgk6Yg

Sport set to play major role in roll-out of new technologies (2004, October 27). Retrieved March 24, 2005, from http://www.euractiv.com/Active ? tcmuri=tcm :29-131149-16&type=News

Television without Frontiers. (1997). European Parliament Directive 97/36/EC, No L202 *Official Journal of the European Communities*, 60–76. Available at http://europa.eu.int.

The sport and new media revolution. (2001). *SportBusiness.com*. Retrieved January 24, 2005 from http://www.sportbusiness.com

The sports market media rights review. (2006, October). Sportcal Global Communications, (5). Retrieved from http://www.sportcal.com/pdf/media_rights_review/issue_5_low_res%20.pdf

Tsiotsou, R. (2005). The effect of European Union regulations on marketing practices: The case of European football. *Journal of Euromarketing*, 15(1), 75–93.

Turner Sports. (2008). NBA TV celebrates the 2008 holiday season [Press release]. Retrieved from http://news.turner.com/article_display.cfm?article_id=4163

Turner, P., & Cusumano, S. (2000). Virtual advertising: Legal implications for sport. *Sport Management Review*, 3(1), 47–70.

TV Channels broadcasting EURO 2008. (2008, June 11). Retrieved from http://www.euro2008info.net/tv-channels-broadcasting-euro-2008.html

UEFA EURO 2008 review. (2008). Retrieved from http://www.euro2008.uefa.com /MultimediaFiles/Download/PressConference/Competitions/MediaServices/73 /54/33/735433_DOWNLOAD.pdf

Virtual advertising guidance note—Electronic imaging systems or "virtual" advertising. Rule 19.2.4. (2000). Retrieved from http://www.ofcom.org.uk/static/archiv e/itc/itc_publications/codes_guidance /programme_sponsorship/virtual_ad _guidance.asp.html

Wilson, B. (2007, July 11). Sport puts up fight to protect rights. *BBC News*. Retrieved from http://news.bbc.co.uk/2 /hi/business/6268854.stm

Wilson, B. (2006, November 19). Mobile TV sports viewing is on the move. *BBC News*. Retrieved from http://news.bbc .co.uk/2/hi/business/6153536.stm

World Cup prompt for African mobile broadcasting. (2009, May 8). *SportBusiness .com*. Retrieved from http://www.sport business.com/news/169365/world-cup-prompt-african-mobile-broadcasting

Ten percent growth in UK internet TV viewers [Web log]. (2009, March 18). *Worldtvpc.com*. Retrieved from http:// www.worldtvpc.com/blog/10-growth-in -uk-internet-tv-viewers/

XFMedia wins Europa League rights. (2008, October 24). *SportBusiness.com*. Retrieved from http://www.sportbusiness .com/news/168153/xfmedia-wins-europa -league-rights

9

The College Sport Research Institute: Where Theory and Practice Lead to Action

RICHARD M. SOUTHALL, MARK S. NAGEL, AND DEBORAH J. SOUTHALL

BACKGROUND: THE LOST NCAA CONFERENCE

In 2002, John Thelin noted there had recently "been a groundswell of excellent scholarly works dealing with intercollegiate athletics" (p. 410). He contended college-sport research presently had both endurance and significance since such disciplines as history, economics, law, literary analysis, and political science were being brought to bear on the serious study of college sport.

In 2006, apparently unaware of Thelin's identified groundswell, and noting a lack of such quality research, the National Collegiate Athletic Association (NCAA) announced an academic conference to encourage scholars to study college sport (NCAA). According to media accounts, NCAA President Myles Brand, a philosopher who was president of Indiana University before taking the reins at the NCAA, was a driving force behind the conference. The initial conference solicited academic papers and established a panel of experts to review submissions through a blind-review process.

A few months later it was reported that Dr. Brand—citing a lack of quality papers—had cancelled the proposed conference. Brand noted, ". . . having been in the academy for 40 years, I think I can tell the difference between a good paper and something that's not high quality, [and I] saw too many of the latter and too few of the former" (Lederman, 2006, para. 14). Some scholars who had been retained to review papers were concerned about the "individual" review process that was undertaken by Brand, especially since as a former faculty member he would have likely encountered and understood the importance of blind review by multiple scholars for an academic conference.

Having cancelled their first academic conference, in January 2008 the NCAA convened invited scholars from sociology, history, literature, economics, and business for a symposium with a rhetorical theme: "College Sports: A Legitimate Focus for Scholarly Inquiry?" (Powers, 2008). After raising concerns among many academics when the first conference was cancelled, the symposium also elicited negative reactions from many observers since the NCAA staff executed the "academic" symposium with complete control over format, purpose, topic areas, and—most importantly—participants.

In addition to the symposium, the NCAA announced a new journal: *Journal of Intercollegiate Sport* (*JIS*), supported by NCAA start-up funding (Human Kinetics, 2010a). According to the journal's website, "The purpose of the NCAA funding is to foster cross-disciplinary research on intercollegiate sport and promote the integration of athletics with the academic missions of NCAA member institutions" (Human Kinetics, 2010a, para. 3). The journal solicits nontechnical manuscripts that are "cross-disciplinary in nature and have clear practical applications" (Human Kinetics, 2010b, para. 2).

During the same time period in which the initial NCAA conference had been cancelled and the "invited" academic symposium was created, Dr. Brand consistently dismissed any criticism of the NCAA or big-time college sport as Brand characterized critics as uninformed. He additionally utilized offhand comments, such as: "They have their facts wrong," as well as formal discussions to dismiss criticism, such as during the 2007 State of the Association address, in which Dr. Brand noted:

> There is little that frustrates me more than critics of college sports who get the facts wrong . . . I challenge the critics of college sports, in the media and on campus, to get their facts right. . . . Meeting the challenges of intercollegiate athletics requires an informed, engaged faculty. (Brand, 2007, para. 16, 19, 45)

By sponsoring an annual academic colloquium and a non-technical peer-reviewed academic journal, the NCAA was in effect expanding its athletic brand into the academic and scholarly-inquiry business. This development was questioned by some scholars, who expressed concerns that the NCAA, as an athletic trade association, might not be an objective party in such scholarly inquiry.

With the NCAA's moving to fill a perceived void in the scholarly landscape, college-sport researchers had several options: (1) Boycotting the NCAA sponsored journal and symposium; (2) Acquiescing to the NCAA's new role as the sole stimulator and disseminator of research related to intercollegiate athletics, and submit manuscripts and presentations to *JIS* and the NCAA symposium; and (3) Forming an independent college-sport research institute that would host an annual scholarly conference on college sport and publish a peer-reviewed academic journal.

THE COLLEGE SPORT RESEARCH INSTITUTE

Against this backdrop, in 2007 a group of college-sport researchers chose the third alternative, and the College Sport Research Institute (CSRI) was the result. Since its inception, one of CSRI's primary missions has been to support independent data collection and analysis related to college-sport issues. At the same time formal mission statements, goals, objectives, and strategies were conceptualized, a basic organizational structure was established.

Basic CSRI Organizational Structure

The College Sport Research Institute has three primary functions: (1) Host an annual conference that allows a forum for faculty, students, and the general public to discuss research related to college sport; (2) Publish a peer-reviewed academic journal related to issues in intercollegiate athletics; and (3) Conduct and support independent college-sport research. In order to accomplish these tasks CSRI has a basic organizational structure, which includes a director, an associate director, three assistant directors, two journal co-editors, general counsel, an advisory-committee coordinator, and a six-member executive board.

CSRI Mission and Goals

The desire to support faculty and student engagement in college-sport research is central to the College Sport Research Institute's mission. Specifically, CSRI exists to:

> Encourage and support interdisciplinary and interuniversity collaborative college-sport research; serve as a research consortium for college-sport researchers from across the United States; and disseminate college-sport research results to academics, college-sport practitioners, and the general public. (College Sport Research Institute, n. d., para. 1)

In order to serve as a national clearinghouse for college-sport research and support independent, organized and focused cross-disciplinary research regarding college sport, the institute hosts an annual academic conference and publishes a peer-reviewed academic journal (*Journal of Issues in Intercollegiate Athletics—JIIA*).

In support of its mission, the College Sport Research Institute has the following goals:

- Create public awareness of socio-cultural, economic, and political issues in college sport, and provide a forum for open discussion of these issues within the college-sport community;
- Build relationships within local, regional and national communities to generate funding for independent college-sport research;
- Generate local, regional, and national awareness of the College Sport Research Institute and The University of North Carolina at Chapel Hill as a leader in college-sport research; and
- Educate students, scholars, athletic administrators, college athletes, coaches, and the general public regarding college-sport issues.

WHERE THEORY AND PRACTICE LEAD TO ACTION

Metadiscrete Experiential Learning

In support of its research mission and specific substantive goals related to this mission, CSRI also provides an opportunity for undergraduate and graduate students to be immersed in a year-round metadiscrete experiential learning environment. Consistent with its mission, CSRI's internship program allows interns a total-immersion setting in which they are involved in CSRI's day-to-day management and operation, as well as the planning, organizing and managing of the institute's annual Scholarly Conference on College Sport and Tee off for Tar Heels Benefit Golf Tournament. CSRI interns, as well as University of North Carolina at Chapel Hill (UNC) graduate and undergraduate sport-administration students take part in this entrepreneurial-based learning laboratory.

A full appreciation of CSRI's entrepreneurial nature requires a basic understanding of experiential learning theory and how CSRI has gone beyond previous experiential learning concepts and embodies metadiscrete experiential learning. Experiential learning has a long educational history. Rogers and Freiberg (1994) detailed two distinct learning typologies: *cognitive* (meaningless) and *experiential* (significant). For Rogers and Freiberg, much of what passes for knowledge, such as rote memorization of multiplication tables or sport trivia, is cognitive and essentially meaningless. However, in a sport-management context, applied knowledge—such as learning about fundamental elements of event management in order to effectively manage a sport event—is significant because such experientially grounded learning addresses students' needs and wants. Such experientially based learning allows students to directly experience sport management through its cogent qualities: personal involvement, self-initiation and evaluation, and pervasive self-effects.

Most notably, experiential learning helps students develop the capacity to reflect on their learning experiences and attach appropriate significance through such reflection (Southall, Nagel, LeGrande, & Han, 2003). It also allows teachers to constantly upgrade and modify instruction methods to meet their students' needs and subject-area developments (Southall, et al., 2003). In experiential learning settings, a faculty member more appropriately takes on role of a *facilitator*. This facilitation includes developing a positive learning climate, clarifying the students' goals and objectives, organizing and making available learning resources, balancing intellectual and emotional learning components, and discussing students' feelings and thoughts, while not dictating their attitudes and beliefs (Rogers & Freiberg, 1994).

Lagace and Longfellow (1989) found that student perceptions can be improved using engaged student participation within course work, as opposed to total reliance on traditional lecture. By 2000, participatory (i.e., experiential learning) projects had been identified as a critical element in student preparation for sport industry careers (Sport Management Program Review Council, 2000). Since that time they have emerged as a common feature in many sport management academic programs (Irwin, Southall, & Sutton, 2007; McKelvey & Southall, 2008).

Similarly, client-based projects are reported to provide a more comprehensive learning experience than other participation exercises (Milner, 1995). Specific to sport management curriculum, Southall, et al. (2003) proposed a *metadiscrete* learning model which deconstructed the arbitrary and unnecessary disconnect between sport-industry practitioners and sport-management faculty. Such a model, in which staff from partnering sport businesses serve as instructional leaders and facilitators alongside sport-management faculty, "enhances student understanding of entrepreneurship, sales, sponsorship, event management, and marketing research within the context of the university's sport management program" (Southall, et al., p. 23). Greater knowledge gain is possible because in a metadiscrete experience, the roles of teacher and practitioner are not separate and distinct, but are dual aspects of the same function. These roles may be more akin to that of *mentors*, with both individuals assuming a more involved relationship with a learner. Applying a metadiscrete learning model to managing the day-to-day operations of a research institute, as well as the planning, organizing, and managing of an academic conference and benefit golf tournament are logical applications of the theoretical elements of experiential learning.

APPLYING A METADISCRETE
LEARNING MODEL TO CSRI

Students' enhanced educational opportunities available in a metadiscrete experiential learning setting are best achieved when provisions for both student and faculty theoretical and practical knowledge needs are met. Faculty mentors involved in CSRI are motivated by the primary goal of determining how to best meet intern and student needs, while insuring CSRI, conference, and golf-tournament success. Meanwhile, the students' and interns' motivations are much more focused on "their" singular event (either the conference or the golf tournament), and are necessarily more short-term oriented. Recognizing this distinction, while still striving to insure CSRI's long-term survival within a metadiscrete model, is a challenge. Against this backdrop, the following section provides a detailed look at several staff opportunities currently available through CSRI.

The day-to-day operations of the College Sport Research Institute involve cooperative student/faculty interaction designed to provide students with practical operational experiences in real-world business settings. Through their participation as CSRI staff members, interns and students are able to demonstrate, develop, and refine specific sport-industry skills and competencies under the day-to-day guidance and supervision of CSRI managers, directors, and associated faculty. CSRI also serves to enhance UNC's sport-administration program's relationships with the sport industry, other college and university sport-management programs, college-sport researchers, and the general public. CSRI's existence is consistent with the UNC graduate sport-administration program's vision statement: "UNC Sport Administration . . . Where theory and practice lead to action."

Every organization should create a structure appropriate to its mission, resources, and opportunities. CSRI's organizational design represents an approach, in which CSRI interns, graduate students, and associated faculty members may simultaneously serve as staff, mentors, advisors, and managers in specific functional areas. In addition, while the College Sport Research Institute office is located on the University of North Carolina at Chapel Hill campus, the institute is a nation-wide entity with faculty-mentors. While the interaction between CSRI executive board members and CSRI staff, interns, and UNC students are often filtered by CSRI faculty-mentors, a great deal of interaction still occurs. In addition, while faculty-mentors and faculty board-of-directors may have direct contact with various publics, much of such public contact is initiated by CSRI interns and UNC sport-administration students (See Figure 9.1.).

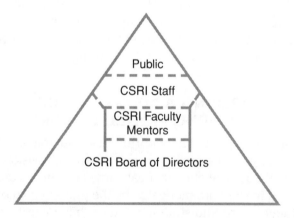

FIGURE 9.1. **College sport research institute filtering structure.**

CSRI faculty mentors assume roles relative to their individual strengths and levels of practical experience. Critical to CSRI's development has been the establishment of an organizational structure to not only encourage faculty-mentor, staff, intern, and student interaction, but delineate specific operational functional areas and management structure. Figure 9.2 illustrates such a structure.

Recognizing regular communication is critical to any organization's success; such communication is encouraged through weekly management-level meetings of the CSRI Director, CSRI Office Manager, and Director of Development and Member Relations, as well as regularly scheduled meetings that include these principals as well as conference co-directors, interns, functional-area directors, and faculty mentors. In addition, regular functional-area staff meetings are held. These meetings allow all CSRI organization members to meet on an ongoing basis to discuss the institute's overall direction, as well as specific long- and short-term goals, current and future projects, or pressing issues. It is important to note all CSRI staff, interns, and students are encouraged to approach UNC sport-administration faculty members, as well as all institute executive board members, whenever they feel the need to ask questions, obtain guidance, or receive reinforcement relative to CSRI duties or responsibilities.

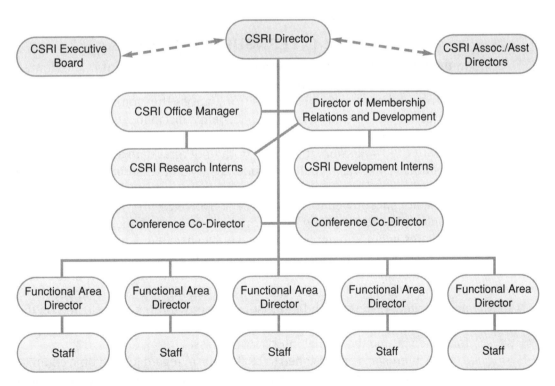

FIGURE 9.2. **College sport research institute operational organizational structure.**

To reinforce CSRI's metadiscrete nature, CSRI-related projects are coordinated with sport-administration course curriculum brainstorming and discussion sessions. These sessions—consistent with the UNC sport-administration program's vision—provide vital learning opportunities for students and faculty to tie sport-management theory to CSRI practice. To identify experiential learning opportunities, faculty members both formally and informally continually discuss when it is appropriate to incorporate CSRI-related activities into course curriculum.

Once an organizational structure was developed, the next step was to formulate policies and procedures designed to support CSRI's mission and goals. Some of the established policies and procedures established include: (a) intern-selection process, (b) membership and new-business development guidelines, (c) conference-planning procedures, and (d) strategic marketing plan.

In any business venture, management recognizes that staff turnover, though often inconvenient, is inevitable. By design, most CSRI interns and undergraduate students transition every semester. In addition, at the present time the positions of CSRI office manager, director of membership, and conference functional-area directors occur annually. Recognizing these limitations, annual and semester orientations strive to limit new CSRI organization members having to "reinvent-the-wheel," while still allowing them to actively engage in a metadiscrete learning experience.

CSRI INTERNSHIP PROGRAM

In the following section, we outline and discuss the recent implemented CSRI Internship Program. This internship program allows students/individuals from colleges and universities from across the United States and/or other countries, as well as from any academic discipline, the ability to gain practical research, development, or event management experience. Consistent with CSRI's mission and goals, both undergraduate and graduate college students, as well as college graduates who have an interest in college sport, college-sport research, sport event-management, or member development are encouraged to apply. College Sport Research Institute (CSRI) internships are offered during fall, spring, and summer semesters. Interested candidates submit an application packet by specified deadlines. Internship program information is posted on the institute's website and also disseminated via academic listservs, e-mail announcements to CSRI-member faculty, and a CSRI conference forum. On an ongoing basis intern applications are solicited, reviewed, and internships offered. Interns are selected on the basis of a general assessment of applicants' qualifications and their performance during the formal interview process.

CSRI internships are designed to be flexible, in regard to both time commitments and areas of interest and exposure. The minimum time commitment for research and event-management interns is 20 hours/week. Because development internships are paid positions—based on a percentage (20%) of developed memberships, donations, or sponsorships—the minimum time expectation for these internships is 30 hours per week. Internships can be tailored to accommodate specific internship course requirements.

Internship applicants must submit an application packet that includes: (a) A current resume specifying current academic standing and documenting the applicant's cumulative GPA; (b) A letter of interest detailing previous work and educational experiences, and their rationale for applying; and (c) Three letters of recommendation, at least one of which is preferred to be from a college professor.

In addition, CSRI interns and their supervisors complete written mid-semester and final evaluations. These evaluations not only provide opportunities to discuss identified strengths and areas of improvement of individual interns, but also allow for ongoing evaluation of staff and faculty mentors. The mid-semester evaluation is designed to ensure productive intern behaviors are reinforced or corrective-action plans are documented. The ongoing nature of the evaluation process is designed to mirror most sport industry environments.

All CSRI interns are required to maintain an ongoing portfolio, designed to document their CSRI work experience and serve as an interview presentation tool. During their exit interviews (held after the student has received their grade, if the internship is a for-credit experience), each intern is asked to offer specific suggestions for improving CSRI policies and procedures. To facilitate this process, each intern orientation involves a two-stage process. The first stage is a meeting with the CSRI office manager, director of membership and development, and institute director. This meeting involves an overview of the internship expectations, CSRI policies and procedures, and specific intern duties and areas of responsibility. Each intern orientation also includes a meeting with graduate-student functional-area directors to discuss conference organization and planning. In addition to these intern orientations, each year incoming UNC graduate students are involved in an orientation and on-boarding process that involves many of the same elements as internship orientations.

CSRI MEMBERSHIP DRIVE

While CSRI receives limited institutional support from The University of North Carolina at Chapel Hill, such support and revenues generated from conference registration fees to its Scholarly Conference on College Sport (SCCS) are not enough to cover CSRI operating expenses. As a result, other forms of income are necessary to ensure CSRI's survival and growth. As an independent research institute, CSRI is not supported by entities such as the NCAA. In reality, CSRI is no different from orchestras, museums, and other non-profit research organizations in that it needs additional support from community members. In addition to seeking support from foundations and government funding, CSRI needs support from faculty, students, and the general public interested in college sport research.

While CSRI is continually seeking foundation and government support, such funding is both limited and takes a long time to generate. As a result, CSRI has also undertaken an entrepreneurial approach to revenue generation, by developing and instituting an individual membership drive.

During the CSRI internship program's initial semester, CSRI interns were integrally involved in the membership drive. The following section outlines and discusses this project in detail.

Components

After two years of existence, in 2009 CSRI was at a proverbial "crossroads." While no directors, editors, or executive board members drew any salaries, the institute's daily operational costs (office staff salaries, internship stipends, office and research equipment/supplies, etc.), and expenses associated with hosting the CSRI conference were more than generated revenues. Simply put, conference registration fees did not offset operating expenses, making contributed income and volunteer time essential to CSRI's survival.

As part of the initial membership campaign, a series of membership "levels" were created. These levels were set as follows: (a) Distinguished Partner ($1,000 and up), (b) Executive Partner ($500–$999), (c) Premier Member ($250–$499), (d) Supporting Member ($100–$249), and (e) Contributing Member ($40–$99).

Each level had various associated member benefits. In order to allow prospective members to examine these benefits, a membership grid was developed (See appendix A.). This graphic representation was designed to allow CSRI interns to discuss the associated benefits with prospective members on the phone while the future members had the matrix on their computer screens. It was also hoped the grid would provide sufficient information for individuals who visited the CSRI website to make a decision to join.

Implementation

On a daily basis CSRI development interns were in contact with prospective members. The prospective member database was developed from a variety of sources, including the CSRI registration list from the previous two conferences, as well as various academic organization lists. In addition, the interns visited sport management program websites. Such prospecting allowed interns to learn a great deal about prospects' research interests and teaching areas. This allowed the interns to be better prepared to discuss CSRI and the appropriateness of a prospect becoming a CSRI member.

During a typical day, each CSRI development intern made between 20–30 phone calls to CSRI member prospects. About two-thirds of these calls were initial contacts with either potential members or sponsors, with the remainder being follow-up calls. The interns quickly learned they actually communicated (via a phone conversation or answered e-mail) with only about five people each day. The other 15–25 daily contacts involved leaving voicemails or composing e-mails to which they would (hopefully) receive responses.

The interns universally reported that almost every single conversation went well and the prospect at least expressed interest in or support of CSRI and the conference. As one intern reported, "Every contact seems to have a positive attitude about CSRI after the conversation, and I probably get around five people per week who either sign up as members or say that they intend to. I also get at least one referral from each new member" (Hunter Culbertson, personal communication, May 28, 2010).

Results

The initial 2010 CSRI membership drive resulted in 116 CSRI members donating approximately $11,000.00. These funds help pay for operational and conference-related expenses, including the salaries of the CSRI office manager and CSRI director of development and member relations. In addition, the generated income was utilized to provide stipends for all three CSRI interns. Moving forward, CSRI is committed to fulfilling its research and service mission, while also providing educational opportunities for selected interns.

DISCUSSION

CSRI is now three years old. What began as an idea among colleagues has developed into a recognized research institute that is fulfilling its stated mission to

> encourage and support interdisciplinary and interuniversity collaborative college sport research, serve as a research consortium for college sport researchers from across the United States, and disseminate college sport research results to academics, college sport practitioners, and the general public. (College Sport Research Institute, n.d., para. 1)

CSRI has proven it can consistently host one of the academy's largest sport-management conferences, the quality of which, in terms of its venue, program, and presentations, has greatly exceeded the expectations of both supporters and initial skeptics. The institute's journal—*Journal of Issues in Intercollegiate Athletics*—has shown consistent growth, with an increasing number of quality articles published each year. In addition, CSRI research focusing on such areas as college sport broadcasts, college athlete graduation rates, and men's basketball roster turnover has received national recognition. CSRI is now seen as a respected source for solid research on college sport.

However, CSRI must continue to be entrepreneurial in order to generate revenues necessary for its survival and growth. Future plans include expansion of the CSRI membership base, to include current and former college coaches, former college athletes, and members of the general public who recognize the need for independent college sport research. CSRI would also like to eventually provide grants to scholars who develop innovative college sport research. CSRI has also investigated opportunities to conduct seminars in other countries regarding the unique nature of American college sport. However, since CSRI must maintain its independent nature, there are no plans to seek corporate support or funding from the NCAA or other college-sport trade associations.

As CSRI evolves one thing will remain consistent: CSRI will remain a student-centered metadiscrete experiential learning laboratory. That is what makes CSRI a unique research entity and keeps it moving forward, always forward.

References

Brand, M. (2007, January 6). In all, fairness. *2007 State of the Association*. Retrieved May 31, 2010, from http://www.ncaa.org/wps/wcm/connect/public/ncaa/about+the+ncaa/who+we+are/myles+brand+legacy/legacy+of+leadership/2007+ncaa+state+of+the+association

College Sport Research Institute. (n.d.). Mission. Retrieved May 31, 2010, from http://www.unc.edu/depts/exercise/csri/mission.htm

Human Kinetics. (2010a). About JIS. Retrieved May 31, 2010 from http://hk.humankinetics.com/JIS/journalAbout.cfm

Human Kinetics. (2010b). Mission. Retrieved May 31, 2010 from http://hk.humankinetics.com/JIS/journalMission.cfm

Irwin, R. L., Southall, R. M., & Sutton, W. A. (2007). Pentagon of Sport Sales Training: A 21st Century Sport Sales Training Model. *Sport Management Education Journal, 1*(1), 18–39.

Lagace, R. R., & Longfellow, T. A. (1989). The impact of classroom style on student attitudes toward sales careers: A comparative approach. *Journal of Marketing Education, 11*, 72–77.

Lederman, D. (2006, November 22). NCAA sidelines a scholarly conference. *Inside Higher Ed*. http://www.insidehighered.com/news/2006/11/22/ncaa

McKelvey, S., & Southall, R. M. (2008). Teaching sport sponsorship sales through experiential learning. *International Journal of Sport Management and Marketing, 4*, 225–254.

Milner, L. M. (1995). Telemarketing for the business school as a sales course project. *Journal of Marketing Education, 17*, 73–80.

National Collegiate Athletic Association. (2006, January 31). Conference to explore role of sport in American culture. *NCAA News Release*. http://www.ncaa.org/wps/ncaa?ContentID=4916

Powers, E. (2008, January 11). Scholars and sports. *Inside Higher Ed*. http://www.insidehighered.com/news/2008/01/11/ncaa

Rogers, C. R., & Freiberg, H. J. (1994). *Freedom to learn* (3rd ed.). Columbus, OH: Merrill/Macmillan.

Southall, R. M., Nagel, M. S., LeGrande, D., & Han. M. Y. (2003). Sport management practica: A metadiscrete experiential learning model. *Sport Marketing Quarterly, 12*(1), 27–36.

Sport Management Program Review Council. (2000). *Sport management program standards and review protocol*. Available from the National Association for Sport and Physical Education, 1900 Association Drive, Reston, VA 20191.

Thelin, J. R. (2002). Academics on athletics. *The Journal of Higher Education, 73*, 409–419.

Appendix A

Giving Level	Contributing Member	Supporting Member	Premier Member	Executive Partner	Distinguished Partner
Minimum Gift Required	$40–99	$100–249	$250–499	$500–999	$1000 and Up
Enhanced welcome kit at Conference Registration	CSRI	CSRI	CSRI	CSRI	CSRI
Registration Discount to SCCS	$50	$50	$75	$100	Complimentary
Year-long recognition on member page of CSRI website	CSRI	CSRI	CSRI	CSRI	CSRI
Recognition in SCCS Program	CSRI	CSRI	CSRI	CSRI	CSRI
10% discount on CSRI Merchandise	CSRI	CSRI	CSRI	CSRI	CSRI
CSRI logo golf shirt or laptop bag		CSRI	CSRI	CSRI	CSRI
Recognition in SCCS Program				1/4 page	1/2 page
Complimentary entry in Annual Tee off for Tar Heels Golf Tourney					CSRI
Complimentary invitations to Annual CSRI Recognition Dinner				1	2
SCCS = Scholarly Conference on College Sport					

10

Entrepreneurial Price Lining Strategy in Sports

CONWAY LACKMAN, DORENE CILETTI, JOHN LANASA, AND MARYELLEN KELLY

Franchising's rich history documents the entrepreneurial spirit involved in balancing risk and value. As costs rise for MLB franchises, especially small market teams, every effort should be made to optimize sports marketing's five P's (product, place, promotion, price, and public relations). As the price of tickets has escalated in recent years, pricing strategy is increasingly more important. With attendance a critical issue for most teams, and especially small-market teams, pricing policies that consider demand and variable pricing are increasingly utilized. Gennaro (2007) suggests that while baseball has moved away from a one-price policy per seat type, it has not fully explored the benefits of segmentation in pricing. We begin by briefly reviewing franchising, moving toward entrepreneurial aspects of sports franchises, ultimately addressing the issue of strategic price lining in sports.

LITERATURE REVIEW

Entrepreneurial Aspects of Sports Franchises

Entrepreneurs have been drawn to franchise arrangements for centuries. The roots of franchise behavior have been traced back to the United Kingdom's pub network and the intervention of King Edgar in 957. His establishment of a formal business format, business standards, and financial arrangements is considered the birth of franchising (Spinelli, 2004). Two major types of franchise systems exist in the United States. Product franchising, first seen around 1840, retains the distribution systems built by manufacturers as alternative ways to bring their products to the public. Business format franchising, popularized in the 1950's, includes organizations like restaurants, food and non-food retailing and business services. Sports franchises as "outlets which can be a vehicle for entrepreneurial activity" (Spinelli, 2004) are considered forms of business format franchising. Spinelli (2004) and other franchise experts offer this general formula for evaluating the risk and reward of franchise investment:

> Franchise fee + PV of Franchise Royalty Payment = PV of the increased net income from the value of the franchise trademark where PV = the present value of a sum of money.

Traditional franchise investors have a variety of ways to raise the franchise fee and royalty payments, such as asset loans, in which the lenders will evaluate the real estate, the equipment, the fixtures, and the inventory of the organization. Blum (2002) noted a preference for conventional lenders to prefer lending to franchisees that are purchasing versus leasing a specific location. Lending based on cash flow (including ticket sales, concessions, sponsorship, space rental, etc.) is another method, in which a lender applies some type of formula (such as multiple of earnings) in order to assess the loan risk. The ability of the potential or current franchisee to document appropriate cash flow is critical to the lending process.

In sport, team franchises cooperate within leagues and exert market power, yet face pressure to simultaneously cooperate and compete (Amaldoss, Meyer, Raju, & Rapoport, 2000). In the United States, professional major league sports are structured as monopolies "that by and large have been created and protected by public policy" (Noll & Zimbalist, 1997, p. 89) which creates "scarcity in teams in order to maximize the value of established franchises" (p. 65). As Wakefield (2007) notes, providers of "other goods and services . . . must abide by federal antitrust laws; professional sports, in large part, do not. The logic presented is that the leagues must maintain control for the integrity of the sport, as they seek to protect the social welfare of fans" (p. 10). As with franchising, leagues determine rules, make revenue decisions, and determine new team admission, drawing compensation from those who enter the league, as new teams—typically expansion teams—pay to enter the industry, which is counter to most other industries (Noll & Zimbalist, 1997), yet in line with franchising. Disparity truly exists between MLB sports franchises in small vs. large markets, because revenue varies significantly between teams in these markets.

Sports franchises, as previously noted, following the model of business format franchises, demonstrate value through the "operation, testing, and documentation of a viable business idea" (Spinelli, 2004) and function in a dynamic relationship with the master organization. Feedback between the master organization (in this case, major league baseball) and the franchisee is considered the key to success in areas of marketing plans, documented and reinforced procedures, process assistance, and business development. The development, implementation, and constant review of ticket pricing strategy is vital to the financial health of the small market franchise, particularly with an estimated 40% of major league tickets unsold yearly (Shaikin, 2007).

Escalator and Product Positioning

For small market baseball teams, there is no other concept more important than the escalator concept (Mullin, Hardy, & Sutton, 2000). For the small team, the objective is to position the product in such a way that new or existing segments move up the escalator. The frequency dimension of the escalator is a way of defining frequency of use markets from non-users to heavy users (Mullin et al., 2000). When defining the rungs on the escalator ladder, a combination of demographic and psychographic analysis can be utilized. To define only the demographic data is not enough. It is important to understand the buying behavior and motivation of the consumer. By understanding the buying motivators, the team can implement strategies, such as pricing as a competitive strategy, that will move consumers up the escalator (Mullin et al., 2000).

For a franchise to be successful, the characteristics of groups along the escalator from non-consumers to heavy consumers must be defined. For example, people attending one to six games can be defined as light users. However, these users have demographic and psychographic similarities to that of the heavy users and cannot be differentiated only by demographics (Mullin et al., 2000). By identifying the demographics along with psychographics and implementing marketing strategy consistent with use requirements, the franchise can provide services or experiences that attract a market that previously has been underserved.

TICKET PRICING AND DEMAND

In major league baseball (MLB), the pricing policy termed variable ticket pricing (VTP) is a topic of increasing interest. VTP is often focused on seating categories—for example, 24 categories of seats are offered by the Los Angeles Dodgers—and demand is determined for seating much like real estate, with increasing prices for high demand seating and reduced prices (through discounts or packages) for those with lower demand (Shaikin, 2007). VTP is analogous to the pricing practices of the airline industry with its practice of offering lower prices to seniors, advance purchasers, and certain weekday travelers with the goal (much like sports events) of filling up empty seats. Teams are investigating pricing strategies that attempt to move customers from light users to moderate users, as well as fill seats because seat inventory is perishable, through numerous options, such as Friday night two-for-one ticket specials, or using fan-provided email addresses to send out timely discount offers to increase game-day attendance. Even so, Gennaro (2007) argues that MLB pricing policies are inefficient, as current segmentation does not fully address demand. Fullerton (2010) suggests price "is perhaps the most criticized aspect" (p. 534) of marketing strategies for sports organizations.

Strategic use of the secondary ticket market can provide another alternative for consideration in pricing, as it "illustrates fans' willingness to pay prices that are considerably different from the actual face value of the ticket" (Drayer & Shapiro, 2009, p.5). This market has been legitimized over the last several years, as organizations such as Stub Hub, and even leagues themselves, provide additional security that promotes consumer confidence in such ticket purchases. While this study does not focus on the secondary ticket market, it is worth noting that additional pricing and segmentation opportunities exist within this market.

A key consideration for baseball is attendance, especially for small market teams. Revenue disparity is one of the main concerns regarding the ability of small market teams to remain competitive (Zimbalist, 2003). With luxury taxes, sponsorship opportunities, and broadcast revenues helping to offset the high cost of operations, the major source of sales revenue is still attendance to help meet franchise goals of increased sales and profitability for the small market team. An increase or decrease of 10% can have significant results for the small market franchise. Consider the college student segment: Many students have very limited disposable income, thus the importance of pricing strategy and other targeted promotions that would attract this segment of the market. It should also be noted that students make up a significant market for potential revenue. In addition to moving this segment into the moderate user category (theoretically up the escalator), price lining can address the perishability of seats unsold during a game. If the demand curve for tickets within a segment is determined to have different price elasticities than other segments, revenue and profit maximization can be better served through price lining.

Studies to date show overall ticket demand to be inelastic (Fort, 2004; Pan, 1999; Fort & Quirk, 1996). One study (Dale, van Iwaarden, van der Wiele, & Williams, 2005) examined ticket demand segments (fan categories) and found that the 55 and older segment held a higher perceived value of attending a game than the younger segment of those under 55, suggesting the younger segment might have more elastic demand than the older segment. However, no effort to estimate price elasticity was attempted. A growing disconnect between customers and prices—particularly in lower income segments—is demonstrated by Dortch (1996). The study suggests that lower income segments are likely to be price elastic, a contention supported in the Lackman Ciletti, & Lanasa (2007) study. Unlike the research by nine of 14 studies in the literature (see Table 10.1), the product category in the segment definition is homogeneous, consisting of a single seat category available to the general public, which serves the purpose of eliminating measurement problems that increase estimation error.

Sports ticket demand elasticity and pricing strategy is addressed in the literature in the traditional microeconomic framework of long run profit maximization. Fort's (2004) model in this framework argued that ticket pricing was inelastic. Porter (2007) challenged Fort's finding based on the interpretation of the impact of non-price variables on the model. Lackman et al.'s (2007) approach stays within the microeconomic profit-maximizing model, and is focused on the revenue side (function), an integral part of the model, so the analysis enriches the revenue escalation model by providing an empirical base for assessing the results of revenue escalation strategy using revenue maximization pricing as opposed to profit maximizing pricing.

Estimating Sports Demand Functions

The literature reveals the problems inherent in estimating sports demand functions required to estimate price elasticity, which determines optimal pricing. The key problems include

- product definition (i.e., every day-game or event game),
- unavailability of segment data, and
- presence of non-price variables (i.e., concessions that are complementary or joint demand products).

The major studies in the MLB pricing literature as shown in Table 10.1 fall into the following juxtaposed categories:

- profit vs. revenue maximizing goals
- time series (TS) vs. cross sectional (CS) data analysis
- secondary (S) vs. primary (P) data
- price inelastic vs. price elasticity (ep) findings
- total market vs. market segment
- product vs. demographic segmentation
- product (i.e., pricing application by event (E) vs. single seat quality everyday pricing (ED))
- narrow (N), 1–2 independent variable vs. multivariable (M)
- single team (S) vs. multiple team (M)

Pricing Goals

Table 10.1 reveals that a preponderance of MLB pricing studies posit profit maximization. This contention (e.g., profit maximization) rests on the assumption that marginal costs are not above zero. This condition yields the proposition that profit maximization equals revenue maximization. In Lackman et al. (2007), evidence shows marginal costs are above zero, and therefore, revenue maximization pricing is different from that of profit maximization. The implication is not subtle.

TABLE 10.1. **Price elasticity studies in MLB**

Study	Goal	Data(1)	ep	Market	Product	Ind.Var	Team
Noll 1974	profit	TS/S	< 1	yes	E	N	M
Scully 1989	profit	TS/S	< 1	yes	E	M	M
Boyd & Boyd 1996	profit	CS/S	1 >*	yes	ED	N	M
Fort & Quirk 1996	profit	TS/S	< 1	yes	E	N	M
Marberger 1997	profit	CS/S	< 1	yes	E	N	M
Pan 1999	profit	TS/S	< 1	yes	E	N	M
McDonnald 2000	profit	TS/S	< 1	yes	E	M**	M
Alexander 2001	profit	TS/S	< 1	yes	E	M	M
Cameron 2002	profit	CS/S	< 1	yes	E	N	S
Fort 2004	profit	TS/S	< 1	yes	ED	N	S
Dale 2005	profit	TS/S	na	no	ED	N	S
Porter 2007 (2)	profit	TS/S	> 1	yes	E	N	S
Rascher et al. 2007	profit	CS/S	< 1	yes	ED	N	M
Lackman et al. 2007	profit	CS	< 1	yes	ED	M	S

(1) All the studies used ex post data.
(2) Porter replicated Fort's 2004 study yielding the opposite finding (i.e., *ep* > 1)
*although ep ranged from .9–1.3, the median *ep* > 1
** more than 50 independent variables.

Under the preponderant assumption that revenue and profit maximization are not equivalent, pricing would always be at the unitary elasticity point (*ep* = 1). Under an elasticity assumption, revenue maximization would occur in the elastic portion of the demand function (Rascher, McEvoy, Nagel, & Brown, 2007). The studies reviewed in the literature use a linear demand function, which produces more conservative (lower) price elasticities than non-linear forms. Regarding data, 10 of the 14 studies used ex post time series data, and all used secondary data.

Price Elasticity

Only Boyd & Boyd (1996), Porter's (2007) rework of Fort (2004), and Lackman et al. (2007) found *ep* > 1. Dale (2005) inferred the same findings, but did not estimate price elasticity. By defining the product as single seat category available to the general public, the commonality of the three studies where elasticity was greater than 1 makes it tempting to assume the *ep* > 1 findings depend on this definition. However, Rascher (2007) used this definition and found *ep* < 1. Regarding number of independent variables incorporated into the model, 10 of 14 were narrow models (i.e., used only price or price and concessions) and all found *ep* < 1. Regarding single vs. multiteam studies, four studies focused on one team, but only Porter's (2007) rework of Fort (2004) and Lackman et al. (2007) found *ep* > 1.

Implications of Price Elasticity for Pricing Policy and Revenue

A fundamental element of pricing policy is the relationship between pricing decisions and revenue results. Integral in this relationship is the magnitude of price elasticity. As the matrix below (Table 10.2) illustrates, price increases with a market condition of elasticity greater than 1 cause revenue to fall, in conflict with the goal of the organization, and represents a decision error. Similarly, a price increase when elasticity is less than 1 also generates a revenue fall and decision error.

To illustrate the consequences of such pricing decision errors based on erroneous elasticity assumptions, we examine the case of the small MLB franchise in the Lackman et. al. study (2007). This study focused solely on the college student segment of the market.

Table 10.3 below illustrates the estimated revenue gains from correctly estimating price elasticity as *e* > 1. For this franchise, on a base revenue of $3,041,425 in 2007 at an average price of $18.05 per ticket, a price cut of

TABLE 10.2. Changes in revenue from pricing decisions under varying price elasticities

	Revenue	Change
Price Decision	*e* > 1	*e* < 1
Raise	decrease	increase
Cut	increase	decrease

TABLE 10.3. Price lining strategies (e > 1)

	Revenue ($000)	Price ($)	Quantity
Price—actual	3,041,425	18.05	168,500
Price—Rev Max	3,208,240	16.85	190,400
Difference	+166,815		
% Difference	5.5	(6.65)	
Elasticity	−1.25		

TABLE 10.4. Price lining strategies (e < 1)

	Revenue ($000)	Price ($)	Quantity
Price—actual	3,041,425	18.05	168,500
Price—Rev Max	2,824,446	16.85	167,624
Difference	(216,979)		
% Difference	−7.13	(6.65)	

6.65% to $16.85 in the targeted segment increases revenue by 5.5% to $3,208,240. This price was estimated in this study (Lackman et al, 2007) as the revenue-maximizing price.

For comparable analysis, we illustrate the consequences of such pricing decision errors, in this case, a price increase, based on erroneous elasticity assumptions, again using the case of the small MLB franchise in the Lackman et al. study (2007). Table 10.4 below illustrates the estimated revenue losses from incorrectly estimating price elasticity as $e < 1$ in the targeted segment. In this case, we use a specific elasticity defined as the average elasticity estimates (0.8) computed in the literature studies that found inelastic demand conditions.

For this franchise, on a base revenue of $3,041,425 in 2007 at an average price of $18.05 per ticket, a price decrease of 6.65% would decrease revenue by 7.13% to $2,824,446.

CONCLUSION

Pricing decisions have significant implications for the success of MLB franchises. Integral to successful pricing decisions are accurate estimates of price elasticity in sports markets. The importance is exemplified by the numerous studies in this area as shown in Table 10.1. The studies also show the mixed results of price elasticity estimates. These mixed results understandably stem from the different data used, market definitions (i.e., total market vs. market segment), assumptions regarding marginal costs, and the product definition (i.e., single seat vs. event pricing). This chapter reiterates the importance of elasticity in pricing decisions and the dependence of the decisions on market strategies, for example, total market vs. market segmentation strategies.

Based on the literature, a range of price elasticity estimates confronts decision makers in sports. The specific revenue implications of pricing decisions based on erroneous elasticity estimates is estimated using a case of a small market MLB team. The case demonstrates an approximately $4 million revenue difference between a pricing decision using accurate vs. inaccurate price elasticity estimates.

Managerial Implications

Previous studies of MLB ticket sales found price to be inelastic when considering total market. These findings provided a basis for MLB executives to raise ticket prices. Ticket sales studies found price to be elastic in particular segments when taking a market segment approach. Such studies suggest that MLB executives can target elastic segments and pursue ticket price reductions that provide additional revenue to the organization. Decision makers should avoid pricing decisions based on erroneous elasticity estimates. When evaluating price lining strategies in a price elastic market segment as in Table 10.3, a price cut increased revenue in the target segment by 5.5% or

$166,815. While this may seem a small revenue gain by MLB standards, it does not mean that other targeted elastic segments won't produce more dramatic revenue increases. In the same example, we posit a scenario where demand is estimated to be inelastic and price is decreased by the same magnitude.

From an entrepreneurial perspective, the development, implementation, and constant review of ticket pricing strategy is vital to the financial health of the small market franchise. Decision makers should not neglect consideration of market definitions based on particular segments of the total market, as elasticity estimates differ based on market definition, and the success of pricing decisions is largely determined by elasticity estimate assumptions.

References

Alexander. D. (2001). Major league baseball: Monopoly pricing and profit-maximizing behavior. *Journal of Sports Economics, 2*, 341–355.

Amaldoss, W., Meyer, R., Raju, J., & Rapoport, A. (2000). Collaborating to compete. *Marketing Science, 19*, 105–126.

Blum, J. (2002, October 1). Financing: How lenders evaluate your franchise. *Franchising World*. Retrieved 11/9/2008 from http://www.allbusiness.com/retail-trade /315106-1.html.

Boyd, D., & Boyd, L. (1996). The home field advantage: Implications for the pricing of tickets to professional team sports. *Journal of Economics and Finance, 12*(2), 23–32.

Cameron, S. (2002, May 27). Bruins to set prices hourly. *SportsBusiness Journal*, 1–50.

Dale, B., van Iwaarden, J., van der Wiele, T., & Williams, R. (2005). Service improvement in a sports environment: a study of spectator attendance. *Managing Sports Quality, 15*, 470–484.

Dortch, Shannon (1996, April). The future of baseball. *American Demographics, 18*(4), 22.

Drayer, J., & Shapiro, S. (2009). Value determination in the secondary ticket market: A quantitative analysis of the NFL playoffs. *Sport Marketing Quarterly, 18*(1), 5–13.

Fort, R., & Quirk, J. (1996). Over-stated exploitation: Monopoly versus revenue sharing in sports leagues. In J. Fizel, E. Gustafson, & L. Hadley (Eds.), *Baseball Economics: Current Research*. Westport, CT: Praeger Publishers.

Fort, R., & Quirk, J. (1995). Cross-subsidation, incentives, and outcomes in professional sports teams. *Journal of Economic Literature, XXXIII*, 1265–1299.

Fort, R. (2004). Inelastic sports pricing. *Managerial & Decision Economics, 25*, 87–94.

Gennaro, V. (2007, August 28). Ticket pricing: Let's get creative, people. *The Hardball Times*. Retrieved from http://www.hardballtimes.com/main/article/ticket-pricing-lets-get-creative-people.

Henderson, J., & Quandt, R. (1994). *Microeconomic Theory*, New York: McGraw-Hill.

Hoy, F., & Shane, S. (1998). Franchising as an entrepreneurial venture form. *Journal of Business Venturing, 13*(2), 91–94.

Kaufmann, P. J. & Dant, R. P. (1999). Franchising and the domain of entrepreneurship research. *Journal of Business Venturing, 14*(1), 5–16.

Kaufmann, P. J., & Stanworth, J. (1995). The decision to purchase a franchise: A study of prospective franchisees. *Journal of Small Business Management, 33*(4), 22–33.

Lackman, C., Ciletti, D., & Lanasa, J. (2007, November). Price lining strategy in sports marketing: Case of a small market MLB franchise. *Sport Marketing Association Annual Conference*.

Marberger, D. (1997). Optimal ticket pricing for performance goods, *Managerial and Decision Economics, 18*, 375–381.

McDonald, M. & Rascher, D. (2000). Does bat day make sense? The effect of promotions on the demand for Major League Baseball. *Journal of Sport Management, 14*, 8–27.

Mullin, B., Hardy, S., & Sutton, W. (2000). *Sport Marketing* (2nd ed.). Champaign, IL: Human Kinetics Publishers.

Noll, R. (1974). *Government and the sports business*. Washington, DC: The Brookings Institution.

Noll, R., & Zimbalist, A. (1997). Sports, jobs, and taxes: The real connection. In Noll, R. & Zimbalist, A. (Eds.), *Sports, Jobs, and Taxes* (pp. 494–508). Washington, D.C.: The Brookings Institution.

Pan, D., Zhu, Z., Gabert, T., & Brown, J. (1999). Team performance, market characteristics, and attendance of Major League Baseball: A panel data analysis. *The Mid-Atlantic Journal of Business, 35*, 77–91.

Porter, P. (2007). The paradox of inelastic sports pricing. *Managerial & Decision Economics, 28*, 157–158.

Rascher, D., McEvoy, C., Nagel, M., & Brown, M. (2007). Variable ticket pricing in Major League Baseball. *Journal of Sport Management, 21*(3), 407–437.

Scully, G. (1989). *The Business of Major League Baseball*. Chicago: University of Chicago Press.

Spinelli, S., Bygrave, W., & Zacharias, A. (2004). Chapter 11: Franchising. *The Portable MBA in Entrepreneurship: 3rd Edition*. John Wiley & Sons, Hoboken, NJ.

Varian, H. (2000). *Microeconomic Analysis*, New York: W. W. Norton & Company.

Wakefield, K. L. (2007). *Team sports marketing*. Oxford, UK: Butterworth-Heinemann.

Zimbalist, A. (2003). *May the Best Team Win*. Washington, DC: The Brookings Institute.

Entrepreneurs, Organizations, and the Sport Marketplace: Subjects in Search of Historians

STEPHEN HARDY

THE NEW SPORT INDUSTRY: NEW QUESTIONS AND NEW APPROACHES

Last year the *Chronicle of Higher Education* ran a feature story explaining that sport history has gained "new respectability." As noted in this article, no longer will the chancellor of the University of Wisconsin at LaCrosse suspect that sport historians spend their time trading baseball cards! Such veiled praise notwithstanding, these are heady times for the field. Quality articles and monographs on sport and leisure are on the increase. New lines of research have branched out to such an extent that Nancy Struna recently characterized the literature as a "glorious disarray."[1]

While I agree with the thrust of Struna's perceptive essay, on closer inspection one finds that most of the recent work may be synthesized under the rubric of social history. This has resulted in publications that focus on two often-complementary elements of interpretation: long-term *social forces* that have nudged sporting practices in certain directions, and the *social functions* of sport within this context. Among the former, one finds the rise of cities, technological revolutions, immigration, the changing roles of women, and the maturing of capitalism. Among the latter, status, ethnic identity, social control, and boosterism.[2]

The result of this research has been a greater appreciation of both the context and significance of baseball, football, hockey, tennis, horseracing, boxing, and other sports as they were experienced in history. At the same time, however, it is important to remember that the social history of sport does not constitute the totality of sport history. As this essay attempts to outline, a number of important topics demand attention from perspectives that are closer to business and economic history. These topics require a shift in attention from the significance of consumption to the structures of production, from the broad sweep of social forces to the minute elements of decision making. In general, they focus on the ways in which entrepreneurs have developed a special, perhaps singular, industry that has produced a particular part of the past. They demand a closer look at why certain organizational forms have grown to dominate the production and distribution of games and sports to their consumers; how these organizations have merged into systems of interdependence wherein some units clearly dominate others; and finally what rules, resources, and practices have constituted the structure or logic of the sport industry over time. In short, they call for an appreciation of sport as a special industry, like agriculture, steel, or medicine.[3]

Naturally, such analysis must pay close attention to social and cultural developments in the wider environment of suppliers, creditors, consumers, and critics. Yet this will be important not only to clarify the sport industry's submission to some wider *mentalité*, but also to explore the ways in which entrepreneurs may have insulated themselves from outside forces and thereby either filtered, misread, or distorted the arguments of their constituents. Indeed, even the most successful entrepreneurs like Albert Spalding faced endlessly complex decisions about game rules, contract negotiations, stadium leases, and interleague wars. As simple as Spalding tried to paint reality, he and his colleagues could not hope to understand or control the full consequences their steady stream of decisions would have on the patterns of sport production and consumption. Neil Harris has made similar observations about the organizers of cultural institutions like libraries, museums, and universities. As Harris maintains, one cannot easily pigeonhole their motives into compartments of "social control" or "nationalism," because they were too often consumed with a struggle to understand, if not govern, their complex organizations. The same may be said about the sport industry. To use Harris's words, historians will not appreciate its development until they begin to "clearly reconstruct the old alternatives" and "suggest the kinds of choices [these] institutions represented." Only by reconstructing the old alternatives that decision-makers faced can historians begin to understand how and why baseball, football, golf, tennis, hockey, and other sports developed along the lines they have, and why the industry's system and structure took on its particular shape and logic.[4]

Reconstructing the history of sport as a productive industry will, first, require an inversion of the dominant process of inquiry. Instead of analyzing sport from the outside in, the researcher must consider developments from the inside out. In other words, the starting point will not be the broad processes that concern social historians—developments in social class, urban life, or racism. Rather, the initial focus will be on the central issues as the sport organizations defined them. While only greater research can clarify these, it is a reasonable assumption that they center upon the acquisition and maintenance of facilities, supplies, and players; the staging of events, the minimization of costs, and the garnering of publicity; in short, the concerns of a business. In turn, these will probably revolve around the key functions of management—planning, coordinating, and controlling human, material, and financial resources in order to reach some objectives, either clear or hazy. The historian's questions then become woven less around changing issues in the social environment and more around standard, ongoing issues within the sport industry. Seen from this light, Jules Tygiel's masterful study of the integration of major league baseball is as much an analysis of problems in strategic planning, talent acquisition, and public relations as it is a thorough, if specialized, study of American racism. The brilliance of Tygiel's book lies in its ability to do both.[5]

What follow are suggestions for historical research into the development of the sport industry. These revolve around three main topics: (a) the sport product, (b) the role of entrepreneurs and investors in developing the product, and (c) the types of individual organizations and networks of organizations that entrepreneurs created. Scholars in economics and sport management have already provided important insights into the contemporary industry. Their work, however, often lacks historical perspective.[6] While historians have uncovered considerable evidence about the past business of sports, especially baseball, their research needs synthesis. But this essay seeks not to supplant any approach to research. Rather, it offers a supplemental framework for analysis. Readers will note its limitations: a focus on team sports and, more particularly, team sports in America. At the same time, some of the discussion and sources suggest the potential for wider applications.

THE SPORT PRODUCT: A TRIPLE COMMODITY

Sport history, from the "inside out," begins with an analysis of the sport product, since a particular product's nature usually influences the organizations that produce it.[7] On close inspection, the sport product unfolds as a triple or three-part commodity, and the sport industry divides into segments that generate or distribute one or more of the parts. These parts, which can exist in isolation but which reach full expression in combination, are as follows: the activity or game form, the service, and the goods.

The term commodity demands some consideration here since it must be understood historically. A commodity, as Marx noted, is "in the first place, an object outside us, a thing that by its properties satisfies human wants of some sort or another." But all products are not necessarily commodities. "To become a commodity," Marx explained, "a product must be transferred to another whom it will serve as a use-value, by means of exchange."[8] Sport, then, becomes a commodity when its producers transfer it, via exchange, to a separate group of consumers. Clearly, even today not all sports exist in commodity form. Stickball flourishes largely as use-value, consumed only by its producers. But even here, components of the activity—balls, special bats— may be commodities if they are purchased at Woolworth's or K-Mart. The job of historians is to uncover the process by which the sport product evolved and by which its triple components edged ever closer to pure commodities.[9]

Now, if one considers the game form first, one can sense the subtlety of this evolution. As a game form, the sport product consists of activities embodied in the rules defining the way the game is played, or the "game occurrence," to use John Loy's phrase.[10] Of course anyone can make up a game, as Professor Naismith demonstrated. But this is of little consequence until rule making is organized and controlled by particular groups who regulate the game form's distribution, or who try to regulate it. Can game forms ever exist as a commodity? Indeed they can and they do, especially at the level of high performance sport. For while sandlotters animate their competition with arguments about unwritten rules, organized leagues resort to published rule books, purchased annually by officials, administrators, coaches, players, and fans. This is no mere cottage industry. *The Beadle Dime Baseball Player* sold 50,000 copies annually in the 1860s, and it receives due credit for its part in making the New York game the national pastime. A few years later, "guides" (including rules and statistics) for all sports comprised a substantial segment of Albert Spalding's empire, both netting him vast profits and supporting the influence of governing bodies whose rules he published. Sales of this commodity continue to be strong. In 1984, NCAA Publishing alone sold approximately $50,000 worth of rule books for college sports.[11]

Sandlotters of course play on, in blissful ignorance of technicalities; but the game form has been a commodity for some time. Rule making itself has become more and more difficult, subject to pressures from lobbies like the American Medical Association. Obviously, the particular forms of any sport, in any historical period, are hardly inevitable derivatives of some *zeitgeist*. *They* are the products of conscious decision making that cries out for more historical investigation.[12]

If rule makers create a special product—the game form—that may exist as a commodity, it is also true that their product seldom exists in isolation. Without disregarding sandlotters, it is clear that game forms are usually played in a situation that involves more than simple, expressive use-value for the players. Some utility beyond competition—not expressed or implied in the rules—is appended to the game performance. This utility is the sport service, the second component of the triple commodity.[13]

Sport services have existed historically in many aspects, including education, status, military preparation, urban boosterism, political propaganda, and most extensively, entertainment. Those familiar with the literature quickly recognize the complex histories of these different service utilities: slow and steady accretions over centuries (recognition of games as military preparation and education dates to the ancients) coupled with flashing, revelatory episodes of growth (the use of the Modern Olympics as political propaganda). Further confounding this history, several services have often wrapped around the same game form. Indeed one could easily argue that the most popular team games have been fertile ground for every conceivable service. And of course this provides a clue to their popularity.[14]

While historians have chronicled and interpreted sport services for some time—usually as "social functions"—a reconsideration will be valuable on several theoretical grounds. For instance, it appears that special organizations have emerged to promote and capture the service utilities, and that these service organizations are often distinct from those controlling the game form. This may result in pressure tactics, negotiations, and accommodations between organizations. A case in point would be the 1905–06 football controversy. At one level, this episode became a power struggle between the old rules committee and the emerging organization, the intercollegiate Athletic Association, whose avowed mission was to shape both the game form and the educational service. The results of these and other conflicts and their consequences for the contemporary sports product can only be understood through careful historical reconstruction of decision-making from the inside out.[15]

Such research may also explain more clearly the movement of sport services toward commodity forms. Social functions are not always free. If we want to enjoy the status value associated with the game of tennis, we pay for membership in an exclusive club. If we want the (sometimes dubious) educational values of soccer for our children, we pay the registration fee for the youth league. If we want entertainment from football, we pay for a Steeler ticket. But this all is not the result of a natural or inevitable process. Every sport has experienced a period of discovery when players, sponsors, and promoters have recognized that others might pay to watch or play a game, in essence exchanging money for the chance to derive their personal use-value from their own form of involvement. Historians are especially equipped to uncover the effects of this discovery on the production of the sport product and on the structure of the sport industry.

The third component of the unified sport product involves the goods, the physical objects necessary to the game form that are recognized or regulated in the rules. Balls, goals, sticks, bats, protective equipment, and uniforms normally fall into this category. So do facilities that are requisite to the contest or exercise, such as swimming pools or lined fields or running tracks. Non-essential facilities, like bleachers, grandstands, or press boxes fall under the province of services. Although this segment of the sport industry has received almost total neglect from historians, it appears that sporting goods reached full-blown commodity status faster than either the game form or the service. The consequences of this sprint are considered later in this essay.[16]

As this brief excursus on the sport product reveals, simple definitions of "sport" run a risk of distorting historical reality. This is especially true since different segments of the sport industry must combine to fuse multiple components into a laminated product that embraces a game form, services, and goods. Such orchestration between organizations has never been smooth, nor has it been static. Indeed, it is the dynamic nature of the industry and its products that renders simple definitions of sport historically hazardous.

ENTREPRENEURS AND INVESTORS

This complexity has intensified in the last two centuries, not surprisingly the same time period that saw the movement of the sport product ever closer to a pure commodity. In reassessing these developments, it will make sense to focus initially on the activities of entrepreneurs, whose role was first outlined by Arthur Cole, Fritz Redlich, and Sebastian DeGrazia. All three suggested that profit-seeking entrepreneurs had altered the direction of leisure and sport in the nineteenth century. As Cole put it, "one man's curiosity may become another man's profit." Or as Redlich argued, "what was originally an autonomous trend favorable to business was consciously developed by business so that in the end business domination of leisure time activities was the result." What these authors emphasized was the commercialization of sport and leisure in the increasingly urbanized culture of nineteenth-century America. A logic that promoted spectacle and profit overwhelmed an earlier, more rural ethos of home-backed, wholesome fun.[17]

While there is much to learn by rereading these still insightful works, there is too easy a sweep to their interpretations. Their speculative nature and their limited sources do not allow for a clear investigation of the motives of entrepreneurs in sport or leisure. And while the profit motive has surely nudged sport in certain directions, one cannot say that it has dominated or even controlled the industry's structure. Sports entrepreneurs have often been like Robert Wiebe's version of the robber barons: "Yet as shrewdly as some of them pursued the main chance, they were also trapped by the present, scurrying where they appeared to stalk." One only needs to think of Chris Von der Ahe or Andrew Freedman to see a scurrying sports magnate.[18]

Indeed, one senses that profit-seeking and risk-taking—normally central dimensions of entrepreneurship—have not always been so pivotal in an industry whose production process has often been heavily subsidized by state and philanthropic agencies (think of high school athletics or YMCAs).

Although profit and risk have been and remain important, the hallmark of the sport entrepreneur has more likely been the innovative activity that Joseph Schumpeter emphasized in his *Theory of Economic Development*. This includes:

1. The introduction of a new good or new quality of a good (or service);
2. The introduction of a new method of production or a new way of handling a commodity;
3. The opening of a new market;
4. The acquisition of a new source of raw materials or unfinished goods; and
5. The crafting of a new organizational structure. Any of these activities results in a "new combination" of production. The parallels in the sport industry are instructive.[19]

In Schumpeter's sense, Walter Camp was an entrepreneur; not because he sought profits for Yale, but because he aggressively created and introduced a new game form, resulting in a product that was attractive and profitable. Naismith's creation of basketball was similarly an entrepreneurial activity; but so also was Senda Berenson's introduction of a new quality to the sport. Further, she opened a new market. Along this last line, massive research is needed to identify the obscure entrepreneurial figures who introduced eastern-born football and baseball to new southern and western markets in the nineteenth century. Easier to assess are the entrepreneurial efforts of Branch Rickey, whose minor league system represented a new source of supply, or William Hulbert, who helped effect a radical reorganization of the baseball industry in 1876. Hulbert's accomplice, Albert Spalding, was thereafter an entrepreneur in all phases of Schumpeter's definition. Indeed, one of the many strengths of Peter Levine's splendid biography of Spalding is its focus on the many moments of innovation that "A. G." orchestrated in all three components of the baseball product. If historians are to uncover the development of the sport industry as a special, perhaps unique, system and structure, it will be necessary to outline the key moments of innovation and the key innovators in any given segment or activity. And doubtless these will diverge from commonplace notions about "great moments" or "great heroes" in sport.

While innovation may be a useful starting place, there are other activities often associated with entrepreneurs—risk taking and profit seeking. After all, most innovative projects involve risk and financing, and risk takers usually expect some utility or profit if the project is successful. Who have been the risk takers and financiers of the sport industry?

In his book *Sport: A Cultural History*, Richard Mandell claims that one foundation for the rise of American sport was "the country's banking system," which he says, "was flexibly capable of supplying venture capital."[20] Unfortunately, Mandell does not support this assertion, and it is extremely doubtful that banks were assuming the risks for ventures as tenuous as nineteenth-century sports. Nonetheless, Mandell does prompt a useful question: When did banks begin to accept some risk in financing sport organizations, wherein they recognized as collateral an organization's franchise values or expected profits and not simply its tangible assets? This would mark a significant moment of legitimacy for individual firms, for networks of firms, and for the industry as a whole.

Although historians have not examined bank financing, they have uncovered the early investors and risk takers for many sports and recreations. Basically they may be sorted into three groups: private sponsors, commercial promoters, and the state. Of the three, it appears that private sponsors played the crucial role early in the history of most sports. This term denotes individuals or groups primarily and initially interested in pursuing games as pure fun or as services unrelated to gate receipts. White collar and elite groups come quickly to mind: Knickerbocker ballplayers, Harvard footballers, New York Athletic Club leaders, members of the Country Club. As baseball historians demonstrate, however, petit bourgeois, working-class, and ethnic groups were also early sponsors of sport.[21]

While private sponsors soon recognized the financial benefits of gate receipts and concessions, and thus often contributed to the commercialization of sports, they must be distinguished from commercial promoters as long as their central concerns lay in areas other than profits. For the commercial promoter, on the other hand, sport (in any of its commodity forms) has principally been a means to personal or corporate profit. As one might expect, the distinction between private sponsor and commercial promoter has often been hazy. The motivations of magna like Henry V. Lucas of St. Louis, Deacon White of Edmonton, or the young Art Rooney, Sr.—owners of sports operations that were marginally (if at all) profitable—surely included civic duty, egotism, and a love of sport as well as a concern for some profit. Other historical figures however, are more clearly painted as commercial promoters: John I. Rogers of the Phillies, who swindled his fellow owners out of gate receipts; Cadwallader Colden, who first tried in 1829 to run the Union Course and horseracing on the basis of gate receipts; or Horace Bigelow, who transformed Lake Quinsigamond into a showcase of saleable sports and recreation.[22]

The third major investor in sport development has been the state in its many forms of legislative bodies, appointed commissions, and regulatory agencies. Beginning with its mid-nineteenth century investments in public parks, and later, playgrounds, the state slowly grew (often through public education) to control stadiums, arenas, vast equipment inventories, leagues of teams, and playing and eligibility rules. At its heart, the state's interest in sport has always been its contribution to social order. As recent works on public recreation suggest, however, although state-controlled sport and recreation have probably served the interests of dominant social groups, it is by no means clear that this occurred to the exclusion of the interests of subordinate groups. Workers and ethnic communities found the play areas to be a fertile ground for contention over the control of leisure, if not of work.[23]

Several questions arise about the relationship of special investor and interest groups to the developing sport product. To begin, have private sponsors, commercial promoters, or the state imposed their own particular *stamp* on game forms, services, or goods under their control? What happens to football, for example, when commercial promoters borrow its form from private and state sponsors (colleges and schools) in order to establish their own venture (ultimately, the NFL)? Are there major alterations in the game form, in associated services, or in goods? Are the tendencies similar in other sports? How have investor groups opposed or accommodated each other's interests? One intersection of interests in need of greater research is the expansion of sports facilities in the first half of the twentieth century. Here was a fertile ground for tradeoffs between private or commercial sponsors and the state. Here began the precedents that make public subsidy of private gain a contemporary expectation.[24] Besides the interaction between investor groups, what about the social composition *within* them? Has this changed over time, with corresponding effects on sport? Ted Vincent has raised this important issue in his provocative (if lamentably unfootnoted) book *Mudville's Revenge*. According to Vincent, the early years of professional baseball and basketball were a "democratic and pluralistic era . . . in which a grocer or saloon keeper had as much chance as a millionaire of producing an event that grabbed headlines in the national sporting magazines."[25] Without providing closely detailed evidence, Vincent suggests that the earliest owners of professional teams tended to be petit bourgeois— liquor dealers, pawnbrokers, attorneys, and the like—who had much closer, organic ties with their communities of fans and players. This group was gradually squeezed out, by the higher capital requirements of larger, more permanent facilities, by players' demands for higher salaries, and by the design of rivals. Similarly, Steven Riess has shown that by the early 1900s big league baseball was controlled by "new men of affluence," the owners of traction companies, large breweries, and construction firms. Lyle Hallowell maintains that a similar process occurred in ice hockey, particularly after 1912 when the advent of artificial ice rinks brought both higher capital requirements and higher potential profits to those wishing to try the big league game. Petit bourgeois would be hereafter relegated to investing in the minor leagues.[26]

Did social and economic backgrounds affect the work "styles" of entrepreneurs and investors. Were "new men of affluence" apt to be more conservative or innovative with the sport product? More exploitive with labor? Clearly, more detailed prosopography is needed across sports, but it appears that the greatest innovations (for better or worse) came from the petit bourgeois. This certainly occurred in track and field, if one can believe the account of James Brendan Connolly, America's first Olympic gold medalist. In 1910, Connolly wrote an expose called "The Capitalization of Amateur Athletics" in which he accused the A.A.U.—purportedly the guardian of amateurism—of leading the wave of commercialization that threatened the pure sport. Connolly traced the problem to the material interests of the printers, jewelers, and politicians who ran various regional and local branches of the A.A.U. Ultimately, Connolly claimed, all of them were beholden to Albert Spalding and his employee, James Sullivan, who doubled as the President of the A.A.U.[27]

Connolly's article challenges a commonplace notion about the control of track and field by elite gentlemen. But it reinforces the idea that any one entrepreneur, investor, or group could not hope to achieve unopposed mastery of any part of the sport industry. "Interlopers," to use the language of baseball, regularly have sought their own share of the market, through some innovative combination in game form, service, or good. Their challenges were often the seeds of change.

ORGANIZATIONAL CHANGE: SHAPING FIRMS FOR EXPANDING MARKETS

Innovative entrepreneurs have developed saleable sport products through countless disputes, decisions, and deals. At the same time, however, they have nurtured extended networks of organizations that produce and distribute these products. Unfortunately, historians have not yet begun to investigate systematically the types of organizations that germinated from the seeds of entrepreneurial decisions. This must be remedied, since organizations are often more enduring than the individuals who create them. Indeed they are the skeletons of the industry (although sometimes only in fossil form). As such, they provide an obvious framework for analysis.

Alfred Chandler and others have demonstrated that organizational forms and structures in any industry are influenced by: (a) the nature of the product, (b) the nature of the market, and (c) what Chandler aptly calls the "visible hand" of strategy.[28] If any sport is, in fact, a tripartite product comprised of a game form, associated services, and associated goods, one may begin by examining the different types of organizations operating in the three product segments.

Although there is considerable overlap between the organizations producing and controlling game forms and services, there are also important historical distinctions that await clarification. Thus, while both game forms and services tend now to be controlled by regional or national regulatory agencies (e.g., NCAA, NAIA, NFSHSA, NFL) this has not always been true. As noted earlier, Walter Camp's Rules Committee was concerned with the game form. Its successor, the NCAA, is concerned with both game forms and services. The growth patterns of other regulatory agencies demand scrutiny. Has expansion typically been local to regional to national? Has control extended in a regular fashion from game rules into services and ultimately into goods? Promising research already exists in these areas, but it has not been synthesized.[29]

One thing, however, is historically certain. In team sports, the production of the consumable game form or service has always been tied to a local firm, which is tied in turn to a basically local market. Sport, as we know it, exists as a "joint inverted product"—a *single* product (the game and its associated services) that is the result of interaction between two separate firms (each team). This fact alone distinguishes football, hockey, baseball, and the like from other commodities. Even more distinctive are the firms producing the game. They have remained essentially *local* firms, even as their once strictly local markets have sometimes extended to regional or national dimensions. Teams like the Dallas Cowboys and the Pittsburgh Steelers, that compete to create the most commercialized and modernized games, have persisted as what Alfred Chandler calls "traditional" firms—consisting usually as a single unit or single office, with a single owner or small group of owners, with a single product line, in a single geographic area. One can't stress locality enough, despite the wider distribution of broadcasts and novelties.[30]

For historians interested in examining the production of sport, a central question now emerges. Is it natural or inevitable that the game should have persisted as a by-product of competition between distinct, local, traditional firms? Was there no logical alternative? Of course there was, and it may be credited with spreading the popularity of virtually every modern sport. This was the barnstorming model, in which the competing teams were part of the same "firm" that viewed an entire region, nation, (or in Al Spalding's case) the world as its market. Most team sports have experienced barnstorming along these lines, yet this model of product ownership and distribution has never thrived or endured.[31]

But why not? Single or common ownership of multiple teams, even if they are anchored in different localities, makes greater economic sense than the wasteful competition between separate firms that has long dominated the team sport industry. Surprisingly, however, the great "concentration movement" that swept American industry in the late nineteenth century never seriously threatened the structure of team sports. Sports magnates have suffered severe public scorn when they have been caught investing in more than one franchise in the same league. Andrew Freedman's ill-fated though eminently logical attempt to form a major league baseball trust stands in virtual isolation. Albert Spalding led the fight against Freedman and he had the press and the public on his side. But neither the press nor the public cared much about the "Freedmanism" that Spalding pursued in sporting goods. Why all the concern about a team's autonomy?[32]

While only detailed historical analysis across sports can answer this question, it is likely that the persistence of the traditional firm in team sports is the result of historical conditioning over centuries. As entrepreneurs developed rounders, stoolball, and baseball, or soccer, rugby, and American football, they extended the logic of team competition so that these games became "representational" as well as "recreational." That is to say, the actual competitors not only enjoyed a form of recreation, but they often bore the burden of representing the interests of a larger group of patrons and general followers. Now this is not simply a nineteenth-century phenomenon. Descriptions of folk football in fourteenth-century Britain or *calcio* in sixteenth-century Italy reveal the deep roots of representational sports. The frequent manipulation of modern games by urban or other community boosters in the last century has been a matter of degree not revelation.[33]

Indeed, it appears that the very structure of modern team sports is in important ways "premodern," imbued with a communal or community logic that has supported the persistence of the traditional firm. Even at the most commercialized levels, where homegrown talent is a rarity, there is a sense of suspicion about the absentee owner, but little fret about players hired from the outside. The whole firm, not just the collection of players, has become the representative of community interests. It must remain separate and distinct from its competitors or it can no longer be truly representative. Therefore, although it might have been eminently logical for ownership of multiple teams to have concentrated into the hands of a few, the longer history of sport itself included a premodern sense of community that sometimes rebuffed the modern logic of capitalism.[34]

Rather than a consolidation of firms, there developed networks of separate, traditional firms attempting to create, control, and apportion networks of local markets. This evolution has occurred at all levels of game forms and services, from the pee-wee to the professional. It has occurred both vertically within a single sport (Pop Warner Football, the NFL) and horizontally across sports (the NCAA, NFSHSA).

At least three areas merit attention as historians examine the interaction of firms and the tensions between capital and community that lay therein. The first concerns the disputes over product and market control between firms and between networks of firms. As Guy Lewis and Ronald Smith have ably demonstrated, the 1905–06 football controversy was more than a general question of violence in the game form. It was also a question of who would control the game form; the entrenched eastern interests so well symbolized in Walter Camp, or the emerging Midwest. The well-documented battles between rival leagues in professional baseball, football, and basketball have similarly been part of long-lasting wars for market control.[35]

The results of these struggles present the second subject that merits attention. This consists of the stratification or layering of firms and markets. It appears that every sport has undergone a "shake out" by which firms have been layered into sets or networks of relatively equal strength. As Edward Gross argues in his seminal paper on the subject, this process is a necessity if the weaker firms are to survive at all, because it allows the chance for victory that is so demanded in representational sport.[36]

But while the outcomes are manifest now—competitive divisions in school, college, and amateur sports; layers of minor leagues in professional sports—the decisions that drove these shake outs largely lie hidden in the shrouds of history. To what extent has stratification been the result of the "invisible hand" of the market, by which entrepreneurs succumb to the odds of population density, per capita wealth, existing modes of transportation, alternative services, or entrenched tastes? To what extent has stratification been forced by the "visible hand" of power and manipulation? The quiet death of the Canton Bulldogs or the Syracuse Nationals reflects the former. The flashing birth of the National League in 1876 exemplifies the latter. Economists often compare sports leagues to cartels. This can be a useful model, but cartels are only one product of a larger process of stratification that will be fully understood only when historians examine it through the lens of local sources in a variety of locales: small towns, regional entrepots, dominant metropolises.[37]

At the same time, as the National League's endurance prompts, scholars may profit from a closer look at the third and related subject of stratification studies. This is the creation and growth of the central administrative offices that coordinate the activities of individual firms in a given network. As Robert Stern outlines in his brilliant studies of the NCAA, the history of such offices has often involved a quest for autonomy from the network of firms that gave them birth. Eugene Murdock's recent study of Ban Johnson provides an excellent glimpse of the central administrator thirsting, groping, and battling for control of the network. One of Johnson's important contributions was his strengthening of the central umpire's bureau, an important source of autonomy and a hallmark of administrative power. His ultimate pathetic demise reflects how fleeting network control can be. For every Judge Landis there are ten Happy Chandlers.[38]

Despite their apparent weaknesses, the central offices of the myriad leagues, conferences, and associations dotting the historical landscape of sports have helped to bring order to the marketplace. Without stable systems of competition, sports firms generally die aborning, as baseball's graveyard amply demonstrates. The structure of firms producing game forms and services is largely comprised of complex molecules—benzene rings of compatible atoms. Free floating atoms like the Harlem Globetrotters are exceptions that prove the rule.

Sporting goods present something different. Rather than networks of traditional, local firms, one finds instead the rapid emergence of what Chandler calls the "modern" firm: multi-unit, multifunction, multiproduct, multimarket.

Whereas thousands of tiny organizations compete to produce and distribute game forms and services, a relative handful of firms supply the material components of that competition. While individual communities feel a special, sometimes passionate attachment to their local team, there is no such sentiment for the sporting goods manufacturer or dealer. Why has this occurred, and with what consequences for the integrated sport product?[39]

To date, few historians have considered the sporting goods industry in any depth or breadth. A quick glimpse at the sources, however, suggests that production and distribution were traditional and slow until after the Civil War. Athletes and sportsmen often fashioned their own utensils or balls. Some equipment—largely for hunting and fishing—was imported or manufactured by specialized firms. More frequently, however, one probably found production in the hands of local artisans in metal, leather, or woodworking, who crafted sporting goods as a sideline. Indeed one current product leader, Hillerich and Bradsby Co. of "Louisville Slugger" fame, began this way. J. Frederick Hillerich started his woodturning business in 1859, making bedposts and handrails as well as some ten pins and bowling balls. Only his son Bud's affection for baseball got the firm slowly involved in the turning of bats, and even then (1880) the elder Hillerich resisted such frivolity because he saw better profits in the current market for butter churn booms![40]

While larger scale manufacture of baseball goods appears to have risen in the late 1860s, football remained at a primitive stage. As one analyst tells us, the first Yale-Princeton game (1873) "was delayed an hour and a half because of the failure to obtain a ball. Another delay occurred during the game when the precious ball burst and had to be repaired."[41] These conditions would change rapidly, however, as entrepreneurs saw the potential for profits in supplying and fuelling the demand for sports. The surge of participation in the next decade was the result of as much as the cause of concentrated ownership in sporting goods production and distribution.

Peter Levine's recent biography of Albert Spalding provides important information on this process, as Spalding's firm represents a classic example of expansion and integration. Spalding opened his first store in Chicago in 1876. By 1899 his empire had extended worldwide, his company had integrated both backward into manufacturing and horizontally in marketing and retail. Along the way he had gobbled up numerous competitors. He had 3,500 employees toiling in five large manufacturing plants around the country, each with product specialties: bicycles and steel products in Massachusetts, boats and canoes in upstate New York, uniforms in New York City and Chicago, bats and wooden materials in Chicago, balls and leather goods in Philadelphia. At the other end, he had dispensed with jobbers and began selling directly to retailers under what his brother called the "Spalding one-price policy." The twenty thousand accounts now dealing with Spalding could not cut Spalding prices or they would risk losing their supply of these popular goods. The empire was fully integrated, from Michigan lumber mills to retail outlets. It paralleled the developments in other industries.[42]

While Spalding's was perhaps the dominant company, buying out Reach, Wright & Ditson, and others, it was not a monopolist. Competitors developed by a similar process of horizontal and vertical integration. The Rawlings Brothers began a retail store in St. Louis in 1888, acting as "exclusive agent" for distribution of Reach products in the South and West. Even before reorganizing in 1898, Rawlings moved into manufacturing. On the other hand, P. Goldsmith and Sons started in the Cincinnati area in 1875, making toys and baseball goods. Steady expansion in manufacturing, marketing, and acquisitions created the firm now known as MacGregor. Wilson began its operation turning out goods from a little red school house in Chicago. These were capable competitors for Spalding in the team sports field, but rivals were even stronger for the bicycle market of the 1890s. Here Spalding was an also-ran to the giant Pope and Western manufacturing works.[43]

Much more research is needed before we can safely say that the production and distribution of sporting goods was oligopolistic. Intense competition by newcomers eroded Pope's bicycle profits in the later 1890s. The combination of severe price cutting and high capital costs was ruinous; the attempt at a trust failed. Developments in team sports are even less clear. Nevertheless, it appears that considerable concentration of control occurred there in the five decades after the Civil War. (This of course has continued so that several sporting goods giants are now owned by even larger conglomerates.)

The effects were enormous. Manufacturers, retailers, and the networks between them formed the vast material foundation for the rise of sport. By 1899, the Reach plant in Philadelphia produced an estimated 18,000 baseballs a day. Machines cut and shaped 20 brands of balls for handstitching including a "Deadball," a "Bounding Ball," an "Out of Sight Ball," a "King of the Field Ball," and a "Cock of the Walk Ball." Similar scales of manufacturing existed for other sports products. As the British magazine *Field* explained in 1904, American golf clubs began to dominate the British market, probably because of "the painstaking care with which the American balances, finishes, and constructs the club according to a standardized average pattern in lie, weight, and form." Standardization and mass production were important aspects of the growing industry, but so was marketing. Companies didn't simply meet demand, as Betts has maintained, they created demand.[44]

As Albert Pope wrote in 1895, bicycle manufacturers knew "at the outset" that they must "educate the people to the advantage of this invigorating sport, and with this end in view, the best literature that was to be had on the subject was gratuitously distributed." Bicycle advertising included colorful posters and witty copy distributed through dozens of general and trade magazines. Albert Spalding went a step further, with the creation of the American Sports Publishing Company, through which he published and distributed guide books on dozens of sports. These guides included not only the rules of the leading governing bodies but also important statistics on the participation and records of individuals and teams around the country. Throughout, Spalding's editors sprinkled reminders that Spalding products were the "official" products of the sport in question. When one remembers that by 1899 Spalding claimed to have 20,000 retail accounts, it is clear how significant this distribution system was for the total sport product. Basketball historian Albert Applin is doubtless correct in crediting Spalding's marketing arrangement for much of the dramatic spread of basketball in the 1890.[45]

If the sporting goods industry influenced participation rates, it is equally probable that their innovations in equipment influenced styles of play and, hence, the rules themselves. In 1902, Rawlings ran advertisements for their new line of football equipment designed by their product genius William P. Whitley. Aptly named, "Whitley's Football Armor" included an "armor" jacket "reinforced with cane ribs which, when struck, equally distributes the force of the blow, thus preventing injury to the player." But as with the boxing glove, protective equipment might equally result in more brutal play. This seems to have occurred in football. Lyle Hallowell has made a similar suggestion about hockey, where protective equipment was developed in the early 1900's at the same period as the slashing, hard-checking "Ottawa" style of play. The precise relationships between sporting goods, playing styles, and playing rules await detailed research, but it is clear that playing styles and rules don't always determine the goods. The sporting goods industry, especially the manufacturers, has had greater capital investments, and greater stakes involved than most franchises. They have seldom been passive observers.[46]

CONCLUSION: THE SPORT INDUSTRY AND ITS IMPACT

I have covered a fair amount of ground in this essay, all in order to offer a framework for research into the development of sport as an industry. Whether the sport is football, hockey, golf, or boxing, my framework focuses on the decisions of entrepreneurs who developed organizations to produce and distribute three-part commodities.

If I have argued for the need to reconstruct the sport industry through the perspective of entrepreneurs—or from the "inside out"—this is not to say that these men or women have ever enjoyed autonomy from the forces and issues in the environments that swirl around them. As one historian of entrepreneurs argued, even the most powerful magnates like Rockefeller and Carnegie "made history only within those external constraints they could not change." Given these constraints, however, entrepreneurs have achieved much. I conclude with some questions and propositions about their achievements in sport.[47]

To begin, there appears to be a process of structural development—for products and organizations—that is unique to sport and that may be common to all sports. Loy, Ingham, and Gruneau have all offered important theoretical suggestions about the transformation of *a* set of rules to *the* set of rules. Gruneau has recently extended his model (based on Canadian history) to include stages of bourgeois, corporate, and state control. Guttmann, Ingham, and Adelman had earlier offered notable insights into the organizational differences between pre-modern or folk sports and their modern, rationalized, counterparts.[48]

But while these authors capture much of the larger framework of development, there is need for much closer morphology. For instance, have all sports developed initially under the aegis of private sponsors—often the players themselves—who have been concerned chiefly with non-commercial utilities? Has each sport experienced a transition in which players have lost control of both the process and the product of their labor? Has this transition come before, after, or simultaneous to the moment of commercialization?[49] Has every sport had a "shake out" and subsequent stratification of firms and markets into sets of similar power and capacity? Have these sets regrouped into even more compatible networks of markets, and have they then fashioned central offices to regulate their activities?

It appears that similar life cycles have prevailed. Since these life cycles have been staggered, however, historians may have to rethink their periodizing of the "rise of sport." For instance, professional baseball had assumed much of its modern structure by 1903, at the very time when football, hockey, and basketball were still very much at a primitive stage of development. And despite the presence of the baseball model, the other sports spent decades working through or replicating similar struggles in the marketplace. At what stage, then, is it appropriate to call any of these sports "modern," to use Adelman's term?[50]

Even as one recognizes the distinct chronologies that have accompanied the life cycles of sports networks, one must also recognize a more pervasive process at work: the concentration of control over the product itself. Thus, although the marketplace has remained formally free (anyone can invent a game), the nature of the product (particularly game forms and goods) has since the early 1900s been determined by a narrow range of firms. A handful of rules committees control the game forms played by most people; a few manufacturers supply the goods at all levels; a limited number of professional groups establish guidelines on coaching, training, playing, and management techniques. As Raymond Williams describes this phenomenon of product convergence, "the general effect is of a relatively formed market, within which the buyer's choice—the original rationale of the market—has been displaced to operate, in majority, within an already selected range."[51]

Ultimately, then, one must ask to what extent the rise of an integrated industry of sport, encompassing both production and distribution, has limited our choices of consumption, both in terms of the range of sports we play and in terms of the way we play that limited range. Has the rise of sport as a commodity meant the strangulation of sport as play? Have the fleeting or enduring "alternatives"—sandlot activities, governance by women, the Labor Sports Union—had any impact on this process?[52]

All of these questions merit further attention from historians. For some time we have recognized the outlines of modern sport and we have learned much about its social and cultural significance. But we still need more detailed research in many areas including rules formation, the life cycles of teams and leagues, the introduction of new goods and services. Many of these topics may be profitably explored by concentrating on the activities of entrepreneurs and, following Neil Harris's advice, reconstructing their alternatives and the choices they made.

Editor's Note

This article was first published in the Journal of Sport History, Vol. 13, No. 1 (Spring 1986).

Author's Note

I would like to thank Melvin Adelman for providing an extended review of an earlier draft of this essay. Ronnie Peduzzi and anonymous reviewers also gave me helpful suggestions.

Endnotes

1. Nancy Struna, "In 'Glorious Disarray': The Literature of American Sport History." *Research Quarterly for Exercise and Sport* 56 (1985): 151–160; Karen J. Winkler. "A Lot More than Trading Baseball Cards: Sport History Gains a New Respectability," Chronicle of Higher Education. June 5, 1985, 5,9. For an opposite view—that serious analysis obfuscates the essence of Intellectuals Miss Baseball's Pitch," *New Republic*, September 9, 1985, 8–10.

2. The social history perspective is evident in the best surveys and in literature reviews. See Benjamin Rader, *American Sports: From the Age of Folk Games to the Age of Spectators* (Englewood Cliffs, N.J., 1983), v; John Lucas and Ronald Smith, *Sage of American Sport* (Philadelphia, 1978), vi; Donald Mrozek, *Sport American Mentality, 1880–1910* (Nashville, 1983), xvi; Melvin Adelman, "Academicians and American Athletics: A Decade of Progress," *Journal of Sport History* 10 (Spring 1983): 80–106; Stephen Hardy, "The City and the Rise of American Sport, 1820–1920," *Exercise and Sport Sciences Reviews* 9 (1981): 183–219. For an early treatment of this issue, see Jack M. Berryman, "Sport History as Social History?" *Quest* 20 (June 1973): 65–73. For a useful overview of social history—its topics and methods—see Peter N. Stearns, "The New Social History: An Overview," in *Ordinary People and Everyday Life*, ed. James B. Gardner and George Rollie Adams (Nashville, 1983), 3–21.

3. My orientation in this essay has been especially influenced by several readings of Raymond Williams, *The Sociology of Culture* (New York, 1982); Thomas Cochran. *Business in American Life: A History* (New York, 1972); Louis Galambos; "The Emerging Organizational Synthesis in Modern American History," *Business History Review* 44 (Autumn 1970): 297–290; idem. "Technology, Political Economy, and Professionalization: Central Themes of the Organizational Synthesis," ibid. 57 (Winter 1983): 471–493; Melvin Adelman, *A Sporting Time: New York City and the Rise of Modern Athletics, 1820–70* (Urbana, 1986).

4. Neil Harris, "Cultural Institutions and American Modernization," *Journal of Library History* 16 (Winter 1981): 38–39. For a similar argument, see David C. Hammack, "Problems in the Historical Study of Power in the Cities and Towns of the United States," *American Historical Review* 83 (April 1978): 323–349.

5. Jules Tygiel, *Baseball's Great Experiment: Jackie Robinson and His Legacy* (New York, 1983). For comprehensive views on management and sport management see Peter Drucker, *Management: Tasks, Responsibilities, Practices* (New York, 1974). Guy Lewis and Herb Appenzeller, Eds., *Successful Sport Management* (Charlottesville, VA, 1985).

6. Economic analysis includes: Roger Noll, ed., *Government and the Sports Business* (Washington, D.C. 1974); and idem, "Major League Sports," in *The Structure of American Industry*, 6th ed.,, ed. Walter Adams, (N.Y., 1982); Ralph Andreano, *No Joy in Mudville: The Dilemma of Major League Baseball* (Cambridge, 1965); Jesse Markham and Paul Teplitz, *Baseball, Economics, and Public policy* (Lexington, Mass., 1981); Henry Demmert, *The Economics of Professional League Sports* (Lexington, MA, 1971). Studies from sport management include: Guy Lewis, "The Sports Enterprise, " *Arena Newsletter* 4 (October 1980): 12–17: Bernard Mullin. "Sport Management: The Nature and Utility of the Concept," *Arena Newsletter* 4 (October 1980): 1–11; idem, "Characteristics of Sport Marketing," in Lewis and Appenzeller, *Successful Sport Management*, 101–124.

7. Drucker, *Managment*, 61–65, 77–78; Arthur Thompson and A. J. Strickland, Strategy Formulation and Implementation (Plano, Texas. 1983), 16.

8. Karl Marx, *Capital*. Vol. I, ed. Frederick Engels (1887; repr. ed., Moscow, 1954), 43,48; "Commodity," Dictionary of Marxist Thought, ed. Tom Bottomore, et al. (Cambridge, MA, 1983), 86.

9. I am indebted to the pioneering effort of Richard Butsch. "The Commodification of Leisure: The Case of the Model Airplane Hobby and Industry," *Qualitative Sociology* 7 (Fall 1984): 217–235. See also Chris Rojek, *Capitalism and Leisure Theory* (London, 1985), ch. 5,

which summarizes earlier work by the Frankfort School on this question; and Robert Goldman, "We make weekends: Leisure and the Commodity Form." *Social Text* 8 (Winter, 1984): 84–103.

10. John Loy, "The Nature of Sport: A Definitional Effort," Quest 10 (May 1968) 1–15. See also Allen Guttmann's chapter on definitions in *From Ritual Record: The Nature of Modern Sports* (New York, 1978), 1–14

11. On the Beadle book see Harold Seymour, *Baseball: The Early Years* (New York, 1960), 44. For Spalding see Peter Levine, *A. G. Spalding and the Rise of Baseball* (New York, 1985). NCAA statistics in correspondence from Ruth Berkey, Assistant Executive Director of the NCAA, 8 August 1985, in the author's possession.

12. See Richard Gruneau's comments on the social construction of rule-making in *Class, Sports, and Social Development* (Amherst, MA, 1983), 19–52. For two interpretations of one rule change-baseballs "fly rule"—see Adelman, *A Sporting Time*, 129–31 and Warren Jay Goldstein, "Playing for Keeps: A History of American Baseball, 1857–1876" (Ph.D diss., Yale University. 1983), 80ff.

13. On utilities and services see Max Weber, *Economy and Society*, ed. Guenther Roth and Claus Wittich (Berkeley, 1978), 68. On recreation and sport as a service see, Louis Marciani, "A New Era in Recreation Marketing," *Athletic Business* 9 (October 1985): 31.

14. Fine studies of sport services include: J. A. Mangan, *Athleticism in the Victorian and Edwardian Public School: The Emergence and Consolirdotion of an Educational Ideology* (Cambridge. 1981); Greg Lee Carter, "Baseball in St. Louis, 1867–1875: An Historical Case Study in Civic Pride," Missouri Historical Society Bulletin 34 (July 1975): 253–263; Richard Mandell, *The Nazi Olympics* (New York, 1971). The list could be endless, since most of the published history of sport now considers the service component of sport as the core of its social significance.

15. See Guy M. Lewis, "Theodore Roosevelt's Role in the 1905 Football Controversy," *Research Quarterly* (December 1969): 7 17–24; Ronald Smith has corrected Lewis on several points in "Harvard and Columbia and a Reconsideration of the 1905–06 Football Crisis," *Journal of Sport History* 8 (Winter 1981): 5–19

16. John Betts gave scattered attention to sporting goods in *America's Sporting Heritage* (Reading, MA, 1974) and Peter Levine has excellent material on Spalding in *Spalding*, but in general this subject has been neglected.

17. See Arthur Cole, "Perspectives on Leisure-Time Business," *Explorations in Entrepreneurial History*, 2nd ser. I (Summer 1964): 6; Fritz Redlich, "Leisure-Time Activities: A Historical, Sociological, and Economic Analysis," ibid., 3 (1965): 3–24. reprinted in idem, *Steeped in Two Cultures*, (New York, 1971), 299. See also Sebastian DeGrazia, *Of Time, Work, and Leisure* (Garden City, NY, 1964), 189–211.

18. Robert H. Wiebe, *The Search For Order, 1877–1930* (New York, 1967), 18. Indeed the centrality of the profit motive has been questioned in Carl Betke," Sports Promotion in the Western Canadian City: The Example of Edmonton," *Urban History Review* 12 (October 1983): 47–56; and Wray Vamplew, "The Economics of a Sport Industry: Scottish Gate-Money Football, 1890–1914," *The Economic History Review* 35 (November 1982): 549–567. American magnates may have been more profit-oriented, but their activities demand closer scrutiny.

19. Joseph A. Schumpeter, *The Theory of Economic Development* (1934; repr. ed., Cambridge, MA, 1961), 66. For discussion of Schumpeter and other theorists, see Jonathan Hughes, "Entrepreneurship," in Encyclopedia of American Economic History, ed. Glenn Porter (New York, 1980), I: 214–228; Joseph C. Pusateri, *A History of American Business* (Arlington Heights, IL. 1984), 5–9.

20. Richard Mandell, *Sport: A Cultural History* (New York, 1984), 182.

21. See Adelman, Spurring Time, chs. 6, 7: Stephen Freedman, "The Baseball Fad in Chicago, 1865–1870: An Exploration of the Role of Sport in the Nineteenth-Century City," *Journal of Sport History 5* (Summer 1978): 42–64.

22. On Rodgers, see Seymour, Baseball, 293. On Colden, see Adelman, *Sporting Time*, 51, 53. On Bigelow, see Roy Rosenzweig, *Eight Hours for What We Will: Workers and Leisure in on Industrial City, 1870–1920* (New York, 1984), 172–183.

23. The best introduction to questions of sport and the state is Hart Cantelon and Richard Gruneau. eds., *Sport, Culture, and the Modern State* (Toronto, 1982).

24. For an excellent investigation into the question of state-supported facilities, see Alan Metcalfe, "Urban Response to Demand for Sporting Facilities: A Study of Ten Ontario Towns/Cities, 1919–1939," *Urban History Review* 12 (October 1983): 31–45. See also Judith Davidson, "The Federal Government and the Democratization of Public Recreational Sport: New York City, 1933–1945" (PhD diss., University of Massachusetts. 1983); Steven A. Riess. "Power Without Authority: Los Angeles Elites and the Construction of the Coliseum," *Journal of Sport History* 8 (Spring, 1981): 50–65.

25. Ted Vincent, *Mudville's Revenge: The Rise and Fall of American Sport* (New York, 1981), 13.

26. Steven A. Riess, *Touching Base: Professional Baseball and American Culture in the Progressive Era* (Westport, CT, 1980), 76. Lyle Hallowell, "The Political Economy of Violence and Control: A Sociological History of Professional Ice Hockey" (PhD diss. University of Minnesota, 1981), 106–110.

27. James B. Connolly, "The Capitalization of Amateur Athletics," *Metropolitan Magazine*, July 1910, 443–454, cited in Levine, Spalding, 172. For a model useful to sport historians, see Lary May's analysis of early movie moguls in *Screening out the Past: The Birth of Mass Culture and the Motion Picture Industry* (Chicago, 1983), 167–199. DeGraria, *On Work, Time, and Leisure*, 148, suggests that the leisure industry had special appeal to immigrants.

28. Alfred D. Chandler, Jr., *The Visible Hand: The Managerial Revolution in American Business* (Cambridge, 1977); Glenn Porter and Harold Livesay, *Merchants and Manufacturers: Studies in the Changing Structure of Nineteenth-Century Marketing* (Baltimore, 1971)

29. See, for instance, Robert N. Stern, "The Development of an Interorganizational Control Network: The Case of Intercollegiate Athletics," *Administrative Science Quarterly* 24 (June 1979); 242–265: idem, "Competitive Influences on the Interorganizational Regulation of College Athletics," *Administrative Science Quarterly* 26 (March 1981): 15–31; Alan Metcalfe, "Sport and Athletics: A Case Study of Lacrosse in Canada. 1840–1889," *Journal of Sport History* 3 (Spring 1976): 1–19; Richard Gruneau, "Elites, Class, and Corporate Power in Canadian Sport: Some Preliminary Findings," in *Sociology of Sport*, ed., F. Landry and W. Orban (Miami, 1978), 201–242: Don Morrow, "The Little Men of Iron: The 1902 Montreal Hockey Club," *Canadian Journal of History of Sport* 12 (May 1981): 51–65.

30. Chandler, *Visible Hand*, 3. On the nature of a market, see Philip Kotler, *Marketing Management*, 5th ed. (Englewood Cliffs, 1984). For a useful introduction to mainstream economic theory of sports see Noll, "Major League Sports," 348–387.

31. Besides the standard histories of baseball, see Donn Rogosin, *Invisible Men: Life in Baseball's Negro Leagues* (New York. 1983), which outlines the continued importance of barnstorming to black players. Ronald Ladwig, "A History of Public Entertainments in Ada, Ohio, 1850–1920" (PhD diss., Bowling Green State University, 1978) shows the importance of barnstorming from the viewpoint of the small town.

32. On the concentration movement see Naomi R. Lamoreaux, *The Great Merger Movement in American Business*, 1895–1904 (Cambridge. Eng., 1985), which contains an excellent bibliography. On the baseball "trust," and on the duplicity of magnates like Spalding, see Seymour Baxball I: 317–322; Levine, *A. G. Spalding*, 66.69.

33. A valuable and well-written introduction to early representational sports is William J. Baker, *Sports in the Western World* (Totowa. NJ, 1982), 43–98. See also his excellent bibliographic essay.

34. For the importance of long-term structures, See Fernand Braudel, *On History*, trans. Sara Matthews (Chicago, 1980). Alan Ingham and I have argued for the centrality of a tension between capital and community in the history of modern sport. See our "Sport: Structuration, Subjugation and Hegemony," *Theory, Culture, and Society* 2 (1984): 85–103.

35. On football, see, Lewis, "Theodore Roosevelt's Role," 717–24; Smith, "Harvard and Columbia," 5–19; Lucas and Smith, *Saga*, 229–249. Sources for the baseball wars are Seymour, *Baseball*, I:135–61, 221–62, 307–24; Voigt, *American Baseball*, I:121–69. On basketball, see Albert Applin, "From Muscular Christianity to the Marketplace: The History of Men's and Boy's Basketball in the United States, 1891–1957" (PhD diss., University of Massachusetts, 1982).

36. Edward Gross, "Spats Leagues: A Model for a Theory of Organizational Stratification," *International Review of Sport Sociology* 14 (1979): 103–112.

37. An excellent study of the need for networking is Morris Mott, "The First Pro Sports

League on the Prairies: The Manitoba Baseball League of 1886," *Canadian Journal of History of Sport* 15 (December 1984): 62–69. See also Harold Evans. "Baseball in Kansas. 1867–1940." Kansa s *Historical Quarterly* 9 (May 1940): 175–92. Myron Cope has material on the NFL's shakeout in *The Game That Was* (New York, 1974).

38. Stern, "The Development of a Control Network;" idem , "Competitive Influences;" Eugene Murdock, *Ban Johnson: Czar of Baseball* (Westport, CT, 1982). *The Sporting News* had regular stories on the umpiring problem. The paper also editorialized at times on important administrative skills. See *The Sparring News*, June 25, 1887, on qualities needed for the presidency of the Association.

39. On the nature of the "modern firm," see Chandler, *Visible Hand*, 3, 347, 373–376.

40. "Hillerich & Bradsby Co., Incorporated" (unpublished, undated. release from H & B, in author's possession). For comments on the early days of home and artisan crafting see John Krider, *Krider's Sporriq Anecdotes* (1853; repr. ed., New York, 1966), 70 ff; Seymour, *Baseball*, 7–8, 18; William Clarke. *Boy's Own Book* (New York. 1864), 17, 264; Patricia Click, "Leisure in the Upper South in the Nineteenth Century: A Study of Trends in Baltimore. Norfolk, and Richmond" (PhD diss., University of Virginia, 1980), 187. One exception to this antebellum situation was the billiard industry, dominated by Michael Phelan. See Adelman, *A Sparring Time*, 220–29.

41. Alexander Weyand, *American Football* (New York, 1926), 4.

42. See Levine, *Spalding*, 71–96. Levine found articles of use to me in *The Sporting News*, March 30, 1895; March 31, 1896; July 1, 1899.

43. *The Sporting Goods Dealer*, a trade journal, had histories in the following issues; July 1948 (Rawlings), September 1946 (Wilson), February 1951 (Spalding). On the bicycle industry see David Hounshell, *From the American System to Mass Production 1800–1932: The Development of Manufacturing Technology in the United States* (Baltimore, 1984), 189–216. The Brunswick Company has recently published a history: Rick Kogan, *Brunswick: The Story of An American Company from 1845 to 1985* (Skokie. IL, 1985). I would like to thank Mr. Grant Burden and Miss Alice Flint for help in gathering material on the sporting goods industry.

44. Betts, *America's Sporting Heritage*, 76; Reach plant statistics in *Sporting Goods Dealer*, October, 1899, 4–5; 1904 *Field* article reprinted in special 75th anniversary issue of ibid., October, 1974, 110. On the technical meaning of mass production, see Hounshell, *American System*.

45. Applin, "From Muscular Christianity to the Marketplace," 55; Levine, *Spalding*, 75–78: Albert A. Pope "The Bicycle Industry." in *One Hundred Years of American Commerce*, ed. Chauncey M. DePew (New York, 1895), 551. For the relationships between manufacturers, advertising, and American culture, see Daniel Boorstin, *The Americans: The Democratic Experience* (New York, 1973),89–164, 307–448, 525–556; Stuart Ewen, *Captains of Consciousness* (New York, 1976): Richard Wightman Fox and T. J. Jackson Lears, eds, *The Culture of Consumption: Critical Essays in American History, 1880–1980* (New York, 1983).

46. *The Sporting News*, September 22, 1902; Hollowell. "Political Economy of Violence and Control," 131. On the brutalizing aspects of boxing gloves, see Elliott Gorn, "The Manly Art. Bare-Knuckle Prize Fighting and the Rise of American Sports" (PhD diss., Yale, 1983), 480–481. For comments on exercise equipment and physical culture, see Mrozek, *Sport and American Mentality*, 84–88.

47. Hughes, "Entrepreneurship," 214. For an excellent look at how the political environment could constrain as well as enable cagey promoters, see Steven Riess, "In the Ring and Out: Professional Boxing in New York, 1896–1920," in *Sport in America*, ed. Donald Spivey (Westport, CT, 1985), 95–120.

48. Allen Guttmann, *From Ritual to Record: The Nature of Modern Sports* (New York, 1978); Alan G. Ingham and John Loy, The Social System of Sport: A Humanistic Perspective," *Quest* 19 (1973): 3–23: Richard Gruneau. *Class, Sports, and Social Development*; Alan G. Ingham, "Methodology in the Sociology of Sport: From Symptoms of Malaise to Weber for a Cure," *Quest* 3 (1979): 187–215; Rob Beamish, "Sport and the Logic of Capitalism," in *Sport, Culture and the Modern Stare*, ed. Cantelon and Gruneau, 141–98; Adelman. *Sporting Time*, esp. 3–10.

49. The links between commercialization and the erosion of player control are quite complex. Beamish and Hallowell provide suggestions about hockey, while Adelman and Goldstein consider baseball.

50. Adelman. *A Sporting Time*, 115. On the notion of the cycles, see John Kimberly and Robert Miles, *The Organizational Life-Cycle* (San Francisco, 1980); Henry Mintzberg, "Power and Organization Life Cycles," *Academy of Management Review*, 9 (1984): 207–224.

51. Williams, *Sociology of Culture*, 105. Limited space prevented me from exploring here the emergence of professional organizations. Their role in the industry has been significant in the twentieth century, since professional organizations have had much to say about playing styles, rules, and equipment. For useful works on professions, see Burton Bledstein, The *Culture of Professionalism* (New York. 1976); Thomas Haskell, ed., *The Authority of Experts* (Bloomington, 1984). For interpretations of the Sport professions see Mrozek, *Sport and American Mentality*, 67–102: Hal Lawson "Problem Setting for Physical Education and Sport," *Quest* 36 (1984): 48–60.

52. The question of freedom versus constraint in sport has been ably outlined in the dialogue between Richard Gruneau and Allen Guttmann in the *Journal of Sport History*. See ibid., 7 (Winter 1980): 68–86 and ibid., 11 (Spring, 1984): 97–99. Works dealing with alternatives include Rob Rock, "Sandlot Seasons: Sport in Black Pittsburgh" (PhD diss., University of Pittsburgh, 1983); Joan Hult, "The Governance of Athletics for Girls and Women: Leadership by Women Physical Educators," *Research Quarterly for Exercise and Sport* 56 (Centennial issue,1985): 64–77; Mark Naison, "Righties and Lefties: The Communist Party and Sports During the Great Depression," *Radical America* 13 (July–August 1979): 47–59.

12

NWCA Entrepreneurial Model: A Proactive Approach to Program Eliminations

COYTE COOPER

INTRODUCTION

In college wrestling in the United States, the National Wrestling Coaches Association (NWCA) (founded in 1928) is the sole organization that is dedicated to carrying out entrepreneurial initiatives that advance college wrestling and its membership institutions (NWCA Mission, 2009). In recent years, with the devastating program eliminations realized at the National Collegiate Athletic Association (NCAA) level, the NWCA has focused on developing an entrepreneurial mindset that is conducive to the sustainability and growth of programs at all levels of college wrestling. However, prior to discussing these individual initiatives in depth, an outline of the challenges facing college wrestling and the NWCA will be outlined to help guide the chapter.

CHALLENGES FACING COLLEGE WRESTLING

Since the 1980s, college sport administrators have increasingly adopted a profit maximization model when making monetary decisions within their coinciding athletic departments (Southall & Nagel, 2008; Southall, Nagel, Amis, & Southall, 2008). In short, NCAA Division I athletic departments have chosen to invest more heavily in men's basketball and men's football in order to improve their financial return on investment (ROI) (Marburger & Hogshead-Makar, 2003; Zimbalist, 2003). Thus, while this spending has clearly benefited many high profile sport programs, the decision making process (coined as the athletics "arms race") has decreased the budget allocation available to nonrevenue Olympic sport teams, and as a result many programs such as men's wrestling have realized significant program eliminations (Kahn, 2007; Ridpath, Yiamouyiannis, Lawrence, & Galles, 2008).

While several men's and women's teams have been negatively impacted by the program elimination process, the data supports the notion that men's wrestling has suffered more losses in participation opportunities than any other nonrevenue sport program. In fact, despite the realization of growth in several nonrevenue sports, the number of college wrestling programs fielded by the NCAA decreased by 35.5% (from 363 to 234 programs) between 1981 and 2006 (National Collegiate Athletic Association, 2008). Further, in addition to the 14 program eliminations realized between 2007 and 2008, the following four college wrestling programs were discontinued during the first month of 2009: Lawrence University, Norwich University, Portland State University, and Rose-Hulman Institute of Technology (NWCA Executive Director M. Moyer, personal communication, January 26, 2009). Thus, it seems clear that the trend to eliminate men's NCAA wrestling programs in the United States continues in today's competitive entertainment industry. With that in mind, it seems necessary for the NWCA to understand the unique reasons why athletic directors choose to eliminate NCAA nonrevenue sport programs.

Alternative Justifications for Program Eliminations

In order to understand the rationale for program eliminations, several scholars have surveyed athletic directors to explore the underlying reasons why athletic administrators choose to eliminate nonrevenue sport programs (Gray & Pelzer, 1995; Williamson, 1983). In a pioneer study on nonrevenue program eliminations, Williamson (1983) determined that athletic directors were most influenced by the following factors when discontinuing sport programs: (1) lack of student interest, (2) high cost, and (3) lack of spectator appeal. Similarly, in a more recent follow-up study, Weight (2009) illustrated that budget considerations, donor support, academic achievement, fan support (and region sport popularity), and student-athlete conduct were all factors that influenced athletic director's decisions to eliminate sport programs.

With changes in the landscape of intercollegiate athletics, scholars have emphasized the importance of continuing to understand athletic directors' priorities within their coinciding athletic departments (Weight, 2009). In essence, it is an understanding of these priorities that will allow the NWCA and college wrestling coaches to take a proactive approach to developing a product that is valuable to senior athletic administrators.

NWCA PROACTIVE APPROACH
TO PROGRAM ELIMINATIONS

In response to the program eliminations, the NWCA has launched an entrepreneurial campaign to strengthen college wrestling and its member institutions at all NCAA levels. With a long-term goal of program sustainability and growth in future generations, the NWCA has implemented several unique business strategies to develop college wrestling at the local, grassroots level. While there are a variety of approaches that could be discussed, this chapter will focus on gaining an understanding of the business strategies that are considered top priorities for the NWCA. These priorities are best illustrated in the following three entrepreneurial categories: (1) Investment in Program Elimination Research, (2) Development of a Coaches Leadership Academy, and (3) Investment in Marketing Initiatives. The three strategies will be discussed in-depth in the following sections.

1. Investment in Program Elimination Research

While the reasons for program elimination have been examined, the NWCA has also recognized the need for a proactive research approach when attempting to save college wrestling programs. Instead of focusing on why programs are discontinued, the NWCA has recently partnered with an expert research team to identify the Olympic program elements (see Table 12.1 below) that senior athletic administrators value most within their corresponding NCAA athletic departments (NWCA Executive Director M. Moyer,

TABLE 12.1. **Olympic program elements for consideration in NCAA athletic departments**

Athletic Success:	High levels of individual/team success in sport competition.
Academic Achievement:	High levels of individual/team success in the classroom.
Community Involvement:	Strong team presence in local community service initiatives.
Conduct (Competition):	Proper behavior exhibited by coaches/athletes during competition.
Conduct (Competition):	Proper behavior exhibited by coaches/athletes during competition.
Enrollment:	Improvement in the student enrollment at your academic institution.
Fan Support:	Strong team support by fans in the surrounding geographic region.
Fundraising:	Development of external funds to supplement team's operating budget.
Personal Relationships:	Strong relationships between administrators and coaching staff.
Program Sponsorship:	Low cost to fund the annual operating budget of a sport team.
Revenue Production:	Development of positive revenue streams at athletic competitions.

personal communication). In addition to surveying all NCAA senior admin-istrators, the research team also interviewed head athletic directors to get more intimate information on the program elements that are most valuable to administrators. Thus, the results will be instrumental in helping the NWCA guide coaches in their pursuit to create a product that is valued by athletic administrators.

2. Development of a Coaches Leadership Academy

Once the athletic directors' preferences are determined, it will be extremely important that the NWCA has an educational process in place to effectively train coaches in best practices to save their programs. In August of 2009, the NWCA unveiled an important element of their "Save College Wrestling" campaign when they conducted their inaugural Coaching Leadership Acad-emy for 29 young, promising coaches. With several unique program ele-ments, the underlying theme for the academy was for coaches to develop the "CEO skills" necessary to protect their wrestling programs in the future. Further, in a recent news release issued by the NWCA, the specific objec-tives of the Coaching Leadership Academy were outlined:

> The purpose of the academy was to utilize peer group discussion among college coaches, athletic administrators, and CEOs to develop best practices for protecting and strengthening intercollegiate wres-tling programs through this challenging economy. Specifically, the goal of the Leadership Academy is to help coaches strengthen their CEO skills and better align their programs with educational values of their academic institutions (i.e., improve eligibility and graduation rates) (NWCA News, 2009).

In addition to the identification of academy objectives, the NWCA has also invested heavily in educational practices that will foster engagement among coaches attending the Coaching Leadership Academy. Under the guidance of internationally renowned coaching development expert Dan Gould, the NWCA has created three unique educational components to their leadership academy:

1. Online educational modules designed to help coaches understand gen-eral CEO principles required to protect their programs.
2. Onsite workshops designed to foster collaboration between coaches and mentors to customize general principles (learned in online mod-ules) to meet the unique demands present on each campus.
3. Mentorship programs designed to provide coaches with ongoing sup-port to overcome unique challenges on their respective campuses (NWCA Executive Director M. Moyer, personal communication, Janu-ary 26, 2009; NWCA News, 2009).

Within each of these program components, there are general CEO skills that are presented to help coaches build their programs from a broad-based perspective. However, while there are a wide range of entrepreneurial skills being introduced, the program has three general core areas of competency that coaches must embrace in order to enhance their chances for program sustainability in future years: (1) building key relationships, (2) developing solid fundraising initiatives, and (3) implementing innovative marketing plans. The details of these core competencies are presented briefly below:

❖ *Building Key Relationships*: The ability to build a solid support system in the surrounding athletic department, academic institution, and community. The purpose of this competency is to educate coaches on how to develop a strong cast of stakeholders who value the academic and athletic aspects of the program. Previous research has illustrated that this is a program element that is valued by athletic administrators.

❖ *Developing Solid Fundraising Initiatives*: The ability to develop fundraising strategies that allow the wrestling program to move towards a "fully endowed" model. The purpose of this competency is to educate coaches on how to implement a business plan that will allow programs to realize sustainability in a profit maximization environment. An endowment is something that will position programs well in today's economic climate.

❖ *Implementing Innovative Marketing Plans*: The ability to embrace marketing strategies that allow a wrestling program to grow their consumer interest at the local level. The purpose of this competency is to educate coaches on how to create and distribute a product that encourages the development of consumer interest in the surrounding area. The ability to develop loyalty among consumers has the potential to bring several benefits that are desirable to athletic administrators.

The previous core competencies are just a few of the skills sets that the NWCA would like coaches to embrace in their pursuit to act as "CEOs" of their individual programs. As previous research has illustrated, these core competencies have been designed to overcome deficiencies that have been identified as critical factors by athletic directors (Weight, 2009). Thus, the NWCA has initially formed educational curricula designed to provide coaches with entrepreneurial skill sets that will allow them to enhance their sustainability within corresponding athletic departments.

3. Investment in Marketing Initiatives

There is no question that marketing will play a major role in determining whether wrestling programs are sustainable in future years. This is a primary reason why the NWCA has invested in technologies that are designed to extend the presence of college wrestling through Internet-based mediums. The first step that the NWCA has taken in this technological area is the development and release of the Live Scoreboard program featured on their website (www.nwcaonline.com). In essence, the software is designed to provide consumers with a "one stop" destination for live college wrestling results all across the United States. More importantly, the program serves as a facilitator to extend the reach of college wrestling because media outlets are able to use the program to access up-to-date statistics (see Figure 12.1 below) on college teams and wrestlers (NWCA Executive Director M. Moyer, personal communication, February 23, 2010). Thus, media outlets now have the information necessary to release quality storylines on deadline related to the college wrestling product.

In addition to the Live Scoreboard feature, the NWCA has attempted to improve the college wrestling product by capitalizing on the low cost video broadcast capabilities available via the Internet. In fact, a collaborative partnership with an established online sports broadcast company (Live SportsVideo) has allowed the NWCA to provide college wrestling coaches with a free platform to broadcast their dual meets live all across the United States. Further, the database video service also provides coaches with a consolidated site to feature promotional videos of the programs. The NWCA

School	State	Division	Confer-ence	Last Name	First Name	Elig Year	Gender	Wt Class	Record	Div Record	Div Win %	Rank
Iowa	IA	Div I	Big Ten	Metcalf	Brent	RSSR	M	149	29-0	24-0	100.00%	1

Category	Value Scored	Value Allowed
Wins	29	
Losses	0	
Pins	15	0
Forfeits	2	
Disqualifications	1	0
Defaults	0	0
Tech Falls	5	0
Major Decisions	2	0
Decisions	4	0
Takedowns	43	1
Escapes	8	28
Reversals	2	0
2pt Nearfalls	0	0
3pt Nearfalls	7	0
4pt Nearfalls	0	0
1pt Penalty	2	0
2pt Penalty	0	0
Stall Warning	0	3
1pt Stalling	0	0
2pt Stalling	0	0
Cautions	0	1
Riding Time Pts	0	0
Total Match Points	123	30
Total Team Points	153	0

Opponent Name	Opponent School	Wt Class	Result	Win Type	Score
Carey, Mark	Coe	149	W	FALL	1:45
Schwebke, Jacob	Cornell College	149	W	FALL	4:35
DeJesus, Victor	Iowa Lakes Community College	149	W	FALL	1:46
Bradley, Brandon	North Carolina—Pembroke	149	W	FALL	3:46
Lowman, Kyle	Southern Illinois Edwardsville	149	W	FALL	4:40
LeValley, Kevin	Bucknell	149	W	DEC	3-2
Bradley, Kellen	Rutgers	149	W	TFS	20-50
Mueller, Mitch	Iowa State	149	W	FALL	5:50
Kittleson, Trevor	Northern Iowa	149	W	FALL	3:49
Morrill, Justin	Utah Valley University	149	W	TFS	22-60
Wiest, Brandon	Missouri	149	W	FALL	3:32

FIGURE 12.1. Example of the NWCA live scorebook.
(NWCA scorebooks can be found at http://www.nwcaonline.com/nwcaonline/results/ColScore book /Welcome.aspx)

Coaching Leadership Academy was targeted as an outlet to encourage coaches to use new media to deliver the dual meet aspect of college wrestling to consumers.

Building on the previous Internet-based themes, the NWCA has also invested in a strong social network (e.g., Facebook) and microblogging (e.g., Twitter) presence that will allow them to market themselves to younger generations of consumers. In addition to developing streamlined messages to groups of followers, the NWCA has also focused on an extensive evaluation of their presence to ensure that they are delivering the most suitable wrestling-related content. Further, the NWCA has created educational modules to help coaches understand the basic steps necessary to gain a solid presence on social network and microblogging sites (M. Moyer, personal communication, February 23, 2010). This is another step that the NWCA has implemented to improve the exposure of college wrestling at the grassroots level.

BUILDING ON NWCA ENTREPRENEURIAL EFFORTS

While the NWCA has implemented several critical components to a successful entrepreneurial campaign, there are a number of initiatives that need to be carried out for college wrestling programs to realize sustainability in today's intercollegiate athletic environment. With a solid foundation in place to educate coaches at the grassroots level, the NWCA must continue to identify key areas of emphasis so that programs are able to reach their full potential within their corresponding NCAA athletic departments. In particular, when developing long-term business objectives, the NWCA should consider the following entrepreneurial initiatives: integrating sound research in educational processes, evaluating the core product, and implementing directed marketing plans.

Integrating Sound Research in Educational Processes

In terms of saving individual college wrestling programs, the most important research focuses on determining which Olympic program elements senior administrators value most in their athletic departments. This focus is paramount because athletic directors have the final say when deciding what budget decisions to make; thus, if program elimination is going to take place, then the athletic director and senior administrators will play a major role in what sport is going to be discontinued (Weight, 2009). With this being the case, it is imperative that the NWCA continues to invest in the implementation and understanding of research that allows wrestling programs to avoid future program eliminations.

Once the NWCA has a solid understanding of the program elements that administrators value most, then they can implement the results in their dissemination of educational content for college coaches. For example, if administrators value the fundraising component of nonrevenue sport teams, then the NWCA can develop modules that focus on providing coaches with innovative skill sets to raise money for their programs. Similarly, if academics are deemed more important than athletic success, then coaches have the opportunity to make adjustments in the core values embraced within their program. Further, the NWCA can incorporate this into their Coaching Leadership Academy by emphasizing the academic mission of programs when engaging in strategic planning initiatives. In essence, this research can allow the NWCA to deliver cutting edge educational processes designed to give coaches the skills to succeed in their athletic departments.

In coordination with the development of sound educational methods, the NWCA should also consider putting together an "entrepreneurial board" to guide college wrestling coaches in to the future. With a solid research base, this board could include academic and industry specialists with the skill sets to lead the NWCA in subject areas that are deemed essential in saving college wrestling programs. For example, the entrepreneurial board could include a member dedicated to developing marketing plans for college wrestling coaches to carry out at the local, grassroots level. Similarly, a fundraising member could develop initiatives for coaches to move towards a fully endowed model. In addition, the potential synergy between the board members could help the NWCA and college wrestling coaches to stay on the cutting edge of a proactive approach to sustainability.

Evaluating the Core Product

There is little doubt that consumer interest will always play a role in program sustainability at the local level. In essence, a strong consumer interest in a surrounding community allows a wrestling coach to maximize their attendance at their home dual meets. More importantly, this consumer interest often leads to increased revenue in the form of event sales and fundraising. With that in mind, it is extremely important that the NWCA develops an entertaining core product that appeals to a broad sports audience (Cooper & Weight, 2009). If a solid core product is not established, then the NWCA and college wrestling coaches will have little chance of retaining casual consumers when they carry out innovative marketing initiatives (Mullin, Hardy, & Sutton, 2007).

As previous research has illustrated, several aspects of the core product can be adjusted to improve the entertainment value of college wrestling (Cooper & Weight, 2009). As shown in Table 12.2, the NWCA would be wise to consider the creation of a task force to examine potential areas of improvement in the rules and regulations implemented in college wrestling. With an emphasis on *action* and *simplicity*, the task force could develop a core wrestling product that would allow the sport to grow more effectively from a consumer standpoint in future years. For example, a simple "sumo-like" push out rule could increase scoring in a manner that is understandable to casual consumers who have no previous knowledge of the sport.

While the logistical and technical aspects of rule change are not the purpose of this specific section, focusing on these aspects will support the

TABLE 12.2. The highlighted findings from the study and their implications on college wrestling

Area	Finding	Implications on College Wrestling
Mean Values	Low values illustrated for the implementation of stalling and consistency of referees	Dissatisfaction of "action" based rules can lead to boring matches and less satisfied customers
ANOVAs	Younger generations less satisfied with rules than older generations	Potential impact on future generations interest in college wrestling product
Open-Ended	Suggest "push-out" rule	Increase action by rewarding aggressiveness during matches
	Suggest eliminating riding time	Reduce confusion during matches and aid in attracting casual fans
	Suggest an adjustment in scoring	Reward offensive attempts and improve the entertainment value of matches

Source: Cooper, C. G., & Weight, E. (2009). In Pursuit of Satisfaction and Fortification: Stakeholder perceptions of NCAA Intercollegiate Wrestling rules and regulations. *Sport Marketing Quarterly, 18*, 92–106.

NWCA in realizing its full potential, by way of extending its fan base in future years. Thus, it is extremely important that the NWCA continues to invest in research initiatives that will allow them to develop a consumer friendly product. When this occurs, the NWCA and college wrestling coaches will be in a prime position to develop innovative marketing plans to draw consumers to wrestling events at the local, regional, and national level.

Implementing Directed Marketing Plans

As the NWCA moves in to the future, it will be extremely important that they invest in research initiatives that allow them to develop innovative marketing plans for college wrestling programs. More importantly, it will be critical for the NWCA to act as a facilitator when creating templates that outline basic marketing initiatives for college wrestling coaches to carry out at the local level. In fact, these marketing strategies should be an integral part of CEO training at the annual Coaching Leadership Academy because they will likely be a major determinant to program sustainability in future years. In order to make this experience more efficient, the NWCA should consider the following tips when dealing with marketing:

❖ *Keep it Simple*: There is no question that college wrestling coaches are extremely busy. In addition to running a program from an athletic perspective, coaches are now expected to act as the CEO of their program if they want it to be sustainable. This means that individuals with a lack of expertise are expected to market their program to consumers in their surrounding community. With that in mind, it is extremely important that the NWCA creates marketing plans that are simple and cost efficient for college wrestling coaches. For example, coaches should be provided with a basic promotional database in the marketing plan that includes basic ideas to create interest in their product.

❖ *Make it Practical*: As the NWCA creates its marketing plan, it is extremely important that the ideas are created by a marketing expert that understands college wrestling and the challenges facing its programs. While the marketing plan should incorporate cutting edge strategies, it is also important that the concepts are crafted specifically for college wrestling and its unique needs. Further, this plan must be developed with a highly practical approach in mind.

❖ *Know Consumer Preferences*: As previous research has illustrated, it is extremely important to gain an understanding of consumer preferences when developing marketing plans (Cooper, 2009a; Cooper, 2009b). In essence, this understanding of preferences will allow coaches to create promotions and delivery strategies suited for important groups of consumers. For example, when individual match-ups are a primary reason for attending dual meets (see Table 12.3), college wrestling coaches can create flyers to highlight this element of events.

TABLE 12.3. **Wrestling consumers' responses to sport motivational preferences**

Sport Fan Motives (N = 965)	M	SD
Individual Match-Ups I consume to follow marquee match-ups between top ranked wrestlers.	5.36**	1.03
Achievement I consume because I enjoy following wrestlers' great achievements.	5.36**	0.97
Wrestling Loyalist I consume because I enjoy supporting college wrestling.	5.33**	1.01
Team Affiliation I consume to follow a team competing in college wrestling.	4.90*	1.48
Individual Wrestler Affiliation I consume to follow an individual wrestler competing in college wrestling.	4.63*	1.49
Entertainment I consume for the entertainment options offered in college wrestling.	4.41*	1.56
Social I consume for the opportunity to socialize with other wrestling fans.	4.18*	1.43
Learning Opportunity I consume to learn strategies/techniques from top collegiate wrestlers.	3.96	1.58

Note. The scale ranged from Strongly Disagree (1) to Strongly Agree (6) $^*p < .001$ ($\mu \geq 4$) $^{**}p < .001$ ($\mu \geq 5$)

❖ *Choose Target Markets*: When developing an understanding of consumer preferences, it is important that coaches learn to identify the key target markets for their wrestling programs. More importantly, within this structure, it is necessary for the programs to understand the unique characteristics of each target market so they can develop products and promotions to create loyalty in consumers.

❖ *Use Technology*: With the growth of the Internet, it is critical that college wrestling coaches develop an understanding of how to gain a program presence on the Internet. For example, with the popularity of social network sites, the NWCA should focus on developing basic strategies for coaches to realize marketing success through sites such as Facebook. In addition to being highly innovative, these sites are a strong candidate for wrestling programs because of the fact that you can reach large groups of younger consumers at no cost.

❖ *Be Innovative/Creative*: The final element relates to the ability to create marketing templates with creative ideas that will allow coaches to understand how to effectively attract consumers. As with any marketing plan, it is absolutely critical that the promotional ideas are extremely fun so that college wrestling can build the proper brand image as it moves forward.

In addition to the previous suggestions, it will also be important that the NWCA recognizes the importance of evaluation when carrying out new marketing ideas. More importantly, the NWCA should constantly work with coaches to identify best promotional practices to be implemented on a regular basis to build consumer interest in their product. Consequently, when soliciting the marketing coordinator for the entrepreneurial board, the NWCA should consider an individual with the appropriate skill set to coordinate this collaborative process. This constant improvement in the marketing could be just what college wrestling needs to realize higher levels of program sustainability in future years.

CONCLUSION

The NWCA has become the sole entity responsible for the viability of college wrestling programs in the future. With an entrepreneurial foundation in place, the NWCA must now turn to a more innovative approach if they are going to reach their full potential in the future. In particular, the group must continue to invest in research that will allow them to streamline their CEO educational curricula available in their Coaching Leadership Academy. Further, with an emphasis on creating new consumer interest in college wrestling, the NWCA must also invest in marketing-based content that will allow coaches to build the sport at the local, grassroots level. If all of these entrepreneurial efforts go well, college wrestling could be highly sustainable in future generations.

References

Cooper, C. G. (2009a). An "All-Star" initiative: Maximizing consumer interest at premier college wrestling events. *Journal of Issues in Intercollegiate Athletics, 2,* 64–75.

Cooper, C. G. (2009b). Team segmentation at the Big Ten Wrestling Championships. *Team Performance Management, 15,* 117–127.

Cooper, C. G., & Weight, E. (2009). In Pursuit of Satisfaction and Fortification: Stakeholder perceptions of NCAA intercollegiate wrestling rules and regulations. *Sport Marketing Quarterly, 18,* 92–106.

Gray, G. R., & Pelzer, J. A. (1995). The impact of Title IX on the discontinuation of NCAA Division I wrestling programs. *Journal of Legal Aspects of Sport, 5*(2), 17–122.

Kahn, L. M. (2007). Markets: Cartel behavior and amateurism in college sports. *Journal of Economic Perspectives, 21*(1), 209–226.

Marburger, D. R., & Hogshead-Makar, N. (2003). Is Title IX really to blame for the decline in intercollegiate men's nonrevenue sports? *Marquette Sport Law Review (14),* Rev. 65.

Mullin, B. J., Hardy, S., & Sutton, W. A. (2007). *Sport Marketing* (3rd ed.). Champaign, IL: Human Kinetics.

National Collegiate Athletic Association. (2008). *NCAA Sports Sponsorship and Participation Rates Report.* Retrieved from http://www.ncaapublications.com/productdownloads/PR2010.pdf

NWCA Mission Statement. (2009). *National Wrestling Coaches Association.* Retrieved from http://www.nwcaonline.com/mission.cfm.

NWCA News. (2009). *National Wrestling Coaches Association.* Retrieved from http://www.nwcaonline.com/nwcawebsite/news/09-09-01/Leadership_in_Wrestling_Shines_Bright_at_NWCA_Coaching_Leadership_Academy.aspx.

Ridpath, B. D., Yiamouyiannis, A., Lawrence, H., & Galles, K. (2008). Changing sides: The failure of the wrestling community's challenges to Title IX and new strategies for saving NCAA sport teams. *Journal of Intercollegiate Sports, 1*(2), 255–283.

Southall, R. M., & Nagel, M. S. (2008). A Case-Study Analysis of NCAA Division I women's basketball tournament broadcasts: Educational or commercial activity? *International Journal of Sport Communication, 1*(4), 516–533.

Southall, R. M, Nagel, M. S., Amis, J., & Southall, C. (2008). A method to March Madness: Institutional logics and the 2006 National Collegiate Athletic Association Division I men's basketball tournament. *Journal of Sport Management, 22*(6), 677–700.

Weight, E. A. (2009). The role of the entrepreneurial coach—nonrevenue sport survival within big-time collegiate athletics. *International Journal of Sport Management, 10,* 1–15.

Williamson, S. C. (1983). The ranking of reasons for discontinuing intercollegiate athletic sports as determined by athletic directors at institutions which have discontinued sports. (Doctoral dissertation, University of Northern Colorado, 1983). *University Microfilms International.*

Zimbalist, A. (2003). What to do about Title IX. *Gender Issues, 21*(2), 55–59.

13

Tennis Player Longevity at the Top of the ATP and WTA World Rankings

CARLOS PESTANA BARROS AND MÁRIO TEIXEIRA

INTRODUCTION

To win a tennis match, a tennis player should control or adapt the evolving situation, deploying and managing the limited resources at his disposal, in order to gain or maintain an advantage, or to retrieve a losing situation. The success of players in terms of winning matches and tournaments is reflected in their position in the ATP or WTA world ranking lists, which are updated on a weekly basis. The duration of top-level professional tennis players is a topic of research interest. Duration analysis is an effective sport research tool used by Okhusa (1999, 2001) in baseball; Frick, Pietzner and Prinz (2007) in European football; Frick, Barros, and Passos (2009); and Del Corral, Barros, and Prieto-Rodríguez (2008) all of them in European football as well, while many other major sports have been neglected. Duration analysis is currently being adopted elsewhere in labor economics field such as self-employment search, job search, individual heterogeneity unemployment or financial contracts. (Carrasco 1999; Tribó, 2005; Cueto & Mato, 2006; Collier, 2005; Haurin & Sridhar, 2003; Gonzalo, 2002), in international relations (Box Steffensmeier, Reiter & Zorn 2003; Barros, Passos & Alana, 2005), corporate finance (Holtz-Eakin, Joulfain, & Rosen, 1994; Orbe, Ferreira & Núñez

Antón, 2002; Leung, Rigby & Young, 2003; Falck, 2007), industry (Requena-Silvente & Walker, 2005) and culture (Giles, 2007).

Contrary to previous studies, this chapter applies data obtained from the study of particular determinants of player's longevity at the top of ATP and WTA rankings, thereby enlarging previous research in sports economics. Specifically, we evaluate various hazard models, taking into account the recurrence of players in the top ATP and WTA classifications. For our purpose, we use data from the ATP for top-ranking male players from 1973 to 2007 and from the WTA for female players from 1978 to 2007.

The present research aims to underscore the significance of career length determinants as they relate to various factors: First, tennis players receive intense media coverage and are popular throughout the world, (Gilsdorf & Sukhatme, 2008a,b); because tennis is one of the main contemporary sports in terms of media coverage, it is of interest to analyze such an important sport thoroughly. Finally, there is fierce competition among professional players to attain the highest rankings and tournament seeding, based on skills, incentives and other contextual issues, which are of interest to identify.

The remainder of the chapter is organized as follows: Section 2 presents the contextual setting, followed by a brief literature review in Section 3. Section 4 describes the theoretical framework, while Section 5 explains the methodology and empirical specification. The data and estimation results are presented in Section 6. Finally, the results are discussed and concluding remarks are made in Section 7.

CONTEXTUAL SETTING

In order to achieve success in professional tennis, potential champions will begin working toward their goal in childhood, requiring emotional support in addition to financial investment to meet the immense costs of training, management, and special schooling. The children identified as being the most talented and promising will, with parental guidance, hope to benefit from full-time preparation programs. This may entail, in the case of young Europeans or Asians, a move to the United States, where the most prestigious, established tennis schools for juniors are located. Having become professional at the national level, they will enter junior tournaments and when they are successful, they will achieve international status and obtain membership with the ATP or WTA. This will enable their participation on the ATP or WTA tournament tours, during which they will gain ranking points that reflect their performance.

The ATP formed in 1972 and the WTA created in 1973 were assemble to protect the professional tennis players. High performance protection and development in tennis sports industry, are examples of fields were those associations apply their work. In 1990, the ATP launched its first worldwide tennis tour, which rapidly became the principal global organization of tournaments, at all levels from juniors to veterans. The best-known, highest profile ATP tournaments in the annual calendar are the four Grand Slams, which are supervised by the International Tennis Federation (ITF). Details of the Grand Slams are displayed in Table 13.1.

At present, besides the Grand Slams, there are six ATP events, which in 2004 comprised 206 tournaments: the ATP Masters Series, the International Series Gold, the International Series, the Challenger Series, and the Tennis Masters Cup. Table 13.2 depicts the range of events, with some characteristics.

The season terminates with the Tennis Masters Cup, a tournament for the year's eight highest-ranking players.

With regard to the ranking system, there are two lists published weekly by the ATP: the ATP Entry Ranking, which is a 52-week rolling ranking, and the ATP Race, which shows the year-to-date rankings. It is the former which determines players' qualification for entry and seeding in all singles and doubles tournaments. Although the points are accumulated over the previ-

TABLE 13.1. **The grand slam tournaments**

Event	City	Country	Continent	Inauguration	Month	Surface
Australian Open	Melbourne	Australia	Oceania	1905	January	Acrylic
French Open	Paris	France	Europe	1891	May/June	Clay
Wimbledon	London	UK	Europe	1877	June/July	Grass
US Open	New York	USA	America	1881	August/September	Deco turf

TABLE 13.2. **ATP tournament circuit**

Event	Number of events in 2004	Total Prize Money (USD)	Organizing Body
Grand Slams	4	6,700,000 to 8,300,000	ITF
ATP League (Tennis Masters Cup and Davis Cup)	2	2,100,000 to 4,450,000	ATP
ATP Masters Series	9	2,450,000 to 3,450,000	ATP
International Series Gold	9	615,000 to 1,000,000	ATP
International Series	44	333,000 to 1,000,000	ATP
Challengers Series	146	25,000 to 150,000	ATP and ITF
Satellite de Series tournament*	29	25,000 to 75,000	ATP and ITF
Futures Series**	356	10,000 to 15,000	ATP and ITF

* Was discontinued in 2007. ** Entry-level tournaments for juniors, awarding points for ATP entry ranking

ous 52 weeks, the World Number 1 of the year is the player with the most points at the end of the season.

The ATP Race differs in that the ranking list is based on points awarded solely in the season, with all players starting in January from zero. In order for a player to have an ATP ranking, he must participate in the ATP tournaments.

The WTA is organized on a similar basis to the ATP. Certain major women's events, most notably the Grand Slams, take place in tandem with the men's tournaments. The main difference between the ATP and WTA circuits is that the tournament prize money available to the female players is less than that in the men's events.

Since 1988, there have been four WTA tournament levels: (1) WTA Tournament Tier I—minimum prize $1,340,000, with 10 tier-I tournaments; (2) WTA Tournament Tier II—minimum prize $600,000, with 16 WTA tier-II tournaments; (3) WTA Tournament Tier III—minimum prize $175,000, with 17 WTA tier-III tournaments; (4) WTA Tournament Tier IV—minimum prize $145,000, with 12 WTA tier-IV tournaments.

Table 13.3 presents the list of the players analyzed, ordered from the first time he/she reaches the top position. Some of the players have already retired, while others remain in competition. Naturally, the career prize displayed for those not in retirement is the estimated value until the beginning of 2007.

LITERATURE REVIEW

To the best of our knowledge, no previous paper has analyzed the duration of tennis players' careers. Scully (1994) used a survival analysis to measure the coaching tenure probability. Audas, Dobson and Goddard (2000) analyzed involuntary and voluntary managerial job termination with hazard functions in English professional football. Ohkusa (2001) analyzed the quit decision among baseball players in Japan, using Cox's (1972) proportional hazard model. Ohkusa (1999) also analyzed the quit decision among Japanese baseball players. Kahn (2006) analyzes racial differences in the retention, pay, and performance of U.S. National Basketball Association coaches in the period from 1996 to 2003.

Using a unique database covering match-level data for a period of 25 years (1972–1997) Audas, Dobson, and Goddard (1997, 1999) investigated the reasons for involuntary and voluntary departures of English football managers. With the help of a specific variant of a continuous time duration model (competing risk), the authors were able to correct for the potential bias emerging, as well as distinguish between voluntary and involuntary manager exits. Dawson, Dobson, and Gerrard (2000) examine the length of time it takes for a football manager to find another appointment after being dismissed. More precisely, they seek to establish whether the length of the period of unemployment reduces the probability of re-employment. With a sample of English football managers between 1973 and 2002 (n = 667), they

TABLE 13.3. List of players analyzed

Name	Year top position first reached	Gender (male = 1, female = 0)	Number of times in top position	Year retired	Career prize (USD)
Ilie Nastase	1973	1	1	1985	2,076,761
John Newcombe	1974	1	1	1981	1,062,408
Jimmy Connors	1977	1	9	1996	8,641,040
Björn Borg	1979	1	6	1984	3,655,571
Chris Evert	1979	0	8	1985	8,895,195
Martina Navratilova	1979	0	9	2006	21,400,871
John McEnroe	1980	1	14	2002	12,547,797
Tracy Austin	1980	0	1	1994	2,092,380
Ivan Lendl	1983	1	8	1984	21,262,417
Mats Wilander	1985	1	1	1996	7,976,256
Boris Becker	1991	1	2	1999	25,080,956
Monica Seles	1991	0	5	2007	14,891,762
Stefan Edberg	1991	1	5	1996	20,630,941
Steffi Graf	1991	0	1	1999	21,895,277
Jim Courier	1992	1	4	2000	14,034,132
Pete Sampras	1993	1	11	2002	43,280,489
Arantxa Sanchez Vicario	1995	0	3	2002	16,942,640
André Agassi	1996	0	6	2006	31,152,975
Thomas Muster	1996	1	2	1999	12,225,910
Marcelo Rios	1998	1	2	2003	9,713,771
Carlos Moyà	1999	1	1		12,868,379
Lindsay Davenport	1999	0	8		21,849,317
Martina Hingis	1999	0	5		20,130,657
Patrick Rafter	1999	1	1	2002	11,127,058
Yevgeny Kafelnikov	1999	1	1	2003	23,883,797
Gustavo Kuerten	2001	1	3		14,743,338
Marat Safin	2001	1	3		13,142,980
Jennifer Capriati	2002	0	3		10,206,639
Serena Williams	2002	0	1		18,073,233
Venus Williams	2002	0	3		18,138,781
Andy Roddick	2003	1	1		12,984,526
Juan Carlos Ferrero	2003	1	1		10,974,463
Justine Henin	2003	0	4		19,002,905
Kim Clijsters	2003	0	3		14,764,296
Lleyton Hewitt	2003	1	2		17,271,212
Roger Federer	2004	1	1		38,707,078
Maria Sharapova	2005	0	3		10,231,402
Amélie Mauresmo	2006	0	2		13,582,586

use Cox's proportional hazard regression model to test the risk of re-employment for unemployed head coaches. As in the other studies mentioned above, they insert a bundle of human capital variables such as age, duration of former playing career, international appearances, managerial experience, and the manager's previous win ratio. Audas, Goddard, and Rowe (2006) also analyze head coaches' employment duration in the NHL, focusing on post-succession performance.

Frick et al. (2009) analyzed the determinants of coach dismissals in German soccer (often referred to by the name of the top league, *Bundesliga*), using several hazard models, namely the Cox model, a variance correction survival model (Prentice, William, & Peterson, 1981), the Exponential model, and the Weibull model. Del Corral et al. (2008) analyzed the pattern of player substitutions during matches played in the First Division of the Spanish National Football League in the 2004–2005 season, using an inverse Gaussian survival model. Therefore, most published papers focus on coach career. More in line with the present research, Frick et al. (2009) implemented a Cox survival model to analyze footballers' careers in the Bundesliga.

THEORETICAL FRAMEWORK

This chapter focuses on top ATP tennis players from 1973–2007 and top WTA players from 1998–2007. There are two critical factors that dictate the length of a tennis player's career at the top of the ATP and WTA rankings: player skill set, and the the local sport market. According to Szymanski (2003), of prime importance is player performance (i.e. his/her win percentage in singles and doubles matches).

The empirical part of this chapter will test the following hypotheses:

H1: The relative prize winnings earned by the player determines his/her career length. Players achieving relatively large accumulations of prize money are more likely to remain in the top ATP and WTA positions, because of the opportunity costs related to it. This hypothesis will be tested with the variable *career prize*, that is, the total prize money earned during the player's career. The importance of earnings in individual behavior is well documented in survival models (Frick et al., 2009; Dawson et al., 2000; Porter & Scully, 1982; Idson & Kahane, 2000, 2004). We are, however, the first authors to test this hypothesis in the tennis market.

H2: The career length of the tennis players is also determined by his/her skills. This hypothesis will be tested with the variables *height* and *weight*. That such physical characteristics affect players' performance is one of the few "stylized facts" in the sports economics literature (Frick et al., 2007; Scully, 1992a,b).

H3: Performance has a positive relationship with the career durations of tennis players (i.e., the probability of losing the top position decreases when performance improves). This hypothesis will be tested with the number of singles and doubles matches won. This is an intuitive hypothesis previously tested in sports by Frick et al. (2009), Frick et al. (2007), Tena and Forrest (2007), and Spurr and Barber (1994).

H4: Career duration of players in the top ATP and WTA rankings is positively affected by gender. This hypothesis will be tested by the variable gender. This is the first time that a gender hypothesis has been tested in survival models, which is significant because sports are always gender-defined. Therefore, only by integrating ATP and WTA players can this hypothesis be tested (Hoang & Rascher, 1999).

H5: Top tennis players tend to be those who are recurrently in their career, because they are competitive individuals who strive for professional success. Tennis players who hold recurrent top rankings throughout their careers are driven by a competitive nature and strong desire for professional success. (e.g., Frick et al. 2009). This hypothesis will be tested by the variable *recur*.

H6: Right-handed players tend to have longer careers because they are in the majority among tennis players, in contrast to the small minority of left-handed players. As majorities tend to succeed more than minorities, we expect to observe the longevity of right-handed players to be greater than that of left-handed players. This hypothesis will be tested by the variable *right-handed*.

H7: U.S. tennis players tend to have longer careers. U.S. players tend to form the majority of ATP and WTA players. Therefore, it is expected that their careers last longer than players from other continents. This hypothesis will be tested by the variable *USA*.

RESEARCH DESIGN

In the study of the career durations of top ATP and WTA players, the event we seek to explain is the loss of the top position, more precisely, the premature loss of the top position. Such a decline can either be definitive or temporary. Definitive losers do not regain their position, whereas recurrent losers can gain and lose the top ranking on numerous occasions. Because such repeated events are unlikely to be independent, the Cox proportional hazard model for single event data is inadequate for estimation (Kalbfleisch & Prentice, 2002). Ignoring this dependence might lead to erroneous variance estimates and possibly biased estimates. One possible solution to this problem is to consider only the time period before the first occurrence of an event. However, this specification strongly assumes that the time earlier than the first event is similar to the time before all events. Moreover, this specification implies the rejection of some data.

Two different approaches can be adopted to handle recurrence data; the first approach is to adopt an accelerated frailty model, modeling the association between failure times as a random-effect term, called *frailty*. Frailties are unobserved effects shared by all units in the sample. An alternative approach is to adopt a proportional hazard model, known as the variance-corrected survival model (Box-Steffensmeier & Zorn, 2002). In this model, the covariance matrix of the estimators is adjusted to account for the additional correlation. Models in this tradition are the independent increments model of Anderson and Gill (1982); the conditional risk-set model in either elapsed or gap time of Prentice et al. (1981); and the marginal risk-set model of Wei, Lin, and Weissfeld (1989). All these models are variance-correction models for repeated events and differ in the way they define the risk set and the event time. In this chaper, we adopt the frailty models. Variance-correction models were adopted by Frick et al. (2009).

In the Prentice et al. (1981) model, an individual is not at risk for a later event until all prior events have occurred, and event time is defined as the time elapsed since the previous event.

Formally, let *T* be a continuous non-negative, random variable that measures the passage of time, and let *t* denote a particular realization (duration) of this variable. The distribution of the duration is $F(T) = \Pr[T < t]$ and the corresponding density function is $f(t) = dF(t)/dt$. Duration analysis is particularly interested in the survival function: $S(t) = [1 - F(t)] = Pr[T \geq t]$ and the hazard function $\lambda(t) = f(t)/S(t)$. The hazard function is the rate at which spells will be completed at duration t, conditional upon having lasted that long. The functions *F*, *f*, *S* and λ simple provide alternative ways of characterizing the distribution of T.

It can be shown that $\lambda(t) = -[dlog_e S(t)/dt]$, and one important role of the hazard function is that it provides a basis for defining *duration dependence*. The underlying random variable is said to exhibit positive (negative) duration dependence at some time t^*, if $[dl(t)/dt] > 0$ (< 0). Positive (negative) duration dependence implies that the probability that a spell is about to end increases (decreases) with an increase in the spell length. We begin estimating a Cox survival model. Let $h[t|\mathbf{Z}(t)]$ be the hazard rate at time *t* for a failure with covariate vector $\mathbf{Z}(t)$; the basic Cox model is as follows (Klein and Moeschberger, 2003):

$$h[t|\mathbf{Z}(t)] = h0(t) \exp[\boldsymbol{\beta}^T \mathbf{Z}(t)] = h0(t) \exp[\sum_{x=1}^{y} \beta_x Z_y(t)]$$

where $h0(t)$ is the baseline hazard rate function. The use of a proportional hazards model means that the hazard rate of a subject is proportional to its baseline hazard rate $h0(t)$, which is the basic assumption of Cox's model. In the model, $\boldsymbol{\beta}$ is the coefficient vector and $\mathbf{Z}(t) = [Z1(t), Z2(t), \ldots, Zy(t)]T$ is the covariate vector. $Zi(t), i = 1,2, \ldots, y$, is a *time-dependent* covariate if its value varies with time.

Assuming that there are no ties between the event times, the parameters are estimated by the partial likelihood function is given by:

$$L(\beta) = \prod_{i=1}^{n} \left\{ \frac{\exp(\beta^T z_i)}{\sum_{j \in R(t_i)} \exp(\beta^T z_j)} \right\}^{\delta_i},$$

where is a censoring indicator equal to one if observed and zero if censored and Y is a risk indicator which is equal to one if the individual is at risk for the current event, and zero otherwise.

An assumption of the proportional hazard model is that the hazard function for an individual (i.e., observation in the analysis) depends on the values of the covariates and the value of the baseline hazard. Given two individuals with particular values for the covariates, the ratio of the estimated hazards over time will be constant; hence the name of the method: the *proportional hazard* model. The validity of this assumption may be questionable, particularly when male and female individuals are present in the sample and in view of the fact that the period of analysis spans from 1973 to 2007. Therefore, the impact of the covariate may be dependent on time. There are tests to verify whether the proportional assumption is fulfilled. In this paper, the Schoenfeld test is adopted, Schoenfeld (1981) and the null hypothesis is that the proportional hazard is correct: The P-value of 0.0312 indicated that there was statistical evidence against the null hypothesis that the proportional hazards assumption was correct. Therefore, we adopted a parametric specification: the Weibull model.

In the Weibull model, the baseline is defined by:

$$h_{0k}(t - t_{k-1}) = \alpha_k (t - t_{k-1})^{\alpha_k - 1}$$

where the time-dependent parameter, α_k is estimated separately for each event. Both models are estimated through maximum likelihood (Allison, 1984; Cox & Oakes. 1984; Yamaguchi, 1991).

DATA AND FINDINGS

The data used to study the determinants of top ATP and WTA players' career duration covers the years 1973–2007. The data was obtained from the ATP website (several websites national and international with different types of information, which publishes information on its top ranked players and on wikipedia (http://en.wikipedia.org/wiki/world_number_one_male_tennis _player_rankings) and on the WTP data was obtained in WTP web site and on wikipedia (http://en.wikipedia/wiki/women's_tennis_association).

The dependent variable is always tenure of ATP and WTA players measured in weeks. The estimated coefficients are always in the proportional-hazard metric.

There are 114 players in the sample, who are responsible for 159 events and 42 censored observations (models M2—M4). The frequency of events is shown in Table 13.4.

TABLE 13.4. **Characteristics of the variables**

Variable	Description		Min.	Max.	Mean	Std. Dev.
Dur	Duration in weeks in ATP and WTA top position	dependent variable	1	377	131.13	108.615
Prize	Career prize winnings ($US)	Variable testing hypothesis	1062408	43280489	17851503	9633819
Height	The height of the player in meters	Variable testing hypothesis 2	1.65	1.93	1.80	0.065
Weight	The weight of the player in kilograms	Variable testing hypothesis 2	55	88	73.433	8.708
Singles matches	The number of singles matches won	Variable testing hypothesis 3	11	167	76	48.464
Doubles matches	The number of doubles matches won	Variable testing hypothesis 3	0	177	26	42.784
Gender	Dummy variable— 1 for male, 0 for female	Variable testing hypothesis 4	0	1	0.53	0.500
Recur	Number of recurrences in ATP and WTA top position	Variable testing hypothesis 5	1	14	6.777	3.844
Playright	Dummy variable— 1 if player is right-handed , 0 if left-handed	Variable testing hypothesis 6	0	1	0.7388	0.440
USA	Dummy variable— 1 for U.S. players , 0 otherwise	Variable testing hypothesis 7	0	1	0.452	0.499

Table 13.4 presents the characteristics of the data used in the analysis.

Model 1 (M1) is the Cox accelerated model. However, this model is presented only for the purpose of comparison, because it cannot accommodate multiple failures. Model 2 (M2) is the Weibull accelerated model. Again, this model cannot accommodate multiple failures. Model 3 (M3) is the Weibull accelerated model with gamma distributed frailty. Model 4 (M4) is the Weibull accelerated model with gamma frailty and shared frailty. These two latter models allow for multiple failures interpreted as frailties (Cleves, Gould and Gutierrez, 2004). M3 measures group frailty, for example, an individual who is recurrent in the top position. M4 measures shared frailty, for example, a frailty common to all individuals.

In all four of the models, the results are quite similar in their main effects. Given the model specification, a positive value for the parameters implies

TABLE 13.5. **Event frequency**

No. of Events	1	2	3	4	5	6	7	8	...	14
Frequencies	10	6	7	2	4	1	0	3	...	1

that the career duration increases with increasing values in the respective variable. A negative value for the parameters implies a negative relationship. The results across the four models demonstrate that the parameters have the same signs.

On the basis of the log likelihood statistic and the statistical significance of the theta variable, the Weibull model with heterogeneity provides the superior fit to the data. The rationale for this result is that heterogeneity represents characteristics that influence the conditional probability of the tennis player's career duration which are not measured or observed and, therefore, not taken into account in the measurement errors of the variables. Unobserved heterogeneity has been the subject of concern and analysis in Chesher (1984) and Chesher and Santos-Silva (2002). Heterogeneous behavior is commonly observed in individuals. Therefore, not taking it into account

TABLE 13.6. **Estimation results**

	M1		M2		M3		M4	
	Coef.	s.e.	Coef.	s.e.	Coef.	s.e.(2)	Coef.	s.e.(2)
logPrize	0.600	1.231	0.1005	0.031	0.1005	0.0311	0.0953	0.0334
Height	−0.180	0.275	−0.0253	0.013	−0.0253	0.1382	−0.0238	0.0139
Weight	0.184	0.313	0.0199	0.008	0.0199	0.008	0.0185	0.0091
Singles matches	0.073	0.086	0.0027	0.0005	0.0027	0.0005	0.0028	0.0005
Doubles matches	−0.064	0.772	−0.0029	0.0006	−0.0029	0.0006	−0.0029	0.0006
Gender	−0.349	0.349	−0.0140	0.0725	−0.0140	0.0725	−0.0205	0.0767
Recur	0.247	0.265	0.014	0.0073	0.014	0.0073	0.014	0.0072
Playright	−1.67	0.586	−0.1471	0.0696	−0.1471	0.0696	−0.141	0.0709
USA	0.494	0.961	0.3194	0.0748	0.3194	0.0748	0.3162	0.0739
Constant	—		−2.1707	2.017	−2.1707	2.017	−1.939	2.024
Ln P	—		1.7418	0.779	1.7418	0.0006	1.760	0.092
Theta	—		—		6.34e−09	0.00001	0.0423	0.090
LL	−122.0		−369.3		−425.4		−501.3	

(1)—All models were estimated in Stata 9
LL—Log Likelihood

is likely to lead to inconsistent parameter estimates or, more importantly, inconsistent fitted-choice probabilities. In the present study, this implies that different individuals can have different preferences relative to the career duration. The variance of unobserved individual specific parameters induces correlation across the alternatives in the choice and, accordingly, survival models with heterogeneity are required. Based on the log likelihood of Model 4, it is concluded that shared frailty has a higher statistical representation than group frailty. This may result from the fact that almost all the tennis players in the sample are recurrent in the top position.

The variables are statistically significant only for the Weibull models. As hypothesised, the higher the career prize winnings, the longer the tennis players' careers tend to endure, signifying that money is the main driving force in this sport, validating Hypothesis 1. The player's height is negative, while weight is positive, signifying that an extended career is positively related to height, while players carrying more weight will have shorter or average careers, validating Hypothesis 2.

The number of singles matches won is positive, but the number of doubles matches won is negative, meaning that winning singles matches and tournaments is a crucial determinant of career duration. This result does not validate Hypothesis 3. We found a female advantage in the top ATP career duration, which was statistically significant. Therefore, Hypothesis 4 is not validated. The most recurrent players in the ATP top rankings tend to have relatively long careers, validating Hypothesis 5. Players who are right-handed have shorter careers than those who are left-handed, rejecting Hypothesis 6. Finally, U.S. players tend to have more enduring careers, validating Hypothesis 7.

DISCUSSION

The results support the majority of the hypotheses and are broadly intuitive takin the european perspective, signifying that tall tennis players who concentrate on singles tournaments and achieve higher career prize earnings remain in the market longer. Their competitive urge will ensure that they strive hard to regain the top position, should they be overtaken by a rival player.

In terms of policy implications, the results suggest that leading European, Australian, South American and Asian tennis players should emulate the U.S. players, who achieve the greatest career longevity. Right-handed players should emulate left-handed players competitivness, and non-recurrent players should follow the example of the recurrent players in order to prolong their careers.

Survival modelling has been shown to be a useful technique for the purpose of this research. Several duration or survival models were presented for comparative purposes, including the Cox model, the parametric Weibull model, a Weibull model that accounts for individual player heterogeneity, and, finally, a Weibull model that accounts for heterogeneity and shared frailty. Shared frailty takes into account the recurrent episodes of most players who have occupied the ATP top ranking position. This last model was found to perform best in terms of its explanatory capability. The model results indicate that career duration at the top of the ATP rankings is related positively to: career prize winnings, height, singles matches, recurrent episodes in the ATP top position, being a left-handed player, and being a U.S. player.

How do these findings compare with previous research? The results confirm that prize money is a driving motivation to maintaining the top position. There is no direct comparison possible with the present research because, to the best of our knowledge, no prior research has investigated the career durations of the top-ranked ATP and WTA tennis players. Nevertheless, comparing the present results with research conducted on football, it is verified that common covariates have similar signs (Frick et al., 2009).

References

Allison, P. D. (1984). *Event History Analysis.* Beverly Hills, CA: Sage.

Anderson, P. K., & Gill, R. D. (1982). Cox's regression model for counting processes a large sample study. *Annals of Statistics, 10*, 1100–1120.

Audas, R., Dobson, S., & Goddard, J. (1997). Team performance and managerial change in the English Football League. *Economic Affairs, 17*, 30–36.

Audas, R., Dobson, S., & Goddard, J. (1999). Organizational performance and managerial turnover. *Managerial and Decision Economics, 20*, 305–318.

Audas, R., Dobson, S., & Goddard, J. (2002). The impact of managerial change on team performance in professional sports. *Journal of Economics and Business, 54*, 633–650.

Audas, R., Goddard, J., & Rowe, W.G. (2006). Modeling employment duration of NHL head coaches: Turnover and post-succession performance. *Managerial and Decision Economics, 27*, 293–396.

Barros, C.P., Passos, J., & Gil-Alana, L. A. (2005). The timing of ETA attacks. *Journal of Policy Modelling, 28*, 335–346.

Borland, J., & Lye, J. (1996). Matching and mobility in the market for Australian rules football coaches. *Industrial and Labor Relations Review, 50*, 143–158.

Box-Steffensmeier, J., Reiter, D., & Zorn, C. (2003). Non-proportional hazard and event history in international relations: *The Journal of Conflict Resolution, 47*, 33–53.

Box-Steffensmeier, J., & Zorn, C. (2003). Duration models of repeat events. *Journal of Politics, 64*, 1069–1094.

Carrasco, R. (1999). Transitions to and from self-employment in Spain: An empirical analysis. *Oxford Bulletin of Economics and Statistics, 61*, 315–341.

Chesher, A. (1984). Testing for neglected heterogeneity. *Econometric, 52*, 865–872.

Chesher, A., & J. Santos-Silva (2002). Taste variation in discrete choice models. *Review of Economic Studies, 69*, 147–68.

Cleves, M.A., Gould, W., & Gutierrez, R. (2002). *An Introduction to Survival Analysis Using STATA.* College Station, TX: Stata Press.

Collier, W. (2005). Unemployment duration and individual heterogeneity: A regional study. *Applied Economics, 37*, 133–153.

Cox, D. R. (1972). Regression models and life tables (with discussion). *Journal of Royal Statistical Society*, Series B 34, 187–220.

Cox, D. R., & Oakes, D. (1984). *Analysis of Survival Data.* London, UK: Chapman and Hall/CRC Press.

Cueto, B., & Mato, J. (2006). An analysis of self-employment subsidies with duration models. *Applied Economics, 38*, 23–32.

Dawson, P., Dobson, S., & Gerrard, B. (2000). Stochastic frontiers and the temporal structure of managerial efficiency in English soccer. *Journal of Sports Economics, 1*(4), 341–362.

Del Corral, J., Barros, C. P., & Prieto-Rodríguez, J. (2008). The determinants of soccer player substitutions: A survival analysis of the Spanish soccer league. *Journal of Sport Economics, 9*(2), 160–172.

Falck, G. (2007) Survival chances of new businesses: Do regional conditions matter? *Applied Economics, 39*, 2039–2048.

Frick, B., Barros, C. P., & Passos, J. (2009): Coaching for survival: The hazards of head coach careers in the German *Bundesliga. Applied Economics, 41*(25), 3303–3311.

Frick, B., Pietzner, G., & Prinz, J. (2007). Career duration in a competitive environment. *Eastern Economic Journal, 33*, 429–442.

Giles, D. E. (2007). Survival of the hippest: Life at top of the hot 100. *Applied Economics, 39*, 1877–1887.

Gilsdorf, K. F., & Sukhatme, V. (2008a). Tournament incentives and match outcomes in women's professional tennis. *Applied Economics, 40*, 2405–2412.

Gilsdorf, K. F., & Sukhatme, V. (2008b). Testing Rosen's sequential elimination tournament model: incentive and player performance. *Journal of Sport Economics, 9*, 287–303.

Gonzalo, M. T. (2002). A new look at the UI effect on transition from unemployment into wage employment in Spain: The limited duration of the UI benefits entitlement. *Applied Economics, 34*, 2177–2187.

Haurin, D. R., & Sridhar, K. S. (2003). Rates on reservation wages and duration of search a job. *Applied Economics, 35*, 1469–1476.

Hoang, H., & Rascher, H. (1999). The NBA, exit discrimination, and career earnings. *Industrial Relations, 38*, 69–91.

Holtz-Eakin, D., Joulfain, D., & Rosen, H. S. (1994). Sticking it out: Entrepreneurial survival and liquidity constraints. *Journal of Political Economy, 102*, 53–75.

Idson, T., & Kahane, L. H. (2000). Team effects on compensation: An application to salary determination in the National Hockey League. *Economic Inquiry, 2*, 345–357.

Idson, T., & Kahane, L. H. (2004). Teammate effects on pay. *Applied Economic Letters, 12*, 731–733.

Kahn, L. M. (1993). Managerial quality, team success, and individual player performance in Major League Baseball. *Industrial and Labor Relations Review, 46*, 531–547.

Kahn, L. M. (2004). Differences in the success of NFL coaches by race, 1990–2002. *Journal of Sport Economics, 5*(1), 6–19.

Kalbfleisch, J. D., & Prentice, R. L. (2002). *The Statistical Analysis of Failure Time Data* (2nd ed.). New York: John Wiley and Sons.

Klein, J. P., & Moeschberger, M.L. (2003). *Survival Analysis: Techniques for censored and truncated data* (2nd ed). New York: Springer-Verlag.

Koning, R. (2003). An econometric evaluation of the effect of firing a coach on team performance. *Applied Economics, 35*, 555–564.

Leung, M. K., Rigby, D., & Young, T. (2003). Entry of foreign banks in the People's Republic of China: A survival analysis. *Applied Economics, 35*, 21–31.

Ohkusa, Y. (2001). An Empirical examination of the quit behavior of professional baseball players in Japan. *Journal of Sport Economics, 2*, 80–88.

Ohkusa, Y. (1999). Additional evidence for the career concern hypothesis with uncertainty of the quit period: The case of professional baseball players in Japan. *Applied Economics, 31*, 1481–1487.

Orbe, J., Ferreira, E., & Núñez-Antón, V. (2002). Length of time spent in Chapter 11 bankruptcy: A censored partial regression model. *Applied Economics, 34*, 1949–1957.

Porter, P. K., & Scully, G. W. (1982). Measuring managerial efficiency: The case of baseball. *Southern Economic Journal, 47*, 642–650.

Poulsen, R. (2000). Should he stay or should he go? Estimating the effect of firing the manager in soccer. *Chance, 13*, 29–32.

Prentice, R. L., Williams, B. J., & Petersen, A. V. (1981). On the regression analysis of multivariate failure time data. *Biometrica, 68*, 157–164.

Requena-Silvente, F., & Walker, J. (2005). Competition and product survival in the UK car market. *Applied Economics, 37*, 2289–2295.

Schoenfeld, D. (1981). The asymptotic properties of nonparametric tests for comparing survival distributions. *Biometrica, 68*, 316–319.

Scully, G. W. (1992a). Is managerial termination rational? Evidence from professional team sports. *Advances in the Economics of Sport, 1*, 67–87.

Scully, G. W. (1992b). Coaching quality, turnover, and longevity in professional team sports. *Advances in the Economics of Sport, 1*, 53–65.

Scully, G. W. (1994). Managerial efficiency and survivability in professional team sports. *Managerial and Decision Economics, 15*, 403–411.

Spurr, S. J., & Barber, W. (1994). The effect of performance on a worker's career: Evidence from Minor League Baseball. *Industrial and Labor Relations Review, 47*, 692–708.

Szymanski, S. (2003). The economic design of sporting contexts. *Journal of Economic Literature, 41*, 1137–1187.

Tena, J. D., & Forrest, D. (2007). Within-season dismissal of football coaches: Statistical analysis of causes and consequences. *European Journal of Operational Research, 181*(1), 362–373.

Tribó, J. A. (2005). An analysis of length of labour and financial contracts: A study for Spain. *Applied Economics, 37*, 905–916.

Wei, L. J., Lin, D. Y., & Weissfeld, L. (1989). Regression analysis of multivariate incomplete failure time data by modeling marginal distributions. *Journal of the American Statistical Association, 84*, 1065–1073.

Yamaguchi, K. (1991). *Event History Analysis.* Newbury Park, CA: Sage.

Index

About the Editors

DORENE CILETTI is an assistant professor in the marketing and sports marketing division in the Palumbo • Donahue School of Business at Duquesne University. Her research and teaching interests include sport marketing, marketing fundamentals, and sales. She is particularly interested in sustainability and its integration in sport and in marketing. Her work has covered a range of subjects including the Pittsburgh Steelers, league sustainability communication, the secondary ticket market, communication in selling, and marketing strategies for career development. Ciletti, who earned a PhD and MBA, coordinates student sales competitions for Duquesne, and serves as faculty sponsor for the Pi Sigma Epsilon professional sales and marketing fraternity on campus.

Ciletti's work has appeared in various sports and marketing journals, such as the *International Journal of Sport Communication*, *Journal of Applied Marketing Theory*, and the *Journal for the Study of Sports and Athletes in Education*, and her textbook, *Marketing Yourself*, was a first for the high school market, combining marketing theory and practice with business market knowledge and career development.

She has worked in various capacities, including marketing communications, sales, and research within the financial services, healthcare, and education sectors. In addition to receiving top sales awards, she has implemented corporate marketing strategies, developing and coordinating events, press releases, and design of marketing collateral; served as editor and contributing writer for internal and external corporate newsletters; and developed and conducted sales and marketing training programs.

Actively involved in the community, Ciletti has served for nearly a decade as a Challenger Baseball team coordinator, and she is a board member or advisor for numerous organizations that support inclusion, autism awareness, sustainability, and community development.

SIMON CHADWICK is a professor and chair in Sport Business Strategy and Marketing at Coventry University Business School, where he is also the founder and Director of the Centre for the International Business of Sport (CIBS). Chadwick's research and teaching interests lie in the areas of sponsorship, sport marketing, and commercial strategy in sport, which means that his work covers a diverse range of subjects including football, motor racing, rugby, athlete endorsements, sports branding, fan behavior, the Olympic Games, the Indian Premier League, and Grand Slam tennis tournaments.

Chadwick, who previously worked at the University of London and the University of Leeds, is the editor of *Sport, Business and Management: An International Journal*, is a former editor of the *International Journal of Sports Marketing and Sponsorship* (he continues to serve as an editorial board member for several other sport journals), and has authored and published more than 500 articles, conference papers, and books on sport. His academic research has appeared in journals including *Sloan Management Review*, the *Journal of Advertising Research*, *Thunderbird International Business Review*, *Management Decision, Marketing Review*, and *Sport Marketing Quarterly*. In addition to this book, Chadwick has also recently co-edited *Managing Football: An International Perspective* (Elsevier). He has also been co-editor of *The Business of Sport Management* and The *Marketing of Sport* (Financial Times Prentice Hall), and *International Cases in the Business of Sport* (Elsevier). Alongside his books, Chadwick has created a sport marketing talk series for Henry Stewart Publishing and is editor of a sport marketing book series for Butterworth-Heinemann.

Chadwick is a visiting academic at IESE and Instituto de Empresa in Spain; the University of Paris, France; and the University of Pretoria in South Africa. Among his other research and consultancy activities, Chadwick has worked with numerous organizations involved in sport including MasterCard, Atletico Madrid, the International Tennis Federation, FC Barcelona, UEFA, Tottenham Hotspur, Sport Business Group, *The Economist*, and the British Council. He sits on the advisory board of StreetGames (an organization which takes sport to disadvantaged communities), and is a close collaborator with or advisor for various organizations in sport, ranging from teams, clubs, and governing bodies through to commercial partners, broadcasters, and government ministries.

Chadwick's views on sport are regularly covered by the media; he has been quoted more than 4,000 times in publications across the world including in the *Wall Street Journal*, the *New York Times*, *Forbes*, *Time*, the *Financial Times*, *The Economist*, *Der Spiegel*, *El Pais*, *Le Monde*, and *China Daily*. He also regularly appears on television, where he has commented on sport for broadcasters such as CNN, Bloomberg, Al Jazeera, the BBC, CNBC, Sky, and CCTV.

About the Authors

CARLOS PESTANO BARROS is an associate professor in the Department of Economics at the School of Economics and Management (ISEG), Technical University of Lisbon. His research interests include sport economics.

NICHOLAS BURTON is a doctoral candidate and research scholar at Coventry University Business School, and researcher for the Centre for the International Business of Sport (CIBS). His research interests include ambush marketing, sport sponsorship, athlete endorsements, and sports celebrity branding, with particular focus on the management of sport marketing and sponsorship.

COYTE COOPER is an assistant professor in sport administration at the University of North Carolina at Chapel Hill. His research interests include issues in college athletics, with an emphasis on the challenges facing non-revenue sport teams.

JORIS DRAYER is an assistant professor of sport commerce in Health and Sport Sciences at the University of Memphis. His research interests include marketing and pricing strategies as well as consumer behavior.

GEORGE FOSTER is Paul L. and Phyllis Wattis Professor of Management, and Dhirubhai Ambani Faculty Fellow in Entrepreneurship, at the Stanford Graduate School of Business. His research and teaching includes entrepreneurship/early stage companies; financial analysis, especially in commercial disputes; and sports business management.

SAMANTHA GORSE is a researcher at the Centre for the International Business of Sport and a doctoral candidate at Coventry University. Her PhD research focuses on investigating the impact of corruption in sport on sport sponsorship agreements, while other research interests include sport entrepreneurship, sport law, and governance.

STEPHEN HARDY is a professor of kinesiology and coordinator of the Sport Studies Program at the University of New Hampshire, where he is also an affiliate professor of history. He has taught courses in sport marketing, athletic administration, sport history, and an introduction to the sport industry.

DAVID HOYT is a research associate at the Stanford Graduate School of Business. He has research interests in a wide range of business disciplines.

CAROL IRWIN is an assistant professor of physical education teacher education in Health and Sport Sciences at the University of Memphis. Her research interests include how community initiatives can collaborate with urban school systems' physical education and health education programs to enhance minority children's health indices.

RICHARD L. IRWIN is a professor of sport commerce in Health and Sport Sciences at the University of Memphis. His research interests include sport marketing, promotion and sales.

MARYELLEN KELLY teaches undergraduate and graduate classes in the Palumbo • Donahue School of Business at Duquesne University. Her research interests include non-traditional work arrangements, product management, and business school pedagogy.

CONWAY LACKMAN is an associate professor of marketing in the Palumbo • Donahue School of Business at Duquesne University. He has served as a Fortune 100 marketing research director and teaches marketing research and business to business marketing.

JOHN LANASA is the chair of Marketing, Sports Marketing, Entrepreneurship, Supply Chain Management, and Global Business Divisions, as well as the Director of the Master of Science in Sports Leadership program at the Palumbo • Donahue School of Business at Duquesne University. His research interests include marketing systems, personal selling, sports marketing, education in sports, and retail.

HEATH McDONALD is an associate professor of marketing at Deakin University. His research interests include consumer innovativeness and the marketing of sports, arts and charities.

MARK S. NAGEL is an associate professor in the Department of Sport and Entertainment Management at the University of South Carolina. His research interests include sport finance, management practices of sport organizations, and sport law.

ANNA SEMENS is deputy director of the Centre for the International Business of Sport and Research Fellow at Coventry University. Her research interests include sports agents and intermediaries, labor markets in professional sports, and the economics of major events.

KENNETH L. SHROPSHIRE is the David W. Hauck Professor and director of the Wharton Sports Business Initiative at the Wharton School, University of Pennsylvania. His research interests include sports law, business, negotiations and social impact.

DEORAH J. SOUTHALL is an instructor of sport administration at the University of North Carolina at Chapel Hill.

RICHARD M. SOUTHALL is an assistant professor of sport administration and director of the Graduate Sport Administration Program at The University of North Carolina at Chapel Hill, where he is also director of the College Sport Research Institute (CSRI).

CONSTANTINO STAVROS is an associate professor of marketing at RMIT University. Aside from research interests in marketing communication, he has published on various sport-related topics including relationship marketing, brand management, player transgressions, consumer defection, and athlete econometric modeling.

MÁRIO TEIXEIRA teaches in the Department of Sport and Health at the University of Évora, Portugal. His teaching experience includes public administration, municipal management, strategic planning, leisure and sports tourism, management of sports facilities, marketing, communication, and public relations.

RODOULA H. TSIOTSOU is an assistant professor of marketing in the Department of Marketing & Operations Management at the University of Macedonia, Greece. Her research interests include services marketing (sport and tourism), branding, non-profit marketing, and e-marketing.